Mediation Theory
and Practice

Second Edition

Mediation Theory and Practice

Second Edition

Suzanne McCorkle
Boise State University

Melanie J. Reese
Boise State University
Idaho State Department of Education

Los Angeles | London | New Delhi
Singapore | Washington DC

Los Angeles | London | New Delhi
Singapore | Washington DC

FOR INFORMATION:

SAGE Publications, Inc.
2455 Teller Road
Thousand Oaks, California 91320
E-mail: order@sagepub.com

SAGE Publications Ltd.
1 Oliver's Yard
55 City Road
London, EC1Y 1SP
United Kingdom

SAGE Publications India Pvt. Ltd.
B 1/I 1 Mohan Cooperative Industrial Area
Mathura Road, New Delhi 110 044
India

SAGE Publications Asia-Pacific Pte. Ltd.
3 Church Street
#10-04 Samsung Hub
Singapore 049483

Acquisitions Editor: Matthew Byrnie
Assitant Editor: Katie Guarino
Editorial Assistant: Gabrielle Piccininni
Production Editor: Stephanie Palermini
Copy Editor: Sheree Van Vreede
Typesetter: Hurix Systems Pvt. Ltd
Proofreader: Jennifer Thompson
Indexer: Suzanne McCorkle
Cover Designer: Scott Van Atta
Marketing Manager: Liz Thornton

Copyright © 2015 by SAGE Publications, Inc.

This book was previously published by: Pearson Education, Inc.

Printed in the United States of America

Library of Congress Cataloging-in-Publication Data

McCorkle, Suzanne.

Mediation theory and practice / Suzanne McCorkle, Boise State University, Melanie J. Reese. — Second edition.

pages cm

Includes bibliographical references and index.

ISBN 978-1-4833-4685-4 (pbk. : alk. paper) — ISBN 978-1-4833-1610-9 (web pdf)

1. Conflict management. 2. Mediation.
I. Reese, Melanie. II. Title.

HM1126.M395 2015

303.6'9—dc23

2013043269

This book is printed on acid-free paper.

SUSTAINABLE FORESTRY INITIATIVE

Certified Chain of Custody
Promoting Sustainable Forestry
www.sfiprogram.org
SFI-01268

SFI label applies to text stock

14 15 16 17 18 10 9 8 7 6 5 4 3 2 1

Brief Contents

List of Cases, Views, and Role-Play Scenarios   xiii

Preface   xv

Acknowledgments   xvii

About the Authors   xix

1. Introduction to Mediation   1

2. The Basic Components of Mediation   19

3. Essential Skills for Mediators   37

4. Pre-Mediation Activities   59

5. Ethical Considerations and Tactical Preparations   79

6. The Mediator's Opening Statement   97

7. Storytelling and Issue Identification   115

8. Setting the Agenda for Negotiation   141

9. Problem Solving and Negotiation   153

10. Settlement and Closure   177

11. The World of the Mediator   191

Appendix A: Practice Cases   203

Glossary   231

References   241

Index   247

Detailed Contents

List of Cases, Views, and Role-Play Scenarios   **xiii**

Preface   **xv**

Acknowledgments   **xvii**

About the Authors   **xix**

1 Introduction to Mediation   1

Why Mediation? 2
    Benefits for the Disputants 3
    Benefits for the Mediator 4

How Do People Find Their Way to Mediation? 5
    Family Mediation 5
    Community Mediation 6
    Victim–Offender Mediation 6
    School-Based Peer Mediation 6
    Business Mediation 7
    Government and Court-Annexed Mediation 7

Power, Rights, and Interests 8
    Resolving through Power 8
    Resolving through Rights 9
    Resolving through Interests 11

The Dispute Resolution Continuum 12
    Litigation 12
    Arbitration 13
    Med-Arb 14
    Mediation 14
    Informal Conflict Management 16

A Disclaimer about Mediation Training 16

Summary 16

Portfolio Assignment 1.1: Starting Your Mediator Portfolio 17

2 The Basic Components of Mediation   19

Philosophical Assumptions   20
    Transformative Approach   20
    Problem-Solving Approach   21
Functional Models   22
Integrating Philosophies   23
Variables That Make a Difference in Mediation Models   24
    Pre-Mediation or No Pre-Mediation   24
    Allow Uninterrupted Disputant First Statements or Control When and How Long Each Person
        Speaks   25
    Allow, Require, or Forbid Private Meetings between the Mediator and the Parties   25
    Require an Agenda before Negotiating, Negotiate as You Go, or Slide Back and Forth between
        Issue Identification and Negotiation   26
    Consider the Parts of the Mediation as Functional Phases or as Chronological
        Steps   26
    Focus on the Problem, the Emotions, or Balance Problems and Emotions   26
    Prescribe Automatic First Moves within Phases or Allow Mediator Choice   27
    Allowing or Prohibiting Parties to Speak to Each Other   27
    Writing and Signing or Not Signing Agreements   27
Phases in the Balanced Mediation Model   28
    Pre-Mediation   29
    Mediation Session   30
    Post-Mediation   33
Does Culture Matter in Mediation?   34
Summary   36

3 Essential Skills for Mediators   37

An Overview of Mediator Skills   38
Trusting and Controlling the Process   39
    Trusting the Process   40
    Controlling the Process   41
Listening: A Bedrock Skill for Mediators   42
    Types of Listening   43
    Variables That Affect Listening   43
    Skills for Listening to Content, Emotion, and Relationship   46
Reframing Messages   50
Listening to Nonverbal Communication   52
Clarifying and Asking Questions   53

Open versus Closed Questions   53
Genuinely Curious Questions   54
Honoring Silence   54
Listening Interculturally   55
Ethical Issues and Listening   56
Summary   56
Portfolio Assignment 3.1: Emotional Paraphrases   57
Portfolio Assignment 3.2: The Open-Ended Question   57

4 Pre-Mediation Activities   59

Contacting Disputants 61
Goals to Accomplish During Intake 62
Education Role 63
Information-Gathering Role 67
Assessment Role 69
Setting the Stage 73
Time and Timing 73
Place 74
Environment 75
Ethical Issues for Pre-Mediation Caseworkers 76
Summary 77
Portfolio Assignment 4.1: The Referral Sourcebook 77
Portfolio Assignment 4.2: Intake and Agreement to Mediate Forms 78

5 Ethical Considerations and Tactical Preparations   79

Mediator Roles 80
Ethical Considerations for Mediators 82
Neutrality and Impartiality 83
Competence 84
Dual-Role Relationships 85
Truthfulness 86
Informed Choice 86
Conclusions about Mediator Ethics 86
Disputant Roles 88
Analyzing Stakeholders 89
The Mediation Plan 90
Common Causes of Conflict 91
Conflict Causes and Mediator Moves 93
Cultural Awareness 94
Summary 95
Portfolio Assignment 5.1: Ethical Codes of Conduct 96
Portfolio Assignment 5.2: Mediator Supplies 96

6 The Mediator's Opening Statement

Opening Statement Functions 98
Opening Statement Styles 99
  Monologue Style 99
  Interactive Style 100
Opening Statement Dynamics 100
  Length 101
  Order 101
Key Components of the Opening Statement 103
  Welcoming 103
  Introductions 103
  Building Credibility 103
  Establishing Stakeholders 104
  Explaining the Nature and Scope of Mediation 104
  Explaining the Mediator's Role 105
  Explaining the Caucus 105
  Explaining Impartiality and Neutrality 105
  Giving a Confidentiality Pledge 106
  Disclosing Notetaking Purposes 106
  Establishing Ground Rules 107
  Discovering Time Constraints 108
  Explaining the Role of Outside Experts 109
  Securing the Commitment to Begin 109
  Transitioning to Storytelling 110
Building Credibility and Rapport 110
The Relationship between Opening Statements and Mediator Control 111
Notetaking for Mediators 111
Summary 113
Portfolio Assignment 6.1: Creating Your Personal Opening Statement 114
Portfolio Assignment 6.2: Creating Your Personal Notetaking Form 114

7 Storytelling and Issue Identification

Theories of Storytelling 117
  Symbolic Interaction 117
  Attribution Theory 118
  Emotional Intelligence 119
Functions of Storytelling 120
  The Individual 120
  The Mediator 122
Mediator Strategies in Storytelling 126
  One Storyteller at a Time 126
  Co-Constructing Stories 127

General Inquiry Approach 127
Whole Picture Questions 128
Being Columbo 128
Specific Inquiry 129
Establishing Agreed-on "Facts" 129
Weighing the Importance of Disagreements 129
Perspective Taking 130
Humor 130

Conflict Causes and Mediator Moves 131
Overcoming Common Pitfalls during Storytelling 132
Pitfall 1: Unchecked Power Differences 132
Pitfall 2: Allowing Blaming and Attacking 133
Pitfall 3: Acting on Overstatements or Generalizations 133
Pitfall 4: Taking Sides 134
Pitfall 5: Permitting Interrupting and Bickering 134
Pitfall 6: Mismanaging Emotional Outbursts 134
Pitfall 7: Letting One Party Monopolize Time or Control the
Process 136
Pitfall 8: Being Overwhelmed with Evidence 137
Summary 138
Portfolio Assignment 7.1: The Vision Quest 138
Portfolio Assignment 7.2: Reframes 138

8 **Setting the Agenda for Negotiation**   **141**

The Mediator's Notes Are the Building Blocks of the Agenda 143
When to Shift to the Agenda Step 143
Components of the Agenda 144
The Commonality Statement 144
The Agenda List 146
Sequencing the Agenda List 146
Who Decides the Order of the Agenda? 146
Methods of Choosing the Sequence 147
Adding an Issue for Continuing Relationships 149
The Language of the Agenda 150
Framing the Agenda Mutually 150
Framing the Agenda Neutrally 151
Summary 151
Portfolio Assignment 8.1: Methods of Ordering the Agenda 152
Portfolio Assignment 8.2: Transitioning to the Agenda 152

9 Problem Solving and Negotiation

153

The Two Worlds of Negotiation 154
Directiveness vs. Intrusiveness 157
Mediator Techniques to Foster Disputant Problem Solving 158
    Starting the Negotiation 158
    Techniques for Cooperative Negotiation 158
    Techniques for Traditional Negotiation 162
Using the Caucus to Respond to Common Problems 167
    Not Bargaining in Good Faith 168
    Hidden Agendas 168
    Reality Check 168
    Lying or Withholding Information 169
    Shuttle 169
Breaking Deadlocks 170
    Analyze the Impasse 170
    Techniques to Break through Impasse 170
Face-Saving 171
Ending the Negotiation Phase 172
Mediator Ethics and the Negotiation Phase 173
Summary 174
Portfolio Assignment 9.1: Questions to Start Negotiation 175
Portfolio Assignment 9.2: Going into Caucus 175

10 Settlement and Closure

177

Why Write Agreements? 178
Is the Agreement Legally Binding or Legally Nonbinding? 178
A Format for Writing Mediation Agreements 179
Choosing the Phrasing of the Agreement 179
    Agreements Use Direct Language 179
    Agreements Are Clear 181
    Agreements Generally Are Positive 181
    Agreements Are Impartial 182
    Agreements Are Concrete 182
    Agreements Arise from the Parties' Words 183
Creating Durable Agreements 183
    Contingency Agreements 183
    Future Clauses 184
    Reality Testing 185
Final Reading and Signing 186

Closing a Nonagreement Mediation 187
Debriefing the Session 188
Summary 188
Portfolio Assignment 10.1: Memorandum of Agreement Form 189
Portfolio Assignment 10.2: The Referral Sourcebook 189

11 The World of the Mediator 191

Variations on Basic Mediation 192
    Co-Mediation 192
    Panels 193
    Extended Pre-Mediation 193
    Mediation and the Internet 194
Mediation as a Profession 195
    Employment Opportunities for Mediators 196
    Standards of Professional Conduct 197
    Professional Mediator Competencies 197
Mediation Skills in Everyday Life 199
The Promise of Mediation 200
Summary 201

Appendix A: Practice Cases 203

Glossary 231

References 241

Index 247

List of Cases, Views, and Role-Play Scenarios

Cases

Case 1.1: A Neighborhood Misunderstanding   2

Case 2.1: My Old Friend Is My New Boss   21

Case 2.2: What's Best for Eli?   24

Case 3.1: The Mistaken Grade   38

Case 4.1: Irreconcilable Differences   60

Case 5.1: The Roommates at Odds   80

Case 5.2: Reverend MacDonald's Mediation   88

Case 7.1: The Privacy Fence   116

Case 7.2: The Catering Dilemma   122

Case 8.1: The Estate Settlement   142

Case 8.2: What a Bad Dog   150

Case 9.1: Not if He Wins   154

Case 9.2: Mrs. Graham and the Train   160

Case 9.3: The Questionable Gift   172

Views

A View from the Field: Small Claims Court Mediation   4

A View from the Field: One Mediator's Ethical Dilemma   85

Role-Play Scenarios

The Cubicle Case   204

The Saving Kids Project Case   207

The Lunchroom Discontent Case   211

Confusion in the Student Project Case   215

The Broken Saw Case   218

The Ad Agency and the Intern Case   221

The Daycare Dilemma Case   226

Preface

Since the first printing of *Mediation Theory and Practice* a decade ago, the field of mediation has found increased institutional stability and legitimacy in a variety of contexts where it once was viewed as outside the mainstream. Mediation practice has fulfilled those early predictions of growth and acceptance, and it continues to shape the traditional conflict resolution landscape in new and exciting ways. The 2nd edition of *Mediation Theory and Practice* is revised and updated to reflect those changes in the alternative dispute resolution field.

While continuing our goal to provide students and practitioners a blend of mediation theory and skill-focused applications, we've included in this edition a greater focus on personal development and ethical practice. New case studies reflecting the expanding practice of mediation, as well the influence of current research, have been added. We maintain the central focus of introducing students to the basics of mediation in an accessible way through narratives and examples. This text aims to address the core concepts necessary for the introduction to mediation class or in the Basic 40 Hour Mediation Training. We continue to challenge students toward practical application and continual improvement. Each chapter contains discussion questions, case analyses, and examples to encourage students to explore the intricacies of the material and to elicit insights about the mediation process.

Chapter 1 explains how people find their way to mediation. By comparing mediation to other forms of dispute resolution, the reader can discern the primary benefits and disadvantages of choosing to resolve issues through mediation. This first chapter introduces the student to the authors' interest-based philosophy of conflict management.

Chapter 2 distinguishes between two approaches to mediation: conciliation and problem solving. We introduce the balanced mediation model as an integration of the two approaches that serves as the training model in this book. We explore variables that make a difference in how a mediation session unfolds.

Chapter 3 begins instruction in the competencies required for beginning mediators. We focus on listening and strategically asking questions as the basic building blocks of a mediator's skill base. A variety of tactics are presented to aid mediators in validating and moving parties through the mediation process.

Chapter 4 details pre-mediation activities and the work of case managers or intake coordinators. Getting parties to the mediation table requires skills in education, information gathering, and assessment.

Chapter 5 overviews the mediator's preparation for a session and ethical considerations. Specifically, the chapter addresses mediator roles and the concepts of neutrality and impartiality. Additionally, Chapter 5 shows how to create a mediation plan based on analysis of the type of conflict being exhibited and information gathered during intake.

Chapters 6 through 10 explore skills to implement the balanced model of mediation, with one chapter dedicated to each phase. Chapter 6 outlines the mediator's opening statement (mediator monologue). We provide a sample opening statement, as well as a discussion of each function of the mediator's monologue.

Chapter 7 presents skills for storytelling and issue identification. Symbolic interaction, attribution theory, and emotional intelligence are introduced as informative about disputants' perspectives during storytelling. We identify specific mediator strategies and pitfalls beginners should avoid.

Chapter 8 lays out how to create and frame the negotiation agenda, featuring tools such as the two-way commonality statement and the general commonality statement. Readers will examine how best to formulate and communicate the agenda, as well as how framing the agenda in neutral terms enhances the process.

Chapter 9 delves into tactics and strategies of negotiation. Mediated agreements arise from the parties rather than from mediator suggestions. This chapter provides the beginning mediator techniques for fostering cooperative efforts as well as techniques for traditional, competitive negotiators. We discuss strategies, such as fractionating apparent differences, creating contingency agreements, and using the caucus to respond to difficulties.

Chapter 10 is a guide to writing the disputant agreements as a Memorandum of Understanding and closing sessions. We explain the skill of agreement writing, with the primary goal being able to make the disputants' agreements clear, durable, concrete, behavioral, and based in reality.

Chapter 11 explores the ever expanding world of the mediator. A review of a variety of mediation contexts and applications is presented, as well as different models of mediation, such as the panel model, co-mediation, and Internet mediation. We discuss volunteer and professional mediation opportunities for service or employment, and the importance of improving conflict situations with the skills and insights addressed in the text.

Throughout the text, vocabulary words are set in bold at their first occurrence and correspond with the definitions provided in the Glossary.

Acknowledgments

The second edition updates were influenced by the feedback from our students, those who used the first edition of *Mediation Theory and Practice,* and our discerning reviewers:

Evelyn L. Ang, MBA, JD, University of Wisconsin-Milwaukee

Kevin James Brown, Oregon Institute of Technology

Joanne Katz, Missouri Western State University

Barbara E. Kirby, Texas Wesleyan University

Bruce C. McKinney, University of North Carolina Wilmington

Sunny J. Rowland, J.D., University of Oklahoma-College of Liberal Studies

Melissa Schroeder, Texas Christian University

C. Brant Short, Northern Arizona University

Barbara S. Spies, Cardinal Stritch University

Stephen Yungbluth, Northern Kentucky University

We also thank the team at SAGE and our editor, Matthew Byrnie, for bringing this project to completion.

About the Authors

Suzanne McCorkle (Ph.D., University of Colorado at Boulder) has served in several capacities at Boise State University: faculty in the Communication department, forensics coach, associate dean and dean of the College of Social Sciences and Public Affairs, and recently as a professor in the Department of Public Policy and Director of the University's Dispute Resolution Program. Dr. McCorkle's other books include *Personal Conflict Management* (Pearson) and *People Skills for Public Managers* (M.E. Sharpe).

Melanie J. Reese (Ph.D., University of Nebraska—Lincoln) is Professor Emeritus and former associate professor at Boise State University. Dr. Reese also served as Faculty Ombudsman at the College of Western Idaho before joining the Idaho Department of Education as the State Dispute Resolution Coordinator for Special Education. Dr. Reese has been a practicing mediator since the late 1980s, involved in cases including divorce, child custody, retail, sexual harassment, real estate, civil court, restorative justice, and estate disputes. Most recently in her work with the Idaho Department of Education, she directs a state-wide dispute resolution office that oversees special education meeting facilitations, mediations, complaint investigations, and due process hearings.

Introduction to Mediation

Why Mediation? 2

Benefits for the Disputants 3

Benefits for the Mediator 4

How Do People Find Their Way to Mediation? 5

Family Mediation 5

Community Mediation 6

Victim–Offender Mediation 6

School-Based Peer Mediation 6

Business Mediation 7

Government and Court-Annexed Mediation 7

Power, Rights, and Interests 8

Resolving through Power 8

Resolving through Rights 9

Resolving through Interests 11

The Dispute Resolution Continuum 12

Litigation 12

Arbitration 13

Med-Arb 14

Mediation 14

Informal Conflict Management 16

A Disclaimer about Mediation Training 16

Summary 16

Portfolio Assignment 1.1: Starting Your Mediator Portfolio 17

WHY MEDIATION?

CASE 1.1: A Neighborhood Misunderstanding

Dana moved from urban Chicago to a small town to be nearer to her grandmother. Prior to moving, Dana lived for 27 years in an apartment with her mom in a rather rough urban neighborhood. Dana was raised to "mind your own business" and not to engage the neighbors in conflict. As she put it, "You never know who is living next to you—they could be dangerous!"

Across the street in her new neighborhood live Tommy and Mary Klimes. The older couple was retired, with a grown son who lived elsewhere in town and an elderly Boston terrier named Button. The couple didn't have a fence, but Button didn't wander too much. Besides, all the neighbors knew Button belonged to the Klimes.

Button didn't like Dana from the first moment they saw each other, and anytime both were outside, Button would bark and run at the new neighbor. Dana felt threatened by the dog. She also was apprehensive about talking to the neighbors directly, so she called the police instead. The police came, stopping first at Dana's house to get her statement and then crossed the street to speak to the Klimes. The Klimes were not given the name of the person who complained about the dog, but later another neighbor told them that the police had stopped at the "new neighbor lady's" house. Tommy, noticing Dana's car in her driveway, promptly walked across the street to introduce himself and apologize for the dog. He rang the bell and knocked, but there was no answer.

Several days later, Button barked at Dana again and came into the street as she got into her car. Again, Dana summoned the police. This time, the Klimes were issued a citation. When Dana returned home from work, the neighbors' son was outside of his parents' home and yelled obscenities at her as she walked into her house. Mr. Klimes heard the comments, came outside, and admonished his son, and then walked across the street to apologize to his neighbor.

However, Dana, feeling threatened, didn't answer the door. Tommy knew she was in there and peeked in the front window to see whether she just didn't hear the bell. Finally giving up, he went home. A few minutes later, the police arrived for the second time that day. Dana had called reporting that her male neighbor was peeping in her windows.

Welcome to the world of **mediation**! You are about to study an activity that spans many **cultures** and thousands of years. Mediation, one form of **alternative dispute resolution (ADR)**, is a process where a **third party** helps others manage their conflict—a worthwhile activity in itself. However, mediation is more than just another alternative to the court system or an offshoot of community problem solving. For many practitioners, mediation is a philosophy of human nature, or as Phyllis Beck Kritek argues, "the resolution of human conflicts is a moral enterprise that is the responsibility of every human" (2002, p. 17).

Individuals trained as mediators find that the skills they learn are applicable to daily communication in their personal and professional lives. People from all walks of life have become mediators—attorneys, counselors, teachers, police officers, human resource professionals, homemakers, college students, and even young children. Some who are trained have found a calling in mediation—an outlet for their lifelong goal of helping people. Others use mediation in their career path or integrate the skills into their existing vocations.

What is it about mediation that appeals to so many different kinds of people and is useful in so many different contexts? Mediation is about empowering people to make their own informed choices rather than having a third party (such as a judge) make a decision for them. Mediation is grounded in the belief that conflict offers an opportunity to build stronger individuals, more satisfying relationships, and better communities. As a student of mediation, you will learn the philosophies and **theories** that underlie mediation, as well as foundational skills any mediator must possess.

We live in a society replete with conflict. We also live in a litigious society. Every day we hear stories about someone being sued for serving coffee that is too hot, having icy sidewalks, or failing to fulfill an agreement. Although litigation has a respectable and important place in society, sometimes there are less adversarial, cheaper, and quicker ways to resolve conflict. As we hear strange tales about neighbors who sue each other about where they put their trash on garbage collection day, we wonder, "Why didn't these neighbors just talk it out?" In a nutshell, that is what mediation offers **disputants**: a chance to "talk it out" in a safe and controlled environment.

Benefits for the Disputants

The situation in Case 1.1 with Dana and the Klimes seems like a simple misunderstanding. However, each party is seeing only a limited picture of reality. In each person's view, the other is acting inappropriately. Dana has legal rights to protection from harassment from her neighbors and their dog. She has the right to involve the police and to press for justice. When the case appeared in court, the judge referred them to the **community mediation** program. The judge wanted to see whether these neighbors could resolve the issues together before assigning time in her already overloaded court calendar. In short, the **parties** in this case were ordered to mediation to work out their dispute, if possible. The judge also believed that the parties' **interests** would be served best in a place where they could explore not only the legal aspects of the case but also the issues surrounding how they experienced the event. In court, only the legal issues would be resolved and a neighborhood could be left in turmoil.

Discussion Question 1.1

WHAT ISSUES in Case 1.1 fall outside the scope of the legal system? What would happen to these issues if the neighborhood misunderstanding case were to be settled in court?

Mediation often is better equipped to explore the relational and emotional issues of a dispute than a formal court proceeding. Research indicates disputants in court-related mediation programs have favorable views of the mediation process, and they have settled their cases between 27 and 63 percent of the time without having to go before a judge. Moreover, people complied with their mediated agreements up to 90 percent of the time (Baksi, 2010; Wissler, 2004).

When the individuals will have a continued relationship, such as in the case of the Klimes and Dana, mediation is particularly appropriate. In this case, the parties met one afternoon with a mediator. A very tense session began. The Klimes explained that they were offended by how Dana treated them; Dana was adamant about the righteousness of her complaints. Through the process of mediation, Dana was able to express her feelings about neighbors and, subsequently, created a way for the Klimes to understand her actions. The Klimes, not having the opportunity in the past to apologize for the dog and for their son's behavior, were allowed to assert their desire for a friendly relationship. The result of this real-world mediation was an offer for Dana to come to the Klimes's house for coffee and to get to know Button, the dog. Dana agreed—but only if she could bring some of the chocolate chip cookies that she baked that morning. With a mediated agreement in hand, the court case was dismissed.

Benefits for the Mediator

Mediation not only adds value for society and to disputants, it also benefits the individuals who learn mediation skills. Those who become mediators express feelings of accomplishment when they help others solve thorny problems. Students of mediation claim they see a microcosm of life during fieldwork practice.

A View from the Field: Small Claims Court Mediation

Roger Cockerille, Idaho 4th District Court Magistrate Judge, tells the individuals sitting in his courtroom waiting for a trial that he orders most of the contested small claims cases to mediation for two reasons: It is their last chance to work things out together before a judge makes a decision that may not please either of them, and about 70 percent of the mediations result in a settlement. Of those who settle, over 90 percent follow through and comply with the agreement they negotiated. If the court makes the judgment, people can appeal, which delays getting the settlement that was awarded. It also is the winner's job in Idaho to collect on the judgment, which means the plaintiff has to find the defendant and try to garnish wages or collect through some other legal means, which is not easy. Many people never see a dime when they "win" in small claims court.

When people arrive at court, they are prepared for a fight. Then they are sent to mediation. While everybody who goes to mediation doesn't have the same experience, many leave transformed. We held a conversation with graduates of the Boise State University Dispute Resolution Program who served as small claims court mediators. Deanna's comment about

(Continued)

being surprised that sometimes money wasn't the **issue** was representative of the group's experiences. "I had a neighborhood case where the people bought a house in the winter and when summer rolled around the sprinkler system didn't work. They tried to fix it, but couldn't figure out how the previous owners had it rigged and couldn't find the other couple. They ended up bringing the former owner to court because it was the only way to find them." During the mediation session, they came to an agreement that the former owner would buy all the replacement parts and train the new owner on how to work the sprinkler system—and they would get together and repair it. They even made plans to have dinner the next weekend. Deanna concluded, "It feels good when you help."

Individuals who mediate cases have the opportunity to complete a voluntary, confidential survey. In 2006, data show that 86 percent of respondents in Idaho's 4th District Court program agreed or strongly agreed that they would use mediation again. Seventy-nine percent agreed or strongly agreed that they thought the mediated agreement would work. Seventy-four percent were satisfied with the mediated agreement. Citizen satisfaction with the program's services is high. The court also can hear more cases more quickly than before the university-court partnership program was established.

Those who study mediation—but never become professional mediators—also accrue benefits. The skills useful to mediators are transferable to everyday life. **Listening**, reframing issues, and problem solving are trademarks of a good mediator and are characteristic of effective leaders. Mediator skills enhance individual competence and can be applied informally at home, work, or in social situations.

HOW DO PEOPLE FIND THEIR WAY TO MEDIATION?

There are many paths to mediation. Mediation can be sought by disputants, recommended by a friend or coworker, or mandated by a third party such as the courts or a work supervisor. Counselors, agency workers, and concerned friends may suggest mediation to help solve problems. Mediation occurs throughout society in many contexts. Families, communities, organizations, courts, and schools are common contexts for mediation.

Family Mediation

Family mediation takes on many forms and can be referred by a variety of sources. For example, a family was having difficulty re-integrating their son who had run away back into the family home. A social worker recommended a mediator to help the family negotiate rules and expectations. In another example, an advocacy agency specializing in resources for the aging regularly refers families to mediation when negotiating elder care issues. A minister recommended mediation to members of her congregation who could not amicably work out the details on an estate settlement after the death of their parent. Divorcing parents in many states are required to mediate parenting plans for their children prior to bringing their case to a judge. Research indicates the disputants in divorce cases see the mediator's ability to provide guidance, empathize, foster a civil conversation, and focus on the facts as critical to success (Cohen, O., 2009).

Community Mediation

One of the early applications of mediation was in promoting community peace. Police who are called about noisy parties or wayward pets may refer the neighbors to mediation. Neighbors who do not get along well, but who would like to, may attend mediation as a way to open lines of communication. On a bigger scale, mediation can address concerns citizens have with police departments, transportation agencies, or across neighborhoods. In one example, community members from a specific racial group felt targeted by police, and a critical incident resulting in the death of a community member exacerbated an already volatile situation. Mediators held community meetings to help parties air concerns and work together to create solutions. Within many cities, community mediation programs are available. Other types of mediation specialists work with faith congregations who are in conflict over management approach, personnel, or doctrinal issues.

Tribal councils perhaps were the original large-group conflict resolution system. For example, Navajo peoples may create a forum for hearing concerns and helping members resolve issues that may affect the public good ("Peacemaking Program," 2012). In discussion circles, issues may be brought to tribal elders or community leaders and addressed communally among the troubled participants, family members, workmates, or those affected by the conflict ("Peacemaking Program," 2012).

Victim–Offender Mediation (VOM)

Victim–Offender mediation (also called Victim–Offender Dialogue and **restorative justice**) holds offenders accountable for their actions and offers a means to bring closure to victims. Judges may refer juvenile or adults to victim–offender mediation so the affected individuals can tell their stories and negotiate a restitution plan rather than a judge deciding the sentence for the offender—a procedure that leaves victims out of the process. In one case, two teenage boys were responsible for vandalizing a city park. The teens were brought face-to-face with a woman who had been responsible for the placement of a defaced monument, commissioned as a memorial to her soldier son who had been killed in action. In the process, the teens learned the effect their actions had for this mom. A meta-analysis of victim–offender mediation studies found VOM reduced recidivism in juveniles (Bradshaw, Roseborough, & Umbreit, 2006). VOM provides a means to help offenders by "holding them accountable in respectful ways that may develop a sense of shame and heightened empathy" (Choi, Green, & Gilbert, 2011, p. 352).

School-Based Peer Mediation

Gaining momentum in the wake of high-profile bullying and violent incidents, peer mediation is employed in many schools. Although school mediation may not be an answer to existing bullying, it may help prevent some situations from deteriorating. In elementary schools, peer-mediators trained in very basic conflict management steps help resolve playground conflicts on the spot without **escalation**, and they have been shown to reduce early stage bullying behavior (Vreeman & Carroll, 2007).

From the early grades to universities, schools instituted programs where students are trained to mediate cases involving peers. Public school teachers refer students in conflict to a peer mediation program. Dormitory roommates may be referred to a campus mediation center to talk about competing study habits and social time issues. Students involved in group projects may seek mediation to work through issues about assignments, leadership, or work accountability.

Business Mediation

Mediation can be included as part of the standard conflict management processes in an organization. Bosses refer employees who cannot work well together to the human resources department for mediation or, if trained, conduct a mediation intervention (a specialized area called **supervisor mediation**). A business threatened with a lawsuit by a dissatisfied customer may suggest mediation rather than going directly to court. When a real estate purchase falls through, the buyer and seller can elect to mediate a fair distribution of the earnest money deposit. Many contracts require mediation of any disagreements between customers and the business provider.

Government and Court-Annexed Mediation

Some situations involve several stakeholder groups who share a common dilemma, such as whether to build a nuclear power plant in their community (Susskind & Field, 1996) or how to manage the declining population of a particular species of animal on public lands. For example, the Department of the Interior uses mediation to involve the public in decision-making processes (Ruell, Burkardt, & Clark, 2010). The Department of Agriculture participates in mediation with farmers who have violated environmental rules or have past due loans. Government officials negotiate the creation and enforcement of rules in a process called **negotiated rule-making** (neg-reg), where businesses, individuals, or other entities who violate regulations meet and create a plan for future compliance (Stephenson & Pops, 1991). Federal regulation requires each state to oversee mediation processes to aid parents and school districts to resolve special education disputes.

In the western United States, mediation and arbitration established who has first rights to scarce water resources. Courts refer many types of civil and criminal cases to mediation, including eviction courts that encourage landlords and tenants to create an amicable plan for departure from a rental unit (rather than having the sheriff force an eviction). Home foreclosure mediation has emerged as a means of keeping families in their homes during an upside down real estate market (Khader, 2010). State taxation entities and the Internal Revenue Service use mediators when negotiating past due taxes (Meyercord, 2010). The **REDRESS©** program has been adopted by the U.S. Postal Services to mediate Equal Employment Opportunity Commission (EEOC) conflicts. Some organizations have professional conflict managers on retainer should a potentially volatile workplace conflict arise. Internationally, mediators meet with cultural and political rivals to negotiate innumerable issues—including matters of war and peace.

In sum, people find their way to mediation because it offers a relatively speedy and efficient way to resolve disputes. Instead of filing a case in the courts or attempting to strong-arm an opponent into compliance, mediation brings the parties together to consider their mutual options. Mediation can be considered an alternative to systems that focus primarily on the rights of individuals and to systems that rely on **power** to determine outcomes.

POWER, RIGHTS, AND INTERESTS

In 1988 William L. Ury, Jeanne M. Brett, and Stephen B. Goldberg proposed that conflict management could be viewed from three perspectives: power, rights, and interests.

Resolving through Power

Power-based approaches to conflict can be summed up with the following adage: "Might makes right." Power is the ability to influence another person. In the scenario earlier in this chapter, Dana could kick the dog and thus exert her superior physical power to put the dog in his place. However, other affected parties also could exert their power. The couple's son may be stronger than Dana and have a physical power advantage. Conversely, Dana's grandmother might be quite wealthy—giving Dana monetary power to obtain a better attorney than the Klimes could afford. If Mary Klimes were the former prosecuting attorney for the city, her power resources could trump those of the others, as networking and influence are very potent resources.

The power approach to conflict resolution is used widely. War, violence, and revenge are extreme examples of the power system. The consequences of the use of power may be highly detrimental to relationships (between individuals, businesses, or countries). Reliance on power to "win" leads to distrust and what Johan Galtung (1969) calls negative peace: peace resulting from forced submission rather than from a change of heart. As illustrated in international conflicts, such negative peace rarely is long lasting. There is some evidence that people who "lose" in disputes may resort to retaliation, sometimes manifested on college campuses through vandalism or theft (Hebein, 1999). In Chapter 7, we will discuss how power comes into play during a mediation session and what a mediator can do to "balance" power for the disputants.

Power, however, can be appropriate in some circumstances. As a parent, it may be necessary to use physical power to control a two-year-old running toward a busy street. The act of forcing, or in this case grabbing the child and removing her from danger, is an act of power. However, reliance on power as a sole source for resolving conflicts would create a tumultuous society, one with people of low power being trampled by those in high power. Fortunately, humans have created other alternatives.

Discussion Question 1.2
WHAT ARE the benefits of resolving disputes with power? What are the possible harms? What might be the consequence of the power approach in the neighborhood misunderstanding case?

Resolving through Rights

The second major approach to conflict resolution is derived from the science of rights, a finely tuned system developed throughout European history and adapted into the U.S. legal system. In this approach, the rights of individuals (as laid forth in the law) are keys to fair and just resolution to conflict. In the U.S. system of justice, the rights of the individuals are outlined in the Constitution, modified by lawmakers, and interpreted by judges. The legal system offers a highly ritualized process for resolving issues that have legal merit (and for dismissing those that do not). In theory, the legal system provides equal access to justice for everyone. All who appear before a judge are governed by the same rules of evidence and legal criteria—regardless of race, creed, or social status. The legal system promises disputants a structured means of resolving their disputes.

However, few would argue that power is not wielded in the halls of justice. Money buys better legal representation. Those who are lacking in resources may find going to court not worth the effort, time, or expense. In one case, a couple had divorced, and then a few months later, they reconciled and resumed their married life (without the formality of remarrying). For six years, they lived together, sharing all expenses. They separated again and created a custody agreement without the courts. Five years after their second separation, the ex-wife sued for back child support from the date of the original divorce 11 years earlier. The amount of money in dispute was $17,000. The cost to each party for attorneys was approximately $8,000. The case was heard over a year later. The ex-husband prevailed, the ex-wife didn't receive any additional support, and $16,000 was paid for attorney fees. Litigation was an expensive way to resolve this dispute for the two single parents living under the poverty level.

TABLE 1.1 Three Perspectives on Resolving Disputes

Approach	Benefits	Disadvantages
Power	<ul><li>Clear winner and loser</li><li>Often expedient</li><li>Power resources usually easy to identify</li></ul>	<ul><li>Negative peace/retaliation</li><li>Lack of satisfaction by one party</li><li>May lead to violence</li><li>Little room for positive expression of concerns</li><li>Power is tenuous and may be lost</li><li>People with low power resources use what power resources they do have to be heard</li></ul>

(Continued)

TABLE 1.1 (Continued)		
Approach	**Benefits**	**Disadvantages**
Rights	• Clear rules for engagement • Specific requirements for evidence • The law is the same for everyone • People can be represented by attorneys • Process may be open to public scrutiny • Precedents are set	• Emotional issues and interests are not allowed • Usually expensive • Usually very time consuming • Quality of legal representation may affect the outcome • Decisions are made by judges or juries • Laws may prohibit creative solutions
Interests	• Open to exploring feelings • Solutions can be unique to the parties • Not limited to precedence or conventional approaches • Structurally flexible as decision making stays with the parties • May be more expedient than litigation • May be less costly than litigation	• May have little or no public scrutiny • Private justice instead of public; therefore open to bias and malpractice by mediators • Some may not be able to negotiate effectively and may be better served by representation • Lack of consistency in outcome • May deter the establishment of important precedents

Some disputes are inappropriate for the courts because they lack legal merit. A court is not the place to settle hurt feelings. When these cases somehow are framed in legal terms and taken to court, relationships may suffer as a result of the adversarial nature of the **rights-based** process. In addition, the **anger**, frustration, and hurt that brought the disputants to court could be deemed not relevant to the findings of legal facts.

Consider the relationship of Dana and the Klimes. In the rights-based system, each would take an adversarial **position** and attempt to convince a judge or jury to rule in her or his favor. While individuals may represent themselves in some courts, more often attorneys speak on behalf of the client—further removing those who have the conflict from the decision-making process. One side would "win" while the other would lose, leaving at least one person feeling unsatisfied with the outcome. At worst, the individuals will invest time waiting for their day in court, spend considerable money on attorneys and fees, and still lack a guarantee that the judge will make a ruling that satisfies either party. Their future relationship could be marred by the escalation of the scenario to the courts and tainted by mistrust and anger. Possible consequences in Case 1.1 include other neighbors choosing sides and continued unpleasant confrontations.

> ### Discussion Question 1.3
>
> WHY DOES society require a rights-based approach to resolving legal conflicts? What kind of conflicts would be best served through a rights-based approach? What type of cases would not be served well through a rights-based approach?

Resolving through Interests

The third approach to conflict provides a forum for issues that do not require resolution in a legal setting. **Interest-based** resolution was popularized by Roger Fisher and William L. Ury from the Harvard Negotiation Project in their book, *Getting to Yes: Interest-based Conflict Management* (2011). An interest-based approach encompasses any process that focuses on the underlying needs of the parties and permits their feelings, concerns, and needs to gain a foothold in the negotiations. The interests of the parties may include issues of power or rights but also the less tangible issues of respect, esteem, and feelings. An interest-based process might be the best choice for disputants who have engaged in a power struggle or who have positioned themselves into inescapable corners. "Those who start negotiation with an unyielding position find it difficult to compromise or think creatively. Changing one's mind is perceived as backing down, creating a loss of face" (McCorkle & Reese, 2010, p. 36). An interest-based mediation process can unlock positions and make more creative thinking possible.

Christopher W. Moore (2003) divides needs into substantive, procedural, and psychological interests. *Substantive interests* relate to tangible or measurable things such as time, specific goods, behaviors, money, or other resources. Two substantive issues for Dana from the case study are trespassing and the dog not being contained. **Procedural interests** arise from stylistic differences about how to communicate with each other, organize tasks, complete work, or structure rules and settlements. The Klimes wanted to meet informally with Dana and talk out the situation. However, through the process of trying to meet with her, Dana felt threatened and an informal interaction was not acceptable to her. Dana pursued legal means to resolve the dispute, but the judge had other procedural interests and sent the case to mediation. **Psychological interests** underlie all of the emotions and feelings that disputants bring to a session. The confusion the Klimes felt over Dana's behavior, their need to be seen as good and nonthreatening neighbors, Dana's feelings of intimidation and her discomfort with the dog, and the desire of all parties to have a peaceful existence are psychological interests. While there are no guarantees that relationships will be improved through interest-based resolution, engaging in a process that explores the motivations of disputants may be less damaging than adversarial approaches.

Kritek (2002) in *Negotiating at an Uneven Table* discusses how interest-based approaches may seem counterintuitive to cultures that rely on "being right" to maintain their power. Humans, however, see the world from many vantage points and have different views of what is "right." Each individual's interests stem from a highly personal perspective on reality. Through interest-based negotiations and the assistance of a mediator, each disputant has the opportunity to view the world as others see it.

When the neighborhood misunderstanding case was referred to mediation, an interest-based process ensued. Through the promptings and guidance of a mediator in a safe context, Dana shared her personal background, feelings of distrust, and genuine fear of the dog and strangers. The Klimes were able to have their apology heard, state their views of what it means to be good neighbors, and express their frustration that Dana would not talk to them when the conflict first occurred. Through interest-based negotiations, each party began to see the other as a partner in fixing the problem. The mediator was able to assist the neighbors in resolving the conflict, and they worked out a plan for Dana to choose other alternatives than the police department when dealing with the dog.

Discussion Question 1.4

WHAT TYPES of disputes would be inappropriate for interest-based resolution? What are the risks to the parties in this approach? What should individuals consider before engaging in an interest-based **negotiation**?

The three approaches to conflict—power, rights, and interests—all have their place in society. While the interest-based approach seems from the previous example to be an ideal choice for resolving disputes, each of the three approaches offers risks and advantages not met by the others. No one approach can be considered appropriate for all cases. Table 1.1 presents some advantages and disadvantages of each approach. The needs of the clients, the issues involved, the power resources of each side, and the concerns for legal precedent should be considered in the determination of the most appropriate approach to conflict management.

The need to explore differences in safe environments while working together toward resolution is underscored by increasing diversity and globalization. As neighborhoods and businesses become more diverse in ethnicity, gender, nationality, age, and lifestyle, it is imperative to develop channels of communication to manage the predictable clashes of **values**, style, and goals that accompany diversity. Parts of the modern mediation movement were born in communities dealing with inner-city racial and social tensions during the turbulent 1960s.

THE DISPUTE RESOLUTION CONTINUUM

Litigation

Litigation, also referred to as **adjudication**, is the process of resolving disputes through a formal court or justice system. In litigation, disputants (either represented by attorneys or representing themselves) appear before a judge or jury to present their case. The case is evaluated based on legal merit and subjected to analysis via the well-defined science of rights. Litigation is a public forum (given the litigants are of legal age), and each case is weighed against existing precedent, constitutional rights, and interpretation of the law. In a jury trial, the case is presented and a judge instructs the jury of the applicable law(s) and the jury's options in making decisions. The jury returns a decision and the judge rules regarding the outcome. In the United States, disputants have the right to appeal the decision to a higher court and continue to appeal to even higher courts through several levels, finally culminating at the Supreme Court of the United States. The other approaches of dispute resolution discussed in this section are considered alternatives to the adjudicative process.

Arbitration

In arbitration an expert third party knowledgeable about the context of the dispute is empowered to make a decision for the disputing parties. The American Arbitration Association defines *arbitration* as "the submission of a dispute to one or more impartial persons for a final and binding decision." The parties can determine in advance of entering into arbitration which issues will be resolved, the type of outcome, and other procedural aspects. Not unlike the judicial process where the judge and jury hold the decision-making authority, arbitrators offer the final solution for the dispute. An **arbitrator** is **neutral** and yet informed enough about the specific issues to conduct investigations and to make a good decision. Arbitrators typically are experts in their area of practice (such as real estate, labor, contracts, or wages). Arbitration usually is less expensive and more expedient than a trial, as well as offering more flexibility in decision making than litigation. Problems may arise from the lack of public disclosure allowed in some arbitration.

Binding arbitration is a process where the decision rendered by the arbitrator is contractual—the parties agree in advance to accept the arbitrator's ruling. If you read the small print on consumer or loan contracts, you may discover that you have agreed to binding arbitration and occasionally the waiver of the right to use other processes.

A situation that led to binding arbitration occurred when a real estate agent met a new client one afternoon who had pictures of a house she wanted to see. The agent showed her the home. An offer on the house was made and accepted by the seller that day. The problem was that another agent had been working for months with this client, and the pictures of the home came from the original agent. Which agent should get the commission from the sale—the agent who had worked with the client the longest or the new one who closed the deal? The case was brought before a Realtor's Association Arbitration Panel. The panel, in a very formal setting, heard from each realtor, asked questions, weighed the evidence, and decided that the agent who first showed the home would receive the commission. Once the panel had made its decision, the parties were required to abide by it. The only recourse was through appeal, and then an appeals board within the association would hear the case.

Another approach is *nonbinding arbitration*. The parties may decide in advance to use the ruling as a suggestion rather than bound by the arbitrator's decision. In the case of a farming dispute, a pilot of a crop-duster plane inadvertently sprayed the wrong fields and killed a half-million-dollar crop. Given the size of this case, the attorneys representing each side engaged in nonbinding arbitration. Hiring a retired judge, they each presented their case and asked him to make an informal decision on the legal merits of the case. This process enabled each side to weigh the strengths and weaknesses of their case and make a more informed decision about how to proceed. The judge sided with the farmer who lost the crops. The result was an offer of settlement by the crop-dusting company to the farmer. The nonbinding arbitration succeeded in keeping the case out of a lengthy and expensive court hearing.

Med-Arb

Med-Arb (mediation-arbitration) is a hybrid process where parties come together to mediate their dispute. However, they agree in advance that if they do not reach an agreement, the third party will move into an arbitrator's role and render a decision (either binding or nonbinding). *Med-Arb* is defined as a process where disputants initially have control of the decision, but they consent to an arbitrated settlement if an agreement is not reached by a preset deadline. In a community resolution program designed to improve relations between the community and the police department, cases are brought to a mediator who neither represents the city nor the community. The mediator may hear a complaint by a citizen alleging a police officer did not follow proper procedure in arresting her juvenile son. In a med-arb situation, the mediator would bring in the parties to see whether a joint resolution could be reached. If the parties could not come to agreement, the mediator would then become an arbitrator who investigates the case and renders a decision. The right to appeal would be part of the process. Figure 1.1 illustrates who decides during arbitration and mediation.

Mediation

For the purpose of this book, we define *mediation* as a process where a mutually acceptable third party, who is neutral and impartial, facilitates an interest-based communicative process, enabling disputing parties to explore concerns and to create outcomes.

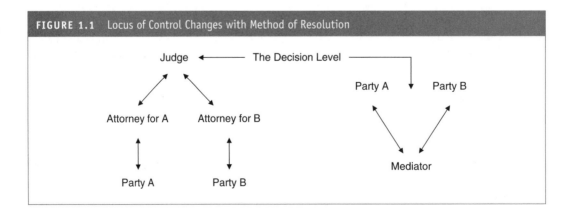

FIGURE 1.1   Locus of Control Changes with Method of Resolution

In the purest form of interest-based mediation, the following standards will be met:

Mutually acceptable: The mediator must be someone whom both parties agree is appropriate for the mediator role.

Neutral: The mediator must be someone who is invested in the well-being of both individuals, but who does not have a preference or affinity for one party over the other.

Impartial: The mediator has no stake in the outcome of the mediation and will not be affected by the decision. The mediator is free from preference toward any possible outcome.

Interest-based: The mediator assists disputants in identifying concerns that affect them and in exploring the specific needs that must be addressed in any outcome.

Communicative process: The mediator facilitates the discussion so parties may understand one another, explore ideas in a safe environment, and approach their problem solving as empowered participants. The mediator strategically applies skills to keep the communication process balanced, fair, and productive.

Parties create the outcome: The mediator does not suggest, lead, or persuade parties to select specific outcomes. Ideas for possible solutions arise from the disputants. The mediator helps them examine the workability and appropriateness of their suggestions.

Discussion Question 1.5

EACH ELEMENT of the definition of mediation is necessary to create the mediation process. What would happen to the mediation if one standard was missing or changed? For each of the standards, explain how removing it would change the nature of mediation.

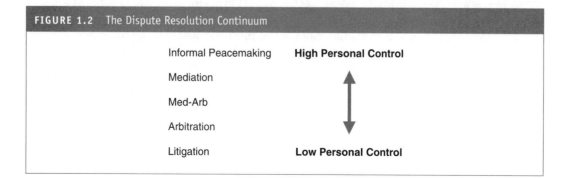

FIGURE 1.2 The Dispute Resolution Continuum

Informal Peacemaking   **High Personal Control**

Mediation

Med-Arb

Arbitration

Litigation   **Low Personal Control**

Informal Conflict Management

Individuals may attempt to resolve disputes directly with the other party. The success of these efforts are dependent on many factors including the skill levels of the parties, the investment in relationship, the urgency in finding an outcome, and the styles the parties employ to resolve their dispute.

Interpersonal conflict management, individual negotiation strategies, and other personal responses to conflict make up the broad realm of informal conflict management. Informal strategies for conflict management are presented in workshops and classes with titles such as Conflict Management, Negotiation, Interpersonal Conflict, Relational Dynamics, and Dealing with Difficult People.

A DISCLAIMER ABOUT MEDIATION TRAINING

The saying "a little knowledge is a dangerous thing" applies to mediation. This book presents the basic theory and foundational skills essential to any competent mediator. No single publication or training program, however, can provide all of the information, skill, and practical experience needed to be a competent practitioner. Most states or territories have standards of practice for mediators, and the information in this book covers only one portion of those standards. We encourage readers to explore the standards of practice in their home state or territory and to engage in supervised practice before venturing out as mediators.

Summary

The process of mediation is not new. In fact, many cultures dating back thousands of years have used some form of mediation in maintaining the health of their societies. Mediation offers disputants interest-based opportunities to play an active part in the resolution of conflict, instead of relying on a third party to make a decision for them. Other approaches to resolving disputes exist, such as rights-based approaches and power-based approaches. There are benefits and disadvantages to each type of resolution process, and all have an important role in society. People from all walks of life practice mediation, either as a career or as part of another vocation.

Disputants come to mediation from many divergent paths. Some are referred, some mandated to attend, and some find mediation on their own. All disputants are looking for satisfaction of their needs, which are categorized into substantive, procedural, and psychological interests.

Litigation, or the adjudication process, is a rights-based approach to resolving conflict. Alternative dispute resolution (ADR) offers paths other than litigation. ADR approaches include arbitration (binding and nonbinding), med-arb, mediation, and personal conflict management. Each method differs in where the locus of control lies for decision making.

Most cultural traditions have some type of ADR process for handling conflicts. In the United States, the ADR movement was influenced by needs of business and government, as well as by cultural and religious traditions. Subsequently, there are many different approaches to mediation—leading to much confusion about what mediation entails. This text covers a pure, interest-based **mediation model**, with roots in the European American traditions of neutrality and impartiality. People who are beginning the study of mediation should be aware of the standards of practice in their state or territory. Becoming a practicing mediator requires much more than taking a class or reading a book.

Portfolio Assignments

Portfolio Assignment 1.1: Starting Your Mediator Portfolio

The mediator portfolio contains information, tools, and worksheets. The "Portfolio" assignments will help each student build a personal toolkit of items to use during a mediation session. These materials will be kept in a three-ring binder with removable pages. Bring the mediator portfolio with you each day you attend training or class.

The first assignment is to secure a three-ring binder and tabs to create sections within the binder. Label the first few tabs as follows: opening statement, forms, mediation techniques, and profession information. Future portfolio assignments will direct you in the content that should be placed in each section.

CHAPTER 2

The Basic Components of Mediation

Philosophical Assumptions   20
   Transformative Approach   20
   Problem-Solving Approach   21
Functional Models   22
Integrating Philosophies   23
Variables That Make a Difference in Mediation Models   24
   Pre-Mediation or No Pre-Mediation   24
   Allow Uninterrupted Disputant First Statements or Control When and How Long Each Person Speaks   25
   Allow, Require, or Forbid Private Meetings between the Mediator and the Parties   25
   Require an Agenda before Negotiating, Negotiate as You Go, or Slide Back and Forth between Issue
      Identification and Negotiation   26
   Consider the Parts of the Mediation as Functional Phases or as Chronological Steps   26
   Focus on the Problem, the Emotions, or Balance Problems and Emotions   26
   Prescribe Automatic First Moves within Phases or Allow Mediator Choice   27
   Allowing or Prohibiting Parties to Speak to Each Other   27
   Writing and Signing or Not Signing Agreements   27
Phases in the Balanced Mediation Model   28
   Pre-Mediation   29
   Mediation Session   30
   Post-Mediation   33
Does Culture Matter in Mediation?   34
Summary   36

Mediation is a term that encompasses a wide array of models, strategies, and outcomes. Because the profession of mediation encompasses so much variety, we cannot simply offer a "mediation model" without first determining the philosophical underpinnings guiding the purpose of mediation. Before we can answer the question "How do we mediate?" we must first establish our reasons for mediating. In this chapter, we discuss assumptions that guide the choices mediators make, compare several models, present the **balanced mediation model** used in this book, and consider how culture impacts mediation.

The phases, steps, or processes recommended for specific mediation contexts are organized into what are termed *mediation models*. Different models of mediation are used throughout the world and vary according to their philosophical approach to **conflict management style**, the emphasis given to specific components, and the unique demands of specialized contexts. What mediation models share in common is that once a model is adopted, it becomes a prescription for what will and will not happen during a mediation session—what is essential and what is forbidden.

PHILOSOPHICAL ASSUMPTIONS

Every choice a mediator makes throughout the process alters the course of the mediation. Determining "why we mediate" provides a direction for those choices. There are two primary philosophical approaches to mediation: the transformative approach and the problem-solving approach.

Transformative Approach

The goal of **transformative mediation** (also called conciliatory mediation) is to build healthy relationships, improve communication between parties, create understanding, and promote healthy communities. Robert A. Baruch Bush and Joseph P. Folger, in their 1994 book *The Promise of Mediation,* capture the spirit of reconciliation in their exploration of transformative mediation.

Bush and Folger (1994) believe every choice is biased on the mediator's worldview and past experience. A major concern for Bush and Folger is the "bias to settle," which they view as a weakness of the problem-solving approach where mediators subtly influence the parties toward settlement. Instead of focusing on the problems to be solved, the transformative mediator should focus on the growth of the individuals.

Transformation mediators assist the parties in discovering their personal values, empower the disputants' inner strengths, and help each person to recognize and empathize with the other party. **Self-determination** (letting the parties make their own decisions) is of paramount consideration (Noce, Bush, & Folger, 2002). Transformative mediators arrive with a mental map and list of questions to help the parties through a journey of self-discovery that may or may not lead to problem resolution. From this perspective, mediators assume that once the parties are transformed, problem solving will follow naturally.

The transformative approach is neither unconcerned with the issues in a conflict nor uninterested in resolution. The hallmark of this approach lies in the mediator's acumen in transforming the conflicting individuals from adversaries to collaborators. The by-product of this approach will be a transformed relationship where the conflict is addressed in light of who the parties are to one another.

CASE 2.1: My Old Friend Is My New Boss

Reymundo and Noah work together in the same department at a warehouse distributing company as supply clerks. They graduated in the same year from Central High School, but they didn't know each other well at that time. While working at the same firm for the last two years, they have become good friends, sometimes getting together after work for a cold drink.

A few weeks ago, the section manager quit. The company posted the job opening, which included a substantial raise and other promotion opportunities down the road. Reymundo and Noah both applied for the job. After saying it was a "close decision," the company promoted Reymundo. The company said that Reymundo had been taking management classes at the university at night and that gave him the edge.

On the first day Reymundo became the section manager, Noah arrived at work 20 minutes after the start of shift. The previous manager always asked Noah to pick up the monthly reports on the 10th of each month. Noah picked the reports up in the main office across the complex without thinking about it because it was the regular routine. When Noah arrived at his workstation, the first words from Reymundo's mouth were "You're late and I can't overlook it just because we're friends." Noah was stunned and thought, "Wow! My former friend has turned into a tyrant already." Noah spent the rest of the day fuming over how he was embarrassed in front of the rest of the staff.

When there was some slack time that afternoon, Reymundo thought he should follow up on the lateness issue and find out more about what was going on—maybe he was a little abrupt that morning. When the afternoon break time arrived, Reymundo asked Noah to step into the break room for a cup of coffee. As he left to go outside, Noah replied, "There is no rule I have to spend my break time with my supervisor."

One week has passed. The friendship seems gone, and the work relationship is stressed. The strain between Noah and Reymundo has started to affect others at work. A special project that Reymundo and Noah were working on has ground to a halt. The general manager of the company sent Reymundo and Noah to mediation.

Problem-Solving Approach

Problem-solving mediation generally assumes that, regardless of the context or the people involved, mediation is about helping people resolve their substantive issues. In the process of helping people resolve their issues, mediators *may or may not* delve into the emotional aspects that caused the conflict and *may or may not* help the individuals improve their relationship and communicative habits. A problem-solving mediator usually subscribes to a model with a more orderly and stately movement from one phase of the process to another, culminating in negotiation and settlement on the problem that brought the individuals to mediation.

Small claims mediation programs typically use the problem-solving approach. These cases involve parties who do not have a long-standing relationship and who may never see each other again. For example, determining restitution for a damaged car fender or settling a disagreement about water rights on adjacent properties might be what brings the parties to **court-annexed mediation**. The problem-solving approach focuses the mediation on the solutions that will resolve the issues that gave rise to the complaint.

Discussion Question 2.1

IS A conciliation or problem-solving approach better for Reymundo and Noah in Case 2.1? If conciliation needs and substantive issues exist in the same case, which should be worked on first?

FUNCTIONAL MODELS

Most mediation models are *functional,* meaning they focus on tasks that must be performed (or results that must be achieved) in a sequential order. At its most basic, a functional mediation model has several steps, with each one requiring unique mediator skills and processes. For example, Kathy Domenici and Stephen W. Littlejohn (2001, pp. 63–98) posit a four-step model with subfunctions embedded within each step:

1. Introduction (of parties, words of encouragement, explanation of process, ask questions prior to beginning)

2. Storytelling

3. Problem solving (defining the problem, agenda-setting, option generation)

4. Resolution (including closure)

There are innumerable varieties of functional models. Some models are very prescriptive and require that a specific skill be applied at a particular point during the mediation session. For example, a model might require a **caucus** where the mediator speaks with each individual separately. Other models may prohibit the mediator from bringing the parties together in the same room. Models have been created for panels of two or three mediators. Cross-cultural models focus on establishing shared understanding (United States Institute of Peace, 2001). Community mediation programs using volunteers with minimal training sometimes adopt a "trust the model" philosophy that involves lock-step phases proven to be effective with relatively simple cases involving neighbors. The therapeutic family mediation model includes an assessment step to detect families with violence or other issues that could make child custody mediation problematic (Irving & Benjamin, 2002). Juvenile victim–offender models include steps that change depending on the age of the offender. Public school or playground peer mediation models are simplified to fit the sophistication level of child mediators. One peer mediation model for grades 6 through 12 (Cohen, R., 2005, p. 209) instructs the adult coordinator to select and screen the cases that are then mediated by students using a five-step model similar to Domenici and Littlejohn's (2001):

1. Agree to solve the conflict

2. Explain the conflict

3. Brainstorm possible solutions

4. Choose a solution

5. Do the solution

INTEGRATING PHILOSOPHIES

James R. Antes, Donna Turner Hudson, Erling O. Jorgensen, and Janet Kelly Moen (1999) observe that mediation models claiming to have steps rarely have strict adherence to their rules. Many factors affect the flow of a mediation session. For example, someone may balk at the end of negotiation because that disputant has unresolved interests that were not discovered earlier. Other anomalies include skipping stages or using the steps out of sequence; reaching solutions without the aid of the mediator; and mediators affecting the substance of the mediation, not just the process. As Antes et al. contend, "good things happen even without reaching agreement" (pp. 288–291). A strict step model may prove too rigid for actual practice.

Antes et al. (1999) suggest the *facets of mediation model* to embrace the conciliation philosophy and to correct the anomalies in a lock-step perspective. The mediator completes a set of nonsequential tasks that address several questions:

- What are we doing here?

- What is this about?

- What is important to self?

- What is important to other?

- What do we do? (p. 293)

The *balanced mediation model* in this book has an inherent problem-solving orientation, but one that is strongly influenced by the desire to engage in **reconciliation** strategies when appropriate. We also acknowledge that mediation phases may progress in a nonlinear fashion. To balance the transformative and problem-solving functions, a mediator must be aware of the many choices to be made throughout the course of a mediation and be aware of the possible consequences to the process of each choice.

CASE 2.2: What's Best for Eli?

Jodi is a single mom of two boys ages six and four. She lives in the small town of Ridgeman—population 2,400. Jodi's six-year-old has an emotional and attention deficit disorder manifesting in high impulsivity and aggressiveness whenever he is frustrated. Eli has hit and kicked his first grade teacher, Miss Davies, on more than one occasion. Although she was not injured, Miss Davies is worried about the safety of her other 23 students and how Eli's behavior may affect the entire class. Miss Davies is a first-year teacher and feels stress from the extra time spent dealing with Eli's behaviors. Eli's special education plan states he is to have an aide available at all times, and the school district hired a young student teacher to fill that role.

In October, Eli was frustrated by a handwriting assignment and threw a pencil at Miss Davies, missing her and hitting a classmate. Miss Davies sent him to the office for the tenth time that year. The Vice Principal suspended Eli for five days and called Jodi, Eli's mom, to pick him up. During the five-day suspension, Jodi and the special education team met to determine how best to handle Eli. The school personnel presented Jodi with the option of bussing Eli to a special school 30 miles away. Confused and overwhelmed, Jodi felt pressured to agree.

Jodi decided to research her legal options. She discovered Eli has a right to a specialist trained to manage emotional disorders and that the school district is required by law to develop a plan to manage Eli's outbursts. She doesn't want Eli to be bussed 30 miles away. Ridgeman Elementary is feeling pressure from other parents not to let Eli back into the classroom. Miss Davies cares about Eli and worries that Eli's return will not be good for anyone involved. As required by law, the State Department of Education provided a special education mediation specialist to help the parties work through these issues.

VARIABLES THAT MAKE A DIFFERENCE IN MEDIATION MODELS

Our analysis of the principles discussed earlier uncovered several variables that—when included or excluded—dramatically alter the flow of the mediated session and the experiences of the disputing parties. The variables and the skills introduced in this chapter will be discussed in later chapters in more depth.

Pre-Mediation or No Pre-Mediation

Some models depend on the mediator (or someone working on the mediator's behalf) to screen the case in advance of the mediation session. The disputants are interviewed during *intake* to discover their issues and the appropriateness of the case for mediation. In other models, **pre-mediation** or screening never occurs and the mediator starts the session cold—with no knowledge of the issues or the disputants. Pre-mediation is a standard procedure in victim–offender mediation where the comfort and safety of the victim is paramount. Some divorce and family mediators use pre-mediation meetings to ascertain family dynamics and safety issues in high-conflict situations. In the case of Reymundo and Noah, in-depth pre-mediation probably would not be used, as the parties can be educated about the process during the opening statement phase. In Case 2.2, the mediator would pre-mediate separately with the parents and the school district to determine issues so the agenda for a meeting with limited time includes the concerns of all parties.

Allow Uninterrupted Disputant First Statements or Control When and How Long Each Person Speaks

Some models (see Beer and Stief, 1997) provide time for disputants to speak without interruption from the other party or the mediator—occasionally with no limits to the length of time a person may speak! Other models assume the mediator will actively, but constructively, interrupt the disputants to validate emotions, clarify ambiguities, reduce negativity, summarize, focus on the immediate task, or divert attacks on the other party. In the case of Reymundo and Noah, allowing uninterrupted comments at the outset probably would lead to an extensive diatribe against the other person—behavior not helpful to the goals of mediation. When accusatory comments persist, the mediator may choose to interrupt the negative trend with emotional paraphrases, reframes, or other skills to moderate emotionality. In the more formal setting with Eli's school in Case 2.2, however, allowing Jodi an uninterrupted chance to share her fears might be appropriate and cathartic.

Allow, Require, or Forbid Private Meetings between the Mediator and the Parties

A *caucus* is required by some models—a **private meeting** during the session between the mediator and each disputant. When time is short, the caucus can be used to speed up negotiation about distributive issues (like money). A few models forbid use of a caucus. Most models present the caucus as an option that the mediator may employ strategically. Even then, how a caucus is conducted varies. Some models require that if a meeting is held with one party, then the mediator must meet with the second party. Other approaches allow mediators to meet with only one person and then to return to the session. What is discussed in caucus in most models is considered confidential communication, although some models may allow the mediator to provide a range of offers to both parties derived from information garnered in caucus. Parties must be apprised of the **confidentiality** parameters of the caucus prior to any disclosure of information.

In the mediation between Reymundo and Noah, the parties were reluctant to talk to each other at the outset. In a private meeting with each disputant, the mediator explored the feelings that were preventing the discussion from moving forward. After discovering that they only had one negative encounter immediately after Reymundo's promotion, the mediator restarted the session with questions to draw out each individual's feelings. In the case with Eli's school, the mediator asked pointed questions to help the district explore its legal obligations in a caucus outside Jodi's presence.

Require an Agenda before Negotiating, Negotiate as You Go, or Slide Back and Forth between Issue Identification and Negotiation

Some mediators establish an agenda of specific issues that will be negotiated, usually after fairly lengthy information giving by the disputants and probing by the mediator. In these models, negotiation of issues is withheld until after the agenda is established, even if one or more of the parties make offers during opening remarks. Other models do not emphasize the establishment of a formal agenda and permit the mediator either to negotiate issues as they arise or to flow from issues identification to negotiation without an agenda.

After the **storytelling** phase, the mediator deduced that two issues needed to be settled between Reymundo and Noah: (1) How could they communicate more effectively at work? and (2) What specifically could each party do to move their special project to completion? In Case 2.2, a very formal agenda was created because of the complexity of the concerns and the legal issues surrounding the case.

Consider the Parts of the Mediation as Functional Phases or as Chronological Steps

Most models present functional steps that emphasize what the mediator should accomplish during a particular portion or phase of the mediation, with an acknowledgment that the phases are not written in stone. A few models, particularly those intended for use by children or mediators with relatively little training, are extremely prescriptive in the presentation of chronological steps—even to the point of a manuscript of what the mediator should say at particular times during the session.

Approaching the mediation process as functional rather than as strict steps allows the mediator leeway in addressing concerns as they arise. For example, it is not unusual during the problem-solving phase for parties to blame each other for the situation. When recrimination occurs during negotiation, the mediator uses **emotional paraphrasing** or other skills to moderate the strong feelings—even though these skills are more common to an earlier phase where storytelling occurs. In Eli's case, Miss Davies was quiet during the early phases of the process, but as the agreement began to take shape, she wanted to tell Jodi about her love for Eli. Recognizing that the teacher's story was important to the relationship between parent and teacher, the mediator interrupted the agreement-writing process to encourage her reflections.

Focus on the Problem, the Emotions, or Balance Problems and Emotions

Models differ on what the mediator is expected to do. Some focus exclusively on substantive issues, such as "How much is the car worth?" or "What is the amount of the cleaning deposit to be returned, if any?" Transformative models focus mostly on psychological or emotional causes of conflict, such as "How did you feel when Reymundo's first words as a supervisor were criticism of you?" or "What concerns you as a parent about Eli riding the bus?"

In Case 2.1, because Reymundo and Noah had a friendship and have an ongoing work relationship, both emotions and substantive issues arise in their case. If the mediator focuses only on the substantive issue of the project, a large portion of the underlying problem would continue to fester. If the mediator focused only on the friendship, opportunities to improve workplace efforts might be missed. Likewise, because Eli will be a student at the Ridgeman School District for several years, building trust between parent and school is wiser than just focusing on the substantive legal facts.

Prescribe Automatic First Moves within Phases or Allow Mediator Choice

A few models contain specific opening moves within particular phases. For example, a model might prescribe that one *must brainstorm* (a problem-solving technique that will be discussed in Chapter 9) at the beginning of the negotiation phase. Most models prefer that the mediator select an opening move to fit the unique circumstance of each situation. In the case of Reymundo and Noah, the mediator chose to start the problem-solving phase with a question directed to both parties: "What ideas do either of you have to improve your work communication that would be good for both of you and the company?" In Eli's case, the mediator could start by asking Jodi what strategies she uses at home to manage Eli's angry outbursts.

Allowing or Prohibiting Parties to Speak to Each Other

Even when the parties are in the same room, a few models don't allow them to speak directly to each other. In other contexts where extreme power imbalances exist, a history of violence is present, or other safety issues arise, mediators may place disputants in different rooms and *shuttle* back and forth between them or conduct the session by phone or via the Web. However, most mediation models prefer face-to-face contact.

In the cases in this chapter, it makes sense to let the parties who have a continuing relationship talk to each other and to keep them in the same room. However, because emotions are high in each of these cases, the mediator may request that the parties only talk to her during the early stages of the session and only allow disputants to converse directly when emotions are calmer.

Writing and Signing or Not Signing Agreements

Agreement formats vary widely depending on the purpose of the mediation. Some agreements must follow specific formats initiated by a company, regulatory agency, court, or program. Other agreements are for the disputants' eyes only. In some states that have adopted the standards in the **Uniform Mediation Act**, written agreements are required or strongly encouraged. Agreements will be discussed in Chapter 10.

In the case of Reymundo and Noah, the mediator recorded the points of agreement, each party signed the agreement before closing the session, and the mediator made copies for each individual. In Eli's school case, the state agency required a written and signed agreement. In workplace and other contexts of mediation, the parties will want to know prior to the session whether the agreement will be private between the two of them, if it will be placed in their personnel files, or if it is open to other forms of public disclosure.

Discussion Question 2.2

REFLECT ON variables that affect a case. What might happen in the Reymundo and Noah mediation if the mediator made any of the following choices?

1. Allowing uninterrupted talk from each party

2. Holding a private meeting with each party

3. Focusing mostly on the emotions of the parties or mostly on the special project

4. Not allowing parties to speak to one another during the mediation

5. Not writing a formal agreement

6. Having the agreement private between the parties or sharing the agreement with their supervisor

---

PHASES IN THE BALANCED MEDIATION MODEL

This book presents the *balanced mediation model* as a useful approach for beginning mediators. The balanced model contains functional phases that were selected to cover the necessary components and skills essential to entry-level mediation or for skill enhancement of practicing mediators. As the mediator enters a specific arena of mediation (victim–offender, community, business, environment, child custody, and so on), the model of mediation practiced in the field may vary considerably from the balanced model presented in this book. However, the balanced model introduces the primary concepts and skills essential to most models of mediation. Chapters 3 and 11 discuss mediator competencies in more detail.

The balanced mediation model (Figure 2.1) is a *phased approach*. We assume, however, that the phases are fluid and that the mediator will return in a cyclical fashion to previous phases as new information, issues, or emotional barriers emerge. In addition, the model offered is a *balanced approach,* focusing on both the relational dynamics of the parties and the content aspects of the issues. The balanced model teaches a variety of skills and options so the mediator can adapt to the unfolding needs of each specific case. This chapter outlines the phases of the balanced model. Each aspect will be discussed in-depth in later chapters.

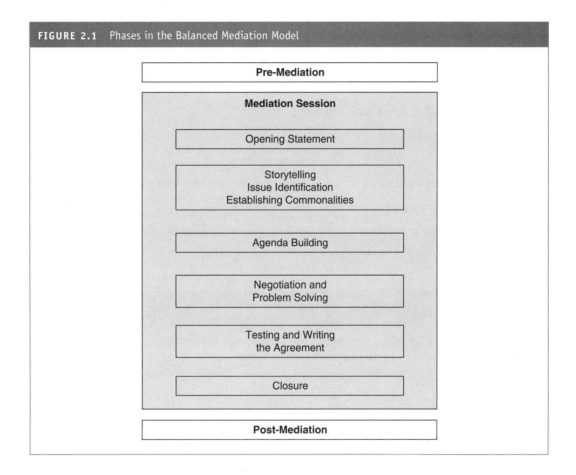

FIGURE 2.1 Phases in the Balanced Mediation Model

Pre-Mediation

Pre-mediation includes all activities that occur before the mediation session begins. Contact with the parties usually is desirable and often is necessary to persuade one or both parties that mediation is a good option for resolving their disagreement. While not all contexts of mediation allow for pre-mediation, mediators should be knowledgeable of, and competent in, pre-mediation activities when the need arises.

Pre-mediation serves three general purposes. First, if one party has contacted the mediator unilaterally, the mediator must approach the other person to determine her or his willingness to mediate. Second, pre-mediation is a time to discover who is involved and should come to the mediation session, develop a preliminary sense of the issues, and determine the presence of power imbalances or other unique personal dynamics. Third, during pre-mediation, the mediator has an opportunity to educate the parties about the process and to begin building trustworthiness and credibility.

Pre-mediation is discussed in Chapter 4. Activities during pre-mediation may include:

- Establishing initial contact with one or both parties
- Determining information about the parties and the conflict
- Gathering of documents about the conflict
- Creating a case file
- Distributing mediation forms and documents
- Screening for appropriateness of issues in comparison with the mediator's skill
- Selecting an appropriate time and place for the session
- Assigning "homework" to the parties to prepare for the session
- Building trust in the mediator and the mediation process

Discussion Question 2.3

CONSIDER THE benefits and drawbacks if the mediator conducted or did not conduct pre-mediation activities in the two cases in this chapter.

Mediation Session

During the session, the mediator leads the disputants through a series of phases. The phases are sequential in the sense that most of the functions of one phase must be accomplished to make success in the next phase more likely. However, it is incorrect to think of the phases as a linear, one-way, lock-step procedure. Mediators often move back and forth across phases, as each unique case requires. This chapter highlights the functions that occur in each phase, with later chapters delving more deeply into the details.

Mediator Opening Statement

The opening of a session is the time when the mediator presents information and establishes a desired tone. The **opening statement**, sometimes called the **mediator monologue**, fulfills several functions. It is important to note that every mediation does not require all items. The opening statement functions to:

- Welcome the parties to the mediation
- Introduce the mediator to the parties and the parties to each other
- Provide information about the mediator's credibility
- Confirm that the right people are at the mediation table

- Explain the nature and scope of mediation

- Detail the mediator's role

- Disclose that there might be private meetings with each party

- Define neutrality and impartiality

- Convey the confidentiality pledge and its limitations

- Reveal the purpose of the mediator's notes

- Establish rules for communication

- State the session length and other logistics

- Establish the role of outside resources or experts

- Secure a commitment to begin

- Transition to the storytelling and issue identification phase

The mediator chooses which functions from the list apply to each specific mediation context. The mediator's opening statement and associated skills are presented in Chapter 6.

Storytelling and Issue Identification

The name of this phase, storytelling and issue identification, is descriptive of the two functions that occur simultaneously once the disputants begin to speak. The mediator encourages disputants to tell their perspectives. As disputants relate what brought them to the point of needing third-party assistance, the mediator inserts a series of skills (discussed in Chapters 3 and 7) to reduce any emotional barriers to settlement. At the same time, the mediator listens to the stories for the relevant facts concerning the disputants' past relationship and the problems at hand, deducing from the facts a list of the issues to be negotiated. The mediator then can create a plan based on the type of issues that stand between the disputants and settlement and strategize how to proceed during the agenda and negotiation phases.

In the Case 2.1, Noah began by saying, "I couldn't believe it when on his first day as a supervisor, Reymundo became a management tyrant." This statement is informative to the mediator in several ways. First, the tone of the phrasing might suggest Reymundo is emotional about the situation, leading the mediator to think of ways to bring the feeling part of the story to the table. Second, Noah is pointing to the issue of respect or friendship as being very important to him. The mediator would note this relational issue to explore later. If, however, both parties were disinterested in a future relationship, the mediator would skip over relationship-building elements and focus more on the substantive issues. For example, in a landlord–tenant case, the parties may have no continuing relationship and will never see each other after an issue about the cleaning deposit is settled. In general practice, mediators often face a dual need to explore substantive and relationship issues, taking their cues from the parties on what is important to them.

As the disputants tell their stories, the mediator also listens for what the two individuals have in common. At strategic points, the mediator will reveal these commonalities to the disputants—trying to stimulate a mutual bond or a motivation to resolve the problem together. In the case of Reymundo and Noah, each claimed that he wanted to be effective at work and treat the other person fairly. Their recognition of this **commonality** of purpose allowed the mediator to bring the two employees to a place where they could problem solve around the issue of effective workplace communication.

Mediators also work to enable the disputants to hear each other's concerns and to create a level of understanding even though they may still disagree about the facts. By focusing on the *interests* of the disputants (their underlying needs), mediators help them gain perspective from the other's point of view. People experiencing conflict often are so caught up in their emotions that they stop listening and literally cannot understand others' feelings or be open to a different point of view. A mediator works to frame one person's story into words that are less threatening and, thereby, easier to listen to (but always being cautious to avoid appearing to take sides). Chapter 7 details skills and mediator choices during storytelling, issue identification, and establishment of commonalities.

Agenda Building

In the balanced mediation model, we highlight setting an **agenda** as a separate phase. Experienced mediators may be successful intermixing storytelling and issue identification with negotiation activities. Novice mediators need to learn to distinguish between the skills of fact-finding and the skills of negotiation, as well as mastering how to set an agenda. The mediator's frame for the agenda links the two disputants together in searching for an outcome that is acceptable to each party. For example, a mediator might say, "From what I have heard thus far, what the two of you say you need is to find is a solution that enables Reymundo to meet his responsibilities as a manager while honoring the friendship the two of you have." The principles and skills to establish an agenda are presented in Chapter 8.

Negotiating and Problem Solving

During the negotiation and problem-solving phase, the mediator determines an order in which to address the issues, whether to treat each issue separately or combine them, and other strategic options. Communication techniques are applied to assist the parties in:

- Generating options for settlement

- Assessing options for settlement

- Making, modifying, rejecting, or accepting offers

The negotiation phase is a good example of how mediation steps are not linear. A return to storytelling and fact elaboration may be prudent if disputants reveal new information about the situation or hidden issues emerge. The tactical choices and skills necessary to assist disputants during negotiation are detailed in Chapter 9.

Testing and Writing Settlement Agreements

Once a tentative agreement is reached on each of the issues on the agenda, the mediator leads the disputants in a revision of each point in the agreement, testing for specificity and workability. Because this book presents the theory and skills of basic mediation, settlement writing is highlighted with its own phase. Poorly written mediation agreements that disputants interpret differently can cause more damage than good. For example, if roommates agree to "respect each other's time for studying," but they do not determine what "respect" means for each of them, the agreement is open to interpretation. If Sarah wants to have a party on Friday night, Elli can say, "That isn't very respectful!" But Sarah could argue that having it on Friday instead of Sunday is very respectful. Only when the agreement is clear, unambiguous, and understood by both parties in the same way should an agreement be solidified. If the disputants do not reach agreement, the mediator will move to closure without a settlement or schedule additional sessions.

A key point in the balanced approach, however, is that writing agreements is not the goal of mediation, nor is it a measure of the mediator's success. Knowing how to assist in agreeing to disagree or closing a session without an agreement is as important as agreement writing. Seasoned mediators recognize that not all mediations end in settlement and lack of settlement does not indicate a failed mediation. Chapter 10 presents the skills of agreement writing and **closure**.

Closure

Once the agreement is signed, the disputants reach an insurmountable deadlock, or the session must end for some other reason, the mediator moves to closure. In sessions ending in agreement, the mediator will praise the disputants for their work, acquire signatures on the agreement form, make all parties a copy of the written agreement (if there is one), and inform the parties of any **post-mediation** actions. In sessions that do not result in settlement, the mediator will summarize any enhanced understanding or points of commonality for the parties or explain other options the disputants can take. Often the closure of a mediation that does not end in agreement starts a new topic of what the next steps are in moving forward from there.

Discussion Question 2.4

HOW DOES an online mediation environment affect the choices a mediator may make in structuring a mediation? What would be fundamentally different in the online context from a face-to-face mediation? Are there some types of mediation that would be inappropriate in an online environment?

Post-Mediation

After the session, several actions may be required. It is atypical for the mediator to have a role in enforcing or monitoring the agreement. However, the mediator may engage in the following activities:

- Follow-up evaluation of the mediator's skillfulness or disputant satisfaction

- Typing final agreements

- Filing case records if required by agencies or courts

- Destroying notes

- Billing the disputants for services, as appropriate

- Discussing the case with superiors or co-mediators

DOES CULTURE MATTER IN MEDIATION?

The approach to mediation described in this book is a European American model. Each culture brings assumptions to mediation. Most European Americans believe that a mediator should be an impartial and neutral stranger. They also expect that the other person in the conflict will be direct about what the problem is and that conversation should proceed in an orderly and rational process where one person speaks at a time. Other cultures may feel these behaviors are odd, rude, or improper. For example, some Native American tribes (as well as other cultures) would prefer someone known to both parties, who cares about each of them and understands their background and values. The use of intermediaries to negotiate conflicts has a long tradition in Hawaii where an extended family member fulfills the mediator or *haku* role. In many cultures, neutrality is not as important as a familiar person who has a stake in making sure the family or community remains peaceful (Ma, 1992).

Although understanding culture and how it impacts mediation is an advanced topic, the pervasiveness of cultural issues justifies its introduction in this basic textbook. Culture theories describe some of the ways groups approach conflict. For example, Mitchell R. Hammer (2002, 2005) argues cultural groups differ in their preferences on how to express emotion during conflict and how directly to speak about issues. Most European Americans and Northern Europeans prefer direct speech and restrained expression of emotion (**discussant cultural conflict style**). Eastern Europeans and some Black Americans exhibit direct speech and more passionate expression of emotions (**engagement cultural conflict style**). Many Southeastern Asian and Native American groups learn to be more indirect in discussing issues (to maintain social harmony) and to be restrained in emotional expression (**accommodation cultural conflict style**). Arab culture suggests exuberant expression of emotion is appropriate while using more indirect communication about issues (**dynamic cultural conflict style**).

Mediators can learn several lessons from the study of Hammer's (2002, 2005) cultural typology. (1) Some disputants believe starting a conversation with a direct expression of the conflict is rude or embarrassing. More pre-mediation work or general background conversation may be needed before getting into the heart of the issue with those who prefer indirect expression of issues. With disputants at the extreme ends of the **directness**-to-indirectness continuum, **shuttle mediation** may be the most efficient method, as the mediator can adapt to each disputant's **style**. (2) When one disputant is from a high emotionally expressive culture and the other is from a low one, the mismatch may make everyone uncomfortable (including the mediator). The high expression of emotion may be frightening to those unfamiliar with cultures that are louder, more exuberant, and use bigger gestures. Conversely, the low expression of emotion may be perceived as a lack of involvement or caring by those who prefer more energetic conversations. The mediator must parse what behaviors mean in their cultural contexts. Is a loud disputant trying to intimidate the other party or just from a highly expressive culture? Some Black Americans prefer a more emotionally expressive style of communication. If a mediator works with two Black American disputants who share a very expressive style, should the mediator follow the narrow strictures of the European American model or allow a more energetic exchange (see Davidheiser, 2008)? A study of culture raises many questions about how a mediator chooses to control the flow of a session.

Geert Hofstede's dimensions provide a starting point for a general study of culture. Using his website, a mediator could compare the general cultural characteristics of two cultures along five dimensions (see www.geert-hofstede.com): **power distance**, **individualistic culture/collectivist culture**, masculinity/femininity, long- vs. short-term orientation, and **uncertainty avoidance**. *Power distance* indicates a group's comfort with social stratification and authority. Disputants from high power-distance cultures may have distinct expectations that lower status individuals should defer to those in higher status, creating an inequitable condition in a mediation session. Likewise, high power-distance individuals will expect more direction from a high-status mediator. The *individualism/collectivism* dimension describes a cultural group's preference for a group identity or individual identity. Highly collective cultures may accept settlements that seem not in their personal best interest if issues are framed in terms of a larger social good. The *masculinity/femininity* dimension indicates a group's preference for competition for material rewards or social cooperation. *Uncertainty avoidance* identifies cultures that tolerate ambiguity and those who are uncomfortable with change or uncertain social situations. Individuals who are uncertainty averse would require very specific terms in any agreement, with contingency clauses to cover options that might arise. *Short- vs. long-term* thinking divides cultures by a value for resolving immediate issues and those who consider the immediate issue to be just one part of social relationships that extend back in time and into the future. Fatahillah Abdul Syuker and Dale Margaret Bagshaw (2013) argued that the use of a Western model of court-annexed mediation with a focus on short-term outcomes led to its lack of success in Indonesia where long-term group harmony is a cultural value. Navajo nation members who are accustomed to a well-known spiritual or community member acting as a mediator who restores peace (Pinto, 2000) might feel uncomfortable with the European American mediation model using a neutral and **impartial** third party.

Mediators should be aware of their personal cultural expectations and preferences, as well as those of their disputants. For example, Molly Inman, Roudabeh Kishi, Jonathan Wilkenfeld, Michele Gelfand, and Elizabeth Salmon (2013) warned that international mediation across cultures may put in-groups with out-groups, causing **stereotypes** and ethnocentrism to flourish. These effects also can arise in small-scale mediation sessions that cross cultural divides. Cultural traits can impact the choices a mediator makes during the process. Morgan Brigg (2003) explains how the Western mediator's goal is to create a place for rational individual expression that moves toward interpersonal peace—a perspective that could perplex disputants from other cultures. Although this book presents a European American approach to mediation, understanding and being open to modifying the model to embrace cultural dynamics is important. Skilled mediators are adept at recognizing and mitigating their personal cultural assumptions, as well as at recognizing when the disputants may be operating from differing cultural worldviews. As you learn the model of mediation presented in this text, challenge yourself to find areas where cultural expectations could affect parties' interpretations of the process.

Discussion Question 2.5

WHAT CULTURES are nearby in your location? How might these cultures' views of how to conduct conflict be different from your personal views?

Summary

The theoretical assumptions a mediator holds affect how a mediation proceeds. Transformative and problem-solving philosophies of mediation present the most striking differences. Conciliation mediation focuses primarily on building relationships and creating understanding between parties. Problem-solving mediation focuses on the process of issue resolution.

Determining "why we mediate" helps mediators make informed choices about the techniques and models they will use. An integrated model of mediation called the balanced mediation model incorporates both a reconciliation and a problem-solving approach. Unlike lock-step models that offer no room for adapting to fit the specific situation, the phases in the balanced mediation model are more flexible. This model is a teaching tool to master the key skills of mediation. The basic mediation model includes pre-mediation, mediation, and post-mediation. During the session, a mediator will proceed through an opening statement, storytelling and issue identification, establishing an agenda, negotiation and problem solving, agreement testing and writing, and closure.

Culture can impact how the disputants perceive each other or the mediator, and vice versa. Mediators should acquire basic culture theory knowledge, as well as specific information about specific cultural groups in their service area. The next chapter presents some basic skills deemed essential for entry-level mediators.

CHAPTER 3

Essential Skills for Mediators

An Overview of Mediator Skills	**38**
Trusting and Controlling the Process	**39**
Trusting the Process	40
Controlling the Process	41
Listening: A Bedrock Skill for Mediators	**42**
Types of Listening	43
Variables That Affect Listening	43
Skills for Listening to Content, Emotion, and Relationship	46
Reframing Messages	**50**
Listening to Nonverbal Communication	**52**
Clarifying and Asking Questions	**53**
Open versus Closed Questions	53
Genuinely Curious Questions	54
Honoring Silence	**54**
Listening Interculturally	**55**
Ethical Issues and Listening	**56**
Summary	**56**
Portfolio Assignment 3.1: Emotional Paraphrases	**57**
Portfolio Assignment 3.2: The Open-Ended Question	**57**

"What makes a good mediator?" is a question often posed by students pursuing mediation training. Mediators juggle many roles simultaneously in the course of their work. First and foremost, though, mediators are good communicators.

Mediators facilitate the process within a session. They ensure that the focus of the discussion stays on target and that the disputants move toward productive outcomes. Mediators listen to the disputants' stories, allow them to vent their frustrations, validate each person's worth or feelings, and provide appropriate feedback. Mediators are conduits of information. They encourage disputants to share information and to understand each other's perspective. Mediators keep communication focused on important and relevant issues. They help disputants discover and express their interests and goals. Mediators are links to additional expertise, data, or resources that may be required to settle a dispute. They know the services available in their community and assist the parties to determine whether outside, objective data are required. Mediators are boundary keepers when they frame issues, moderate emotions, and contain the conflict within a productive range.

Mediators are adept at **multitasking**—simultaneously keeping an eye on the process, emotions, content, individuals, flow of information, power issues, verbal and nonverbal messages, and much more. Acquiring the fundamental tools that enable mediators to succeed is the first step in mastery of the art and practice of mediation. While the array of mediator skills may seem daunting, training and skill practice can build confidence and competence.

CASE 3.1: The Mistaken Grade

The dean of the College of Arts and Sciences referred a student grade appeal to the campus mediation center, hoping that the case could be resolved before it progressed to the formal grievance procedures. Both Valerie Smith, the student, and Mr. Washington agreed to mediate. A student and a professor associated with the mediation center on campus co-mediated the case.

After the opening statement, the mediators asked Valerie to start and to tell them what her feelings were about her grade. Valerie explained in very emotional terms that her work in the technical writing class was the same as the other students, but she received a "C" when other students received an "A." She didn't want to say why she thought that was happening, but it wasn't fair. Mr. Washington, an adjunct professor from a local corporation brought in to teach the class, related that he liked Valerie and enjoyed having her in class, but she hadn't put in as much effort as the other students on the practical project and that even though her grades were good on individual projects, he didn't think she had earned an "A."

AN OVERVIEW OF MEDIATOR SKILLS

To some extent, the skills of entry-level and advanced mediation are the same—the primary difference being the depth of accomplishment in each skill area. In other ways, the skills of

TABLE 3.1 The Mediator's General Attributes and Abilities

- Analyze situations and alternatives
- Use persuasion
- Listen actively
- Gather information through asking questions
- Provide effective feedback
- Show empathy without being patronizing
- Create multiple options
- Understand what can and cannot be mediated
- Master multiple strategies and techniques
- Know how to obtain a commitment to mediate
- Recognize difference between issues and interests
- Work within the mediator's personal limitations
- Comprehend the moral and legal issues in mediation
- Uphold the difference between mediation and other ADR processes
- Create appropriate ground rules
- Recognize how typical conflict types manifest
- Identify when and how to involve another available referral source
- Describe behavior nonjudgmentally
- Ask effective questions
- Deal with power imbalances

Source: Picard, 2002; Singer, 2001.

advanced mediators are quite different. Advanced mediators may specialize in a specific context or type of client, for example, child custody, divorce, victim–offender, real estate, special education, business, taxation, or environmental issues. Each client group and context requires advanced skills that extend beyond those of entry-level, general practice mediation.

Many theorists agree the skills necessary for mediator competency are a blend of theory and practice (Picard, 2002; Singer, 2001). Table 3.1 itemizes a mediator's general attributes and abilities.

Discussion Question 3.1
ARE THERE skills that can't be taught? What personal attitudes, philosophies, and experience do you already possess that will become positive mediator qualities? What new skills do you need to hone?

TRUSTING AND CONTROLLING THE PROCESS

One key competency that a mediator must attend to is *process fidelity*. As discussed in Chapter 2, the mediator must have a strong grasp of the philosophical differences inherent in each approach to mediation. Each model or philosophical choice demands certain skill sets from the mediator. The mediation model offers direction and guidance for orchestrating the session.

Trusting the Process

Trusting the process—the phases in a mediation model—is imperative for mediators. Sometimes even experienced mediators wonder whether things are progressing as they should. There is a constant temptation to jump to the end of the process by engaging in problem solving too early. To determine whether the process is on track, the mediator must be able to assess what stage the mediation is in and what to do next. Trusting that parties eventually will create their own agreements is easier to do when you know that the "process" works. For example, in one divorce mediation, there were a significant number of issues to work through (child custody, alimony, child support, and division of property). The mediation finally was nearing completion, with only one more issue to work through—dividing up one party's 401(k) retirement plan. The mediator, growing weary of a long session, opted to voice an opinion about what the parties should do, saying that they could be done if they just split the retirement fund down the middle, 50/50. The parties said, "Fine." The couple was scheduled to return the next day to pick up a draft of their agreement. Instead, both parties called to say they would not be coming as they decided they didn't like the agreement. Neither party felt ownership over the 401(k) decision. One intrusion by the mediator derailed all their hard work. In this case, the mediator lost focus on *impartiality toward the outcome* and ultimately wasted the time of all parties involved.

Sometimes just initiating the process will resolve the problem. Phillip and Marshall lived near each other off campus and were referred to a college mediation center by the police, who were called because Phillip's dog chased Marshall's daughter out of her front yard. After the mediator presented the opening monologue and his understanding of the issue that brought the two students to the mediation center, Phillip turned to Marshall and handed him a sheet of paper, saying, "Here's my phone number. The dog is supposed to be chained. It shouldn't happen again, but if it does, call me and I'll take care of it or get rid of the dog. I wouldn't want my kids threatened either." The neighbors, who had never met or spoken before, started a dialogue that improved their relationship without the mediator's assistance. While most cases are not this easy, the processes that comprise mediation are crafted for optimal efficiency and effectiveness. Trust the process.

Discussion Question 3.2

PURISTS VIEW the mediator who suggests solutions as overly **intrusive** into the disputants' outcome and either unskilled or unethical. Conversely, some mediation contexts allow intrusiveness. What are the consequences to the mediation process if a mediator offers suggestions, solutions, or opinions?

Controlling the Process

Control of the process is an instrumental skill in mediation. The word "control" sometimes carries negative connotations. For mediation to work, however, the mediator must be in charge. The mediator controls the stage; the disputants retain autonomy over any agreements.

Many experienced mediators can attest to the problems associated with having a disputant "gain control of the process" in the midst of mediation. Once one party begins determining the direction of the mediation, the other party responds to the shift in power with defensiveness, withdrawal, or distrust of the process. A mediator is not acting as a dictator by controlling the process. Instead, he or she is like a captain steering the "mediation" ship down a safe channel. The disputants may try to take the helm of the ship and steer it into narrow side channels, but it is the mediator's responsibility to resist and redirect the session back on course.

Mediators also control the tone of the mediation. **Emotional contagion theory** serves to explain how a mood is established among the parties. One person's behavior influences the emotions of others, as if a mood is contagious. Elaine Hatfield, John T. Cacioppo, and Richard L. Rapson (1993) argue that understanding the nature of emotional contagion theory can aid professionals in shaping the emotional tone of a session. For mediators, recognizing the human propensity to mimic behaviors or adopt the emotional state of those around us can provide an impetus to the mediator's choices in the tone of the mediation and emotional expressiveness. It also offers a warning for mediators to be wary of unconsciously adopting the mood of disputing parties who are depressed, resigned, angry, or exhibiting other strong emotions. A mediator who exudes a tone of calm and genuine care may foster similar responses in the parties.

Like emotional contagion theory, **communication accommodation theory** (CAT) examines how humans subconsciously regulate their behaviors to meet the communication patterns of another person. If a disputant has a slow rate of speech or uses dramatic gestures, the mediator might adapt rate of speech or size of gesture to be similar to the disputant—creating a feeling of kinship and comfort.

Communication accommodation theory also provides a tool to analyze cultural communication among diverse groups. A mediator will have cases where either the disputants have significant cultural differences or the mediator will have cultural dissimilarities from one or more of the disputants. As discussed in Chapter 2, recognizing patterns of behavior when faced with cultural differences is an important skill for the mediator.

When people communicate, CAT posits that one individual's behaviors will converge, diverge, or overaccommodate to the other person. *Convergence* is a strategy of adapting to each other's communication pattern. Our behaviors converge to a common volume, eye contact pattern, or rate of speech. When disputants turn in their chairs so they can see each other more directly, convergence may be occurring. When taken by both parties as sincere, convergence is perceived as thoughtful (West & Turner, 2010).

Divergence occurs when communicators purposefully accentuate a difference in communication to separate their identities. Mediators should be aware of these patterns, especially as divergence can be a method of establishing power. Intentionally using a sophisticated vocabulary when in conflict with a person who uses more earthy terminology may be a divergence tactic that the mediator will need to address. Nonverbal divergence may be expressed by one party engaging in prolonged eye contact with someone who avoids eye contact or orienting the body away from the other disputant.

Finally, *overaccommodation* occurs when one party overadapts to the other's communication style. Frequently, overaccommodation is a reaction to a perceived communicative inadequacy. People may speak more loudly when talking to an individual whose root language is different from their own, as if volume would aid in comprehension. Mediators should be alert to the CAT responses of disputants (or in themselves) to ensure that overaccommodation does not derail the process.

How people manage their disclosure with others also can be explained using **communication privacy management theory**. Sandra Petronio (2002) describes information as personal (known by oneself) or collective (known by self and other). When information is moved from the personal to the collective, rules exist to govern how that information will be used. The parties, however, may bring different ideas to the table about what should remain personal and what can be disclosed.

A mediator can help the disputants by exploring rules for managing information. For example, a parent may be uncomfortable sharing the details of a family crisis that is affecting her son's work in school, but she is torn because she knows that if the school were more aware, it might be understanding of his behavior. A mediator, sensing this tension, could work with the parent to explore options for the optimal level of disclosure, allowing the protection of private information while sharing important elements of the situation or identifying rules about who will have access to the information. In general, private information will only be shared if the mediator has created a safe environment for the parties.

While mediators have control of the mediation process, new mediators often struggle with letting go of a belief they have control of the outcome. A foundational part of mediation is the tenet that parties have control of the decision making—they maintain *self-determination*. This means that a mediator may masterfully employ the requisite skills in a mediation session, and yet the parties may determine that a solution is unreachable. Accepting the limits of the mediator's influence is an important lesson for beginners.

LISTENING: A BEDROCK SKILL FOR MEDIATORS

While mediators must master a series of skills to be successful, no skill is more essential than the ability to listen. North Americans commonly and mistakenly assume that listening is a natural activity requiring little effort or skill. **Hearing** is a physiological activity that occurs naturally when the physical hearing organs function properly, but listening only occurs after the brain receives and processes the message. Hence, people who are deaf and can lip-read or understand American Sign Language cannot hear, but they may listen well. Listening is a mental skill requiring attentiveness and energy. To be competent at listening, one must understand the listening process, which is composed of five elements: reception of messages, attention to the message, concentration on processing the message, message interpretation, and memory (Ridge, 1993).

As Michael P. Nichols observes, "listening is so basic that we take it for granted. Unfortunately, most of us think of ourselves as better listeners than we really are" (2009, p. 11). The assumption that we all are naturally good listeners simply is not true. We tune out messages that are boring or not what we want to "hear." We are sidetracked by thoughts or preoccupations, distractions, daydreams, or anxiety about what we will say when it is our turn to speak. We may attend only to the meaning of the words a person is saying and miss the body language that would help us interpret the speaker's intention.

Disputants can have difficulty listening to each other for a variety of reasons: They may believe they are in the right, they feel misunderstood, or they may doubt the other's sincerity. The mediator has the job of orchestrating an environment where parties can listen effectively. Kerry Patterson, Joseph Grenny, Ron McMillian, and Al Switzler (2002) note, "At the core of every successful conversation lies the free flow of relevant information. People openly and honestly express their opinions, share their feelings, and articulate their theories. They willingly and capably share their views, even when their ideas are controversial or unpopular" (p.20). Until the parties can manage this level of interchange unassisted, the mediator is there to promote a safe and accessible venue for dialogue.

Types of Listening

Several types of listening are identified by communication scholars: **comprehensive listening** (to understand what is said), **empathy/empathic listening** (supporting and helping the speaker to talk through his or her problem and feelings), **critical listening** (evaluating what is said), and **appreciative listening** (listening for enjoyment) (Wolvin & Coakley, 1993). A competent mediator is adept at empathic listening, comprehensive listening, and critical listening. Each phase of the mediation process may require more focus on one type of listening than on the others. For example, empathic listening is essential to the initial storytelling phase; critical listening is vital to the negotiation and settlement writing aspects of a case.

Regardless of the phase a session is in, mediators must listen. The mediator's listening helps the disputants develop trust, provides information on which to base strategic choices about the process, and uncovers the raw content of the issues.

Discussion Question 3.3

IN CASE 2.1, what types of listening would the mediator use? Are the same types of listening skills required in Case 3.1? Is the proportion of time spent on each type of listening different for conciliatory and problem-solving approaches?

Variables That Affect Listening

How people learn to listen (or not listen) has intrigued researchers for decades. In the 1980s, research indicated a difference in North American men and women's listening acuity, with men less adept at listening and less attuned to the nonverbal nuances that enable one to interpret the complexities of human communication (see the discussion in Borisoff & Hahn, 1997). Another study found females adopting a people-oriented style of listening with a focus on emotions and personal stories and men using a more action-oriented style of listening with attention to concise presentations of facts (Johnston, Weaver, Watson, & Barker, 2000). More recent scholars might cast listening as easier for those who are high in **emotional intelligence (EQ or EI)** than those who are high in intellectual intelligence.

For mediators, the question is less about what type of person is more adept at listening over another, and more about what factors inhibit effective listening. In this section, we will explore the variables mediators should be aware of as they work to create an environment where effective listening can happen—among mediators and disputants.

Listening is a complex undertaking. Judi Brownell (2010) explains a skills-based model of listening called the HURIER model. This model identifies six components of listening: (1) *hearing*, (2) *understanding*, (3) *remembering*, (4) *interpreting*, (5) *evaluating*, and (6) *responding*. In each component, barriers can affect the ability to listen effectively. For example, emotional involvement or personal identification with an issue can prevent disputants from comprehending those who disagree with them. High emotions seem to inhibit genuine listening. Where people sit can affect the ability to hear the other clearly. It is incumbent on the mediator to discover the disputants' idiosyncratic listening weaknesses and styles.

Many phenomena impede listening (see Van Slyke, 1999). For example:

- *Thinking-speaking gap:* Using the time between speaking (125–250 words per minute) and comprehending (500 words per minute) to focus on topics other than the one at hand, such as the mediator drifting off to think about the next appointment or what to have for lunch.

- *Selective attention:* Listening only to part of a message.

- *Impatience:* Assuming we know what the disputant is going to say or assuming repetition of a concern is not important. Repetition often means the mediator needs to validate strong feelings or probe for hidden details.

- *Agenda building:* Listening for facts to fit one's preconceived ideas about the case or its resolution.

- *Perceptual bias:* Predetermining meaning based on one-sided data rather than acknowledging that others may have different ideas.

- *Emotional state:* Being so consumed by how you are currently experiencing the event you cannot listen.

- *External distractions:* Letting background noise or movement capture your attention.

- *Communication style:* Focusing on the accent, grammar, or other stylistic features of speech instead of on the speaker's meaning and intentions.

- *Preconceptions:* Letting past interactions with the disputant, including first impressions, contaminate how the mediator interprets messages.

- *Affiliations:* Assuming the disputant will think or behave in particular ways because of groups he or she belongs to (i.e., **constituencies**).

The mediator is a highly skilled listener who uncovers the hidden issues important to the disputants, as well as a skilled communicator who creates an environment where disputants can begin to listen to each other. Erik J. Van Slyke (1999) presents an excellent explanation of why listening is the preeminent variable to settlement of conflicts: "The problem in conflict, however, is not whether the other party listens to us, but rather whether we listen to and understand the other party's perspective. Only after we have listened to the other party will that party want to listen to us. Only after the other party feels understood will he or she want to understand and be influenced by us" (p. ix). Patterson et al. (2002) speak of the "pool of shared meaning" from which parties will work together on problems. Barriers to listening inhibit parties from adding to the pool or benefiting from other's ideas. The mediator is charged with making it possible for each disputant to get ideas on the table.

The stress and emotion in a conflict situation sometimes creates defensiveness. Conflict management scholars use Jack R. Gibb's classic 1961 concept of supportive and defensive communication to explain the destructive communication cycles that manifest during **interpersonal conflict**. Gibb posited that certain types of communication behaviors create **supportive climates** where individuals feel trust, openness, and cooperation. Other communication behaviors lead to **defense-provoking/defensive climates** where individuals feel threatened, wary, combative, and stop listening. The effective mediator will be alert for defensive behaviors and consider strategies to move parties to more supportive alternatives.

TABLE 3.2 Supportive and Defensive Climates

Behaviors Leading to Defensive Climates	Behaviors Leading to Supportive Climates
Blame others	Acknowledge personal responsibility
Speak in generalities without specifics	State issues clearly with specificity
Use provocative language to offend or escalate; attack other's integrity or values	Show sensitivity for word choices
Use threats, hostile joking, sarcasm, pointed questions	Use inclusive words, friendly tone, and sincere inquiry
Adhere to personal agenda	Identify problems as mutual concern
Focus on self-serving options, stick to one solution	Search for fairness that meets each party's needs
Frame solutions as either-or, or forced choice	Brainstorm and explore multiple options
Criticize others, trivialize concerns, belittle ideas	Ask questions to understand, acknowledge efforts and worth of other's ideas
Express superiority of one's view and ideas over the other's	Express value of others and their ideas even when disagreeing
Use manipulation to win	Be open to different approaches

Source: Adapted in part from Borisoff and Victor (1998, pp. 37–73).

The inability of disputants to assume supportive postures keeps them from solving problems. It is the mediator's job to mitigate defensive communicative and, if possible, assist in transporting the disputants who arrive with hostility to a more productive frame of mind. Ideally, the mediator would facilitate a more supportive/less defensive communication pattern for the individuals and a climate conducive to mutual problem solving. For example, when an individual uses phrases that provoke the other party, the mediator might ask the comment to be phrased in another way.

Whether disputants begin with defensive postures that must be moderated or arrive in a conciliatory mood, mediators are required to listen to the disputants. Mediators also need the disputants to be able to listen to each other. Listening—either to the other party or to the mediator—is the only way disputants can understand what is driving the conflict and the only way for the mediator to address what is keeping the parties from being able to settle their conflict. Listening is the most basic mediator skill and was mentioned as critical by virtually all of the practitioners interviewed in a study by Myra Warren Isenhart and Michael L. Spangle (2000, p. 215).

Discussion Question 3.4

CHANGING A climate from defensive to supportive takes more than just being a good listener. Discuss how each of the following variables can affect the climate of the mediation session: environment, seating, clothing choices, power differences, timing, professionalism, level of formality, speaking tone, and topics of conversation. Offer other variables that may affect the climate of the mediation session.

Skills for Listening to Content, Emotion, and Relationship

To accomplish the goals of cutting through defensiveness and uncovering the information that can lead to settlement, the mediator listens for three levels of meaning in the disputants' messages: What emotions are expressed? What is the implied relationship between the disputants? What is the factual content of the case? The dialogue between Sidney and Gino illustrates the three levels of meaning inherent in any message:

CONTENT: Sidney noticed a smelly odor coming from the cat box and says, "I wish the house was fresher."

EMOTION: Sidney is frustrated and disappointed. Gino hasn't cleaned the cat box, and she is worried about being embarrassed when Gino's mother and father arrive for dinner that night and says, "I wish the house was fresher."

RELATIONSHIP: Sidney doesn't feel she can tell Gino directly to clean the cat box. Their communication patterns with one another have defined direct requests as nagging. So, she hints about her discomfort in an effort to persuade him to clean the cat box and says, "I wish the house were fresher."

The words in the messages above are the same. Only by attending to Sidney and asking her about the comment can the mediator determine which level of meaning is the most important at that moment. The mediator uses techniques to encourage, validate, or ask for clarification to uncover hidden levels of meaning.

The mediator's toolbox contains different types of listening skills that can be used separately or together to achieve the desired outcomes. Among these skills are empathic listening, **validation**, **paraphrasing feelings**, and **pure content paraphrasing**. This chapter introduces an array of listening skills for mediators and will integrate them into the phases of the balanced mediation model throughout the book.

Empathic Listening

Empathic listening helps build trust and confidence. *Empathic listening* strives to understand and reflect the perspective of the other person without evaluation. David A. Binder, Paul Bergman, and Susan C. Price (1996) observe that individuals rarely have an opportunity to talk to someone who will not judge them or give advice—an apt description of a mediator. When empathic, nonjudgmental listening occurs, people naturally want to tell their stories. In addition to building trust in the mediator, empathic listening elicits the disclosure of personal information that often is unknown to the other disputant. Empathic listening may involve displaying interest nonverbally, such as leaning forward, nodding, and using strong eye contact. Verbally, the empathic listener encourages the party to continue with her or his narrative, without being judged. Adding an occasional, comment ("Then what happened?") demonstrates a desire to understand the speaker's story.

Validation

When a mediator listens with empathy, the disputant feels *validated*. Mediators learn many techniques to moderate emotions and to elicit feelings of validation in disputants. Disputants come into the mediation session with a need to be heard. Parties may be frustrated because they believe that no one listens to them and that no one understands their concerns. They may feel ignored, disrespected, or victimized. Disputants may exhibit an emotion, such as anger, that is masking an underlying fear that is the real barrier to resolving the conflict. A major role of the mediator is to create a place where parties can speak, be heard, and move toward mutual understanding—to be validated. Ideally, the mediator would orchestrate each party's understanding of the other disputant. At the very least, parties must believe that the mediator has heard and understood their perspectives, emotions, and issues—even if the other party does not. In Case 3.1, Mr. Washington could be validated by repeating his statement: "So, you liked having Ms. Smith in your class." The mediator could validate Ms. Smith by saying, "It must have been surprising when you opened your semester report and saw a grade you didn't expect."

Paraphrasing Feelings

Paraphrasing feelings is a skill mediators apply to moderate emotion or disrupt negative venting about the other party. There are numerous variations of emotional paraphrasing techniques. In general, the emotional paraphrase identifies the feeling underpinning the speaker's message. In a case where a kindergartener had fallen asleep on the school bus, missed her stop, and was taken to the bus yard and left for two hours, the father retold the story in mediation with much anger. The mediator highlighted that emotion with a three-word **feeling paraphrase**: "You were terrified." The identification of the emotion acknowledged the helplessness and fear that drove the angry outburst in the mediation session. One mediator described the well-placed feeling paraphrase as the act of "letting the air out of the balloon." The disputant has put energy into an emotional message that was released when the mediator acknowledged the feelings. Then the disputant was able to focus on other aspects of the issue, such as solutions for the future.

Variations of the standard emotional paraphrase technique sometimes are useful. One variation requires that the mediator interrupt or overlap the disputant's venting. This variation is particularly useful with disputants who want to complain at length and hardly ever create natural pauses. Because the technique overlaps the disputant's speech rather than waiting for the individual to stop talking, this variation of the emotional paraphrase technique only is used when a person is showing intensity or high emotion. A disputant may say, "I can't believe I had to learn from another customer that Jennifer was complaining all over the neighborhood about my business, but never talked to me!" The "heat" behind the statement begs for some mediator response. A validation of the disputant's feelings after the one-sentence remark ("So you were bothered by that") goes a long way to build trust and to identify a potential emotional blockage to settlement. If, in addition to the one-sentence remark, the disputant continues to vent for a long time in the same negative tone, an emotional paraphrase that overlaps the venting may calm the disputant and decrease the amount of time an individual expends seeking acknowledgment. Conversely, when the disputants are calm, interrupting to paraphrase feelings will sound—and be—contrived.

Emotional paraphrasing and validation help disputants identify the feelings behind comments and "humanize" the parties to each another. In conflict, disputants keenly feel personal emotions and frustration, yet rarely do they consider the feelings of the other person. Through feeling paraphrases, the mediator simultaneously validates one party while helping the second person discover a new level of understanding of the situation. The mediator's emotional paraphrasing fosters an opportunity for empathy to grow between the disputing parties.

ACTIVITY 3.1: The Skill of Paraphrasing Feelings

Purpose: To validate the emotions while a disputant is venting and to uncover emotional blockages to settlement.

Useful When: The disputant is visibly emotional, upset, or using emotional language such as "I am angry" or accusations "He doesn't care!" You may use an emotional paraphrase three to four times before a visible lessening of high emotion will occur. If paraphrasing feelings does not moderate emotion after the fourth attempt, move on to another skill.

(Continued)

THE PROCESS

1. Ignore all substantive content for the moment.

2. Focus on the emotional words or tone underlying the comment.

3. Interrupt (speak at the same time as the disputant rather than waiting for a pause) and give the three- to six-word emotional paraphrase.

4. Use words that are as positive as possible without putting the other party in a negative light.

5. Stop talking and listen. If the disputant says, "Yes," or nods and continues, the emotional paraphrase was on target. If the disputant says, "No, I'm not _____, I'm _____," the validation was slightly off. In that case, simply repeat what the disputant just said, "Oh, so you're _____."

6. Stop talking and let the disputant continue relating her or his information.

EMOTIONAL PARAPHRASING FORMULA

Mix and match an opening phrase with a tone/feeling word to fit the disputant's comment.

Opening Phrase +	Word Describing Tone/Feelings
You seem	frustrated, sad, mad, upset
It sounds like you were	concerned, afraid, surprised
That must have been	scary, confusing, disappointing

While some sources give a comprehensive list of words to describe emotions, each mediator need only develop a repertoire of descriptions that he or she can use comfortably while mastering the skill.

Emotionally paraphrase the following comments:

1. "I can't believe it! I hate it when she uses the copy machine and then just leaves when it runs out of paper."

2. "Gerald is just a pit bull. He roars into the meeting and wants to have everything his own way. He just can't let go of his own ideas!"

3. "Noah drives like a maniac and I refuse to ride with him anymore!"

Pure Content Paraphrasing

Pure content paraphrasing is a familiar skill for many people. In *pure content paraphrasing,* the mediator summarizes in a few words the essence of the facts that a disputant relates. Pure content paraphrasing is best applied when the disputants are calm or the mediator is checking the accuracy of factual details. Mediators often will paraphrase facts regarding what a typical day is like in someone's work routine, how houses are related spatially to one another, or the proposed schedule for repayment of a business debt.

Content paraphrasing can be particularly useful when keeping track of many details. For example, one disputant presented the following information: "I had several estimates done on the car. One guy said he could fix the fender for $200, but painting it would be another $250. The other guy said he could do it all for $500, and fix the busted taillight, too. The last guy was sky high and said it would take $900 to fix everything."

A content paraphrase summarizes the facts of the statement, highlighting important details without parroting every word. The mediator could say, "So the range of estimates to fix the car was between $450 and $900." Content paraphrasing is an important tool in verifying important information and clarifying facts. Content paraphrasing can be destructive when applied to emotional statements or facts presented in one disputant's slanted self-interest. It is not productive to content paraphrase the statement, "I really hate Ivan," by saying, "Oh, so you hate Ivan." Content paraphrasing at the wrong time can validate one person's slanted view of reality, to the detriment of the other party. Generally, mediators avoid paraphrasing a disputant's *position*. Hope B. Eastman (2008) cautions that "many mediators underestimate how engaged parties want them to be on substance."

Discussion Question 3.5
HOW CAN we determine which level of a message (emotional, relational, or content) is most critical to validate (if validation is warranted)? What dangers are there if a mediator focuses on the "wrong" level?

REFRAMING MESSAGES

The term **reframing** encompasses a series of listening tools to change a disputant's negatively phrased or unproductive words into more neutral terms. A mediator applies reframing to make information more usable in the session, while affirming the general intent of a comment. Reframing also can be used to summarize a **substantive issue**. After listening to a complaint, the mediator generalizes the disputant's concern without validating any negative words about the other party, positions, or proposed solutions. If the disputant says, "He has to clean up his trashy yard or move out of the neighborhood, or else I'm going to have my attorney file a suit," then the mediator would offer a reframe of the general concern while deleting the **threat** and the positional demand. For example, the mediator might respond with "You like a neat yard" or "You're concerned about how the neighborhood looks." After reframing a comment, be sure to listen for confirmation. If the disputant says "No," probe to uncover the general interest and reframe again.

The theoretical concept behind reframing assumes that each disputant paints a personally biased picture of reality—in the example earlier in this section, cleaning up the yard or suing are one disputant's solutions. Communication scholars know that language is ambiguous. What is a "trashy yard" to one person may be a "work in progress" to another. Even if the appearance of the yard is less than desirable, there are many possible solutions. For example, the neighbors may decide to build a tall, sturdy fence. By reframing the general concern rather than repeating any of the specific solutions or positions, the mediator transforms the frame through which the disputants view the conflict.

Reframing offers an important tool to mitigate the harm that occurs when disputants engage in defensive communication or negative labeling. In conflict, disputants have a tendency to blame others, rely on stereotypes, make faulty attributions about the other party's motivations, and provoke defensiveness. Reframing allows the mediator to take what is valuable from a statement while reducing the "sting" of inflammatory words. For example, during a mediation with a middle-aged male landlord and a 20-year-old female tenant, the landlord bluntly told the mediator, "Kids these days are so irresponsible, and this girl is no exception. She poured it on with honey on how good she'd be even though she didn't have any references. Then she trashed the apartment. You can't trust them!" Imagine being the young woman hearing those comments. Most likely, you would feel defensive or embarrassed. In response, she retorted, "If you weren't such a slumlord, you wouldn't have these problems."

Both parties are sharing valuable information about their perspectives but not in a frame that the other party will be able to accept. She's hurt; he's angry. If the mediator does not intervene quickly to reframe the message, the process could deteriorate. In this case, the mediator combined the skills of validation, feeling paraphrasing, and reframing to meet the goal of directing the process back on track and moderating the emotional climate. The mediator said, "As a property owner, you're disappointed with the way the apartment was left and want to discuss the damages. Being respected is important to both of you, although neither of you are feeling respected right now." Then, the mediator refocused the session on the substantive issue by asking, "Could one of you tell me more about the agreement you had?"

ACTIVITY 3.2: Methods of Reframing

- Negative labeling is replaced with the positive quality the disputant would prefer

  Comment: "He never talks to me. He is a jerk."

  Reframe: "You'd like better communication between the two of you."

- Positions are changed into general issues for exploration

  Comment: "He has to pay me the money he owes me today."

  Reframe: "You'd like this issue settled as soon as possible."

(Continued)

(Continued)

- Negative comments or blaming are transformed into a general concern

  Comment: "The project is failing because he is lazy."

  Reframe: "You're concerned about the project."

Reframing Exercises:

1. Role-play the scenario in Case 3.1. How would you reframe the interests of Ms. Smith or Mr. Washington?

2. Role-play the scenario in Case 1.1. The individual playing the mediator should reframe Dana and her neighbors' interests, rather than repeating their statements of frustration.

LISTENING TO NONVERBAL COMMUNICATION

The skilled mediator listens to more than just words. Mediators also listen with their other senses to detect the underlying tone of the words, contradictions between words and body, and shifts in **attitude**. A mediator may perceive that a person is hurt or angry not from the **denotative meaning** of the words but from the tone of voice. Looking at the other disputant directly and saying in a friendly fashion, "I've always enjoyed the music from your parties," conveys a message where the words and the nonverbal meaning match. Glaring at the other disputant and saying with a sarcastic tone, "I've always *enjoyed* the *music* from your parties," conveys quite a different meaning.

Mediators also "listen" with their eyes to the nonverbal communication of disputants to gauge when they are ready to begin negotiating in good faith. Disputants who are angry may sit with their bodies slightly turned away from each other. When someone speaks calmly and turns his or her body to a more direct orientation to the other party or leans toward the other disputant, it may mean a shift of perception also has occurred.

Because nonverbal communication is ambiguous and open to many interpretations, mediators should check their assumptions through emotional paraphrasing or asking questions. If one party "looks" surprised at the information the other is relating, the mediator might say, "You seem surprised by that remark. Is this new information for you?" Acknowledging how the cue was picked up nonverbally, a mediator could say, "I've noticed that you looked confused when she said she was concerned about your son being left alone at night. Did I read that right?"

ACTIVITY 3.3: Testing Nonverbal Accuracy

With a partner or in a group, test your ability to read others' nonverbal communication. One person should select an emotion from the list below and express it only using nonverbal

(Continued)

communication: eyes, gestures, audible (yet nonlinguistic) expressions, and body posture. Other group members should guess the emotion displayed. Discuss how that same emotion could be shown in different ways.

> shock
>
> sadness
>
> impatience
>
> annoyance
>
> dismay
>
> disbelief

CLARIFYING AND ASKING QUESTIONS

The simple question is not so simple in mediation. The mediator should understand the functions of different types of questions and develop a repertoire of stock questions. Asking the right strategic question at the right moment during the mediation process is a skill that develops with time and practice.

Open versus Closed Questions

Open-ended questions do not have a predicable answer. "What is your house like?" is an *open question* to elicit whatever information the disputant chooses to be important. "Does your house have a basement?" or "How many people live in your home?" are **close-ended questions** that require a specific piece of information as the answer. Open questions suggest a topic of response but do not require a specific item of information. The more "open" the question, the more choice the disputant has in answering.

Generally, open questions should be used *before* closed questions. Open questions elicit a broad sweep of information providing opportunities for an unfiltered and rich response. The broadest of open questions can launch a mediation's storytelling phase, such as "What brought you here today?" or "From your perspective, what is the situation about?" When too many closed questions occur too early in the process, the mediator may "fix" the issues in the disputants' minds in a different way than might have otherwise occurred. In other words, the mediator may unwittingly bias the session. Additionally, disputants may feel they are being interrogated, which risks reducing trust and confidence in the mediator. Finally, closed questions may, in the words of David A. Binder, Paul Bergman, and Susan C. Price (1996), cause the mediator to "miss both the trees and the forest" (p. 56). By focusing too soon on the details, the mediator may miss some of the issues important to the disputants. Closed questions are useful during late storytelling and negotiation phases to verify the mediator's understanding of a disputant's interests, to probe for facts, or to test an agreement.

Discussion Question 3.6

QUESTIONS THAT begin with "why" often lead to feelings of defensiveness. Offer possible reasons for this phenomenon.

Genuinely Curious Questions

Curiosity is a beneficial mediator trait. When a disputant says, "He just doesn't respect me," a curious mediator may wonder what "respect" means to that individual. Based on that curiosity, the mediator may ask "What led you to that conclusion?" or "What do you mean when you use the word 'respect'"? From an attitude of curiosity, a mediator may say, "Help me understand how you arrived at that conclusion." Many times, the answers to **genuinely curious questions** provide insights or information that may not otherwise have been disclosed. Curious questions help individuals think through assumptions they have made unconsciously. At times mediators may even use the word "curious" in framing a question: "I'm curious about something. You said that you feel detached from the work team. What is that like?"

HONORING SILENCE

New mediators might feel they have to be doing something to fill in the silences that occur during the natural course of mediation. Silence happens for many reasons. A person may need to reflect and collect some thoughts before answering. Sometimes, disputants are mentally discarding unproductive gut responses and forming a more thoughtful comment. A mediator can use silence after asking a question to both parties, asking them to make some notes before answering.

Silence is an important part of some cultures' communication patterns. Once a statement has been made, it may be customary for there to be a silent space before the next comment is made. These reflective pauses demonstrate respect by separating the listening and responding functions. Listeners can give their full attention because they are not preparing their responses while another is speaking. As novices become more experienced, they learn appropriate timing and have a better sense of when a pause becomes too long.

In summary, mediators manage a multitude of tasks related to listening. Mediators must:

- Validate the emotions of the parties

- Help the parties explore, understand, and articulate their interests

- Clarify important information

- Determine what type of issue needs attention, such as the emotion, the relationship, or the content (or all three at once)

- Summarize without trivializing the concerns of the parties

- Help parties create a common story that integrates their unique perspectives

- Address power imbalances by encouraging the lower party's participation

- Make sure that both (or all) parties have access to problem solving and decision making

- Recognize and respond to messages sent nonverbally, as well as verbally

- Honor reflective silence

LISTENING INTERCULTURALLY

Andrew D. Wolvin and Carolyn Gwynn Coakley (1996) note that scholars "have come to recognize that culture is a primary determinant of all communication behaviors—including listening" (p. 125). In cases where one or more disputants or the mediator comes from different cultural backgrounds, the mediator must adopt a heightened listening sensitivity to detect potential areas for miscommunication. For example, if one disputant's culture or faith believes that events are fated to occur and the other disputant believes in personal control over one's destiny, statements such as "our car accident was fated to be" could be inaccurately perceived by one party as a ploy to avoid responsibility. In some cultures, it is impolite to say "no," and to **save face**, disputants will agree to a settlement they have no intention of fulfilling. Not looking directly at a person of higher status could be perceived as **avoidance**, lack of engagement, or lying by a mediator with a bias that direct eye contact is the norm. Some cultures encourage negotiating details and never accepting the first offer, while others may find that to be disrespectful. Nodding and smiling may indicate agreement or confusion, depending on a person's cultural upbringing.

Melissa L. Beall (2010) states that while much of the work in intercultural communication focuses on the differences between the cultures, the similarities between cultures are often overlooked. She notes, "What is apparent, however, is that unless the interactants in diverse communication events are aware of both similarities and differences, problems may occur" (p. 226). Those who are unaware of how other cultures listen are more likely to misunderstand communication behaviors.

Mediators should be knowledgeable of what is common in terms of values, communication norms, and idiosyncrasies to the populations they serve, but they should always be aware that those differences may not apply to each individual from any given culture. For example, a mediator could say, "When you nodded there, I'm not sure if that meant that you agreed. Do you agree with the proposal or should we discuss it further?" Approaching disputants with sincere inquiry is generally met with appreciation. Culturally competent mediators continue to learn about the diverse populations they work with and go beyond superficial levels of cultural knowledge (Sockalingam & Williams, 2002).

ETHICAL ISSUES AND LISTENING

While listening is an essential skill, the application of listening skills does more than just guide the mediation session. The techniques discussed in this chapter function to alter the perception of the conflict in the minds of the disputants. In fact, some skills are intentionally designed to create perception changes because the conflict must be *transformed* if the disputants are to have the opportunity to alter their relationship or solve their problem. However, the application of **active listening** skills inherently includes more subtle transformations that may not be consciously intended by the mediator.

Bruce Phillips (1999) comments that "active listening plays an important role in building or sculpting meanings, ideas, insights, and solutions between people, none of which would have been generated individually" (p. 179). How a story unfolds during a session and how the individuals develop their narrative is guided by what the mediator does. The reality built during a session is influenced by what the mediator chooses to select or ignore, the information solicited or discouraged, and the words the mediator chooses to paraphrase, reframe, or reformulate (Heisterkamp, 2006). In particular, Phillips (1999) discusses the inequities that can occur when a mediator uses listening and questioning skills differently with each disputant—perhaps as a result of unconscious bias toward one of the disputants. For example, a mediator may encourage one disputant's perspective merely by using an *open* **reformulation** that seeks elaboration of a comment ("Oh, so you are saying you'd like more cooperation. Tell me more.") and by minimizing the other disputant's perspective through the use of a *closed* reformulation—a paraphrase immediately followed by a topic change or a shift to the other disputant ("Oh, so you are saying you'd like more cooperation. I'd like to go back to another issue you raised earlier about . . ."). The result of the inequitable treatment could subtly frame the issues to advantage one disputant over the other.

As the mediator masters listening and questioning techniques, keep in mind the necessity of consistent and fair application of the skills. The mediator's self-awareness of preferred personal communicative styles and skills in need of improvement are good places to start on the path of ethical listening competence.

Discussion Question 3.7

EXPLAIN HOW actively listening to disputants can affect the course of the mediation. What should mediators do to be ethical in their listening endeavors? What can a mediator do to become more self-aware of his or her communicative biases?

Summary

Mediators must acquire a variety of skills and assume numerous roles. All mediators must have both knowledge and skill competencies. Mediators must understand and trust the processes in the model they are implementing and learn to control the flow of a mediation session. Emotional contagion theory and communication accommodation theory help explain disputant and mediator behaviors that may affect the session. Mediators should be aware of diversity issues and be vigilant to avoid overaccommodation. Communication privacy management theory can explain how parties work to manage the tension between what private information will be shared and what will remain secret. How a mediator develops trust and safety will affect what disputants choose to disclose.

Listening is foremost among mediator skills. Three types of listening are applied in mediation: comprehension, empathic, and critical. Mediator listening skills include empathic listening, validation, paraphrasing feelings, and pure content paraphrasing. Reframing is a tool involving several listening skills that refocuses a message to highlight one specific element. Mediators also "listen" to nonverbal messages and cultural context. Supportive and defensive climates deeply affect listening behaviors, and mediators can learn to recognize defensive creating behaviors and work to aid parties in creating supportive climates to resolve disputes.

Mediators use closed and open questions to elicit information. Questions probe the emotional, relationship, and content aspects of the case. Mediators should look for opportunities to display genuine curiosity as they work to understand the issues.

Finally, mediators must be aware of the ethical implications of how they apply listening and other communication techniques. Inequitable application of skills such as reformulation can create bias.

Portfolio Assignments

Portfolio Assignment 3.1: Emotional Paraphrases

Every mediator needs a list of emotional paraphrases or validations. As you read the textbook or listen to sample mediations, write down every good emotional paraphrase or validation that you hear.

Title the page in your notebook: "Emotional Paraphrases I Can Use." Feel free to use either the format of an emotional paraphrase or general validation (discussed in Chapter 3).

Emotional Paraphrase: "You seem _____.[emotion word]."

General validations: "You were _____ [emotion word] when _____ [event]."

Record at least ten emotional paraphrases or validations.

Portfolio Assignment 3.2: The Open-Ended Question

Asking open-ended questions is a skill. As you read the text and listen to other mediators, be alert for good open-ended questions that apply to many types of mediations.

(Continued)

(Continued)

Create a page in your mediator's notebook called "Open-Ended Questions." List at least four open-ended questions that might be useful during the early phases of storytelling for each of the following contexts:

- Open-ended Questions for Early Storytelling in Business Cases
- Open-ended Questions for Early Storytelling in Roommate Cases
- Open-ended Questions for Early Storytelling in Neighbor Cases

Pre-Mediation Activities

Contacting Disputants   **61**

Goals to Accomplish During Intake   **62**

    Education Role   63

    Information-Gathering Role   67

    Assessment Role   69

Setting the Stage   **73**

    Time and Timing   73

    Place   74

    Environment   75

Ethical Issues for Pre-Mediation Caseworkers   **76**

Summary   **77**

Portfolio Assignment 4.1: The Referral Sourcebook   **77**

Portfolio Assignment 4.2: Intake and Agreement to Mediate Forms **78**

CASE 4.1: Irreconcilable Differences

Roland and Janet have been married for 12 years, have two sons, and have cited irreconcilable differences in their mutual decision to divorce. Complicating the dissolution of their marriage is a community house for helping runaways and teen mothers that they jointly manage. Both put their hearts into growing the community house into the successful program that it has become. Although they no longer will be married, their work relationship will continue (as well as the co-parenting of their sons). The tensions surrounding their separation are now affecting their work. There are major issues that need to be resolved, such as the division of property and financial obligations, as well as the distribution of labor in the agency. Janet has contacted an attorney to begin the divorce proceedings, but Roland decided to contact a mediator recommended by a friend. Roland makes the call to a mediator without consulting with Janet.

ACTIVITY 4.1: The Intake Coordinator's Cold Call

Role-play with a partner the phone call between Roland and the intake coordinator. The person playing Roland can think he knows what mediation is, but he confuses it with arbitration, allowing the intake coordinator the opportunity to explain the mediation process. Place your chairs back to back to simulate a phone call while you talk.

The work of mediation begins before the disputants meet face-to-face. Contact with disputants prior to the session is called *mediation casework* or *intake*. In this chapter, *intake coordinator* and **caseworker** are synonymous names for the individual who conducts the pre-mediation activities.

In larger organizations, different people may fulfill the roles of intake coordinator and mediator. However, the mediator on a case may conduct the intake. Having an intake coordinator who is not the mediator can be beneficial in four ways. First, if someone else manages the initial meeting, the dispute and the disputants are "fresh" to the mediator and preconceived views may not have a chance to solidify. Second, the workload can be shared. Third, individuals who are not talented mediators can develop fulfilling roles as intake specialists. Finally, the disputants may better understand what to expect during the mediation session.

Separating the mediation and intake functions creates four potential disadvantages. Having a mediator and an intake coordinator adds an additional level of complexity. Second, the cost of the service may increase. Third, the mediator cannot begin the trust and credibility-building functions during casework. Finally, in some contexts, such as restorative-justice-based mediation, most of the total time spent with disputants may occur during pre-mediation. Victims are coached on how to approach the offender; offenders are prepared to accept responsibility for their actions and not re-victimize the other party.

CONTACTING DISPUTANTS

As stated previously, people find their way to mediation in a variety of ways. Referrals from counselors, attorneys, and others are common paths to the mediator's door. The courts and other government agencies also send people to mediation—both voluntarily and involuntarily. Mediation can occur when one party initiates the request. Whether by choice, referral, or mandate, disputants seeking assistance may call mediators or fill out service request forms on a website. Even though a disputant may make the first move, he or she may not know very much about mediation. For example, in Case 4.1, Roland called the recommended mediator, but he did not really understand what the process was or whether it was an appropriate fit to work out his dispute with Janet. The intake coordinator explained the mediation process and screened the case for appropriateness.

An organization like the Better Business Bureau, court, or a state educational agency, may provide the forms, information about mediation, and video examples on websites to better serve the public—making the intake coordinator's job a bit easier. A good website can provide educational information about mediation to prospective disputants.

Discussion Question 4.1

LOCATE AN organization in your state that provides mediation services, such as small claims court, the Department of Special Education, or the State Personnel Commission. What information about mediation is available on its website? What information should a website offer to inform the public about mediation processes?

A common job for intake coordinators is the initial contact with the parties. When one disputant does not know that mediation is being contemplated, the contact with that person is labeled a *cold call*. When cold calling, the intake coordinator may encounter suspicion. For example, in Case 4.1, when called by the intake coordinator, Janet may assume that the mediator was working for Roland. Janet's view was that her attorney was her advocate; the mediator was Roland's advocate. Intake coordinators explain the mediation process and work to alleviate fears, anxieties, suspicions, misassumptions, and other obstacles. In essence, intake coordinators are the salespeople for mediation.

ACTIVITY 4.2: The Intake Coordinator's Second Cold Call

Role-play with a partner the cold call between the intake coordinator and Janet. The person who plays Janet should be tentative about mediation, concerned about bias, and insistent on telling her side of the story. The intake coordinator should validate without agreeing using the skills in Chapter 3. Place your chairs back to back to simulate a phone call while you talk.

GOALS TO ACCOMPLISH DURING INTAKE

As expressed in previous chapters, mediation is not a panacea for all disputes; neither are all mediation specialists well matched to all types of disputes. Because the public generally is uninformed about types of mediation, the intake coordinator has multiple goals: educating disputants, gathering information from disputants, and assessing whether the dispute is a match for a specific mediator's skills and the agency's mission. Although we will discuss the functions of education, information gathering, and assessment separately, the intake coordinator fulfills the three roles simultaneously.

TABLE 4.1 Intake Goals

Education Role

- Educate about mediation
- Explain mediator's expertise and credibility
- Communicate mediator expectations (role and process)
- Communicate disputant expectations (behavior and outcome)
- Establish boundaries
- Explore other resources (if necessary)
- Explain fee structure and payment procedures

Information-Gathering Role

- Determine who needs to come to the table
- Initial issue identification
- Demographics of disputants
  - o Culture
  - o Language
  - o Gender
  - o Age
- Types of disputants
  - o Voluntary versus mandated participation
  - o Conflict styles
  - o Communication ability
- Contact information
- Session schedules
- Time constraints and deadlines
- Referral agencies
- Determine ability to pay

Assessment Role

- Determine issue appropriateness
- Assess history of and threat of violence
- Ascertain the decision makers and affected parties
- Determine the appropriateness of mediation over other resolution processes

TABLE 4.1 (Continued)

- Explore advocacy needs
- Review legal issues (restraining orders, parental rights, illegal activities)
- Compare power resources and ability levels (cognitive, communicative)
- Assess disputants' ability to self-determine
- Assess levels of distress and resistance

Education Role

Explain the Process of Mediation

Even disputants who profess to be well versed about mediation should be provided information about the process. Mediation may not be familiar to a disputant who mistakes it for arbitration, litigation, or even meditation. If asked a direct question such as "Do you know what mediation is?" most clients would respond in the affirmative. Instead of asking disputants whether they understand mediation, the intake coordinator briefly explains the process to all new clients.

The education function should be concise and adapted to the disputant's needs. For example, "Mediation is a process where a third party helps people discuss their unique situation and creates a place where the two of them work through possible solutions to meet their needs. The mediator will not make decisions for the parties, but will help them through a process to reach their own decisions." In Case 4.1, Roland, having initiated this call, may be willing to accept the inherent neutrality of the mediator. Janet, however, may require more information and assurances about the balanced nature of the process.

Establish Boundaries

Disputants occasionally try to lure the mediator to their side. Janet or Roland may feel the need to paint the intake coordinator a picture of how things "really are." The intake coordinator views these persuasive efforts as an opportunity to *establish boundaries* by validating concerns without agreeing with positions. The caseworker then encourages the parties to come to the mediation session and discuss what is important to them. To clarify misperceptions, the intake coordinator covers what a mediator will and will not do. For example, "Your mediator is not a judge or decision maker. Instead, you and the other party will examine the issue and make decisions about the solutions that might work for both of you." Some disputants can be very persistent in their efforts to persuade an intake coordinator to their side. A statement that explains neutrality and puts the onus of responsibility back into the disputant's hands is helpful. For example:

JANET: "Roland is being completely unreasonable. You have to at least agree with that!"

INTAKE
COORDINATOR: "My job and the mediator's job is not to pick a side. What the mediator can do is help the two of you explore your challenges in-depth and arrive at a solution that meets the needs of both of you."

The intake coordinator should correct disputants immediately if they make the assumption that the mediator is biased toward one party or the other.

Create Credibility

The value of the mediation process and the credibility of the mediator are conveyed initially during pre-mediation. Sharing statistics about the growth and success of mediation helps people feel more confident. Relating the training and credibility of the mediator begins to build clients' trust. Mediator credibility and disclosures about the process combine to form persuasive reasons to give mediation a try.

Intake coordinators may explain the value of settling issues during mediation before more risky processes are invoked. In Fisher and Ury's *Getting to Yes* (2011), the concept of **BATNA** (the Best Alternative To Negotiated Agreements) is provided as a key negotiation tool. Other scholars created the concept of **WATNA** (the Worst Alternative To Negotiated Agreements). The best (and worst) alternatives for clients sometimes mean proceeding to court or having the conflict continue. Presenting mediation in comparison with other alternatives allows parties to make an informed choice about the process they will choose to settle their issues. If Janet replies that she already has an attorney working on the case so she doesn't need a mediator, pointing out the unpredictability of the courts may be appropriate. Clients also are reassured that the judicial system option will still be open if the mediation outcome is not satisfactory.

ACTIVITY 4.3: Explaining BATNA

In a phone role-play between Janet and the intake coordinator, the intake coordinator explains BATNAs or WATNAs inherent in the situation to Janet. Place your chairs back to back to simulate a phone call.

An ethical mediator, however, never disparages another vocation to bolster the attractiveness of mediation, discourages disputants from contacting attorneys, or uses a high settlement rate in mediation as a club. For example, the intake coordinator may ask, "How do you think this situation might play out if it goes to court?" The answer may offer an opportunity to discuss the benefits of mediation. For cases involving small amounts of money, the intake coordinator can explain that, "In court, even if you do win a judgment, you still have to collect. In general, mediated agreements are kept by the parties more often than those ordered by the courts." Be careful, however, of overstating the success or expectations for resolution in mediation.

Intake coordinators must refrain from giving legal advice, for example, saying, "You seem to have a pretty good case and would probably win in court." Even if the intake coordinator has legal experience, speculation without proper legal credentials and full case analysis is inappropriate and may constitute the **unauthorized practice of law**. Instead, the intake coordinator emphasizes that mediation offers the parties self-determination, which is lost when a judge makes a decision.

Another avenue of persuasion lies in the emotional and relational aspects of the case. Robert A. Baruch Bush and Joseph P. Folger (1994) explain that success in mediation is not measured solely in settlement rates. Success can be evaluated by the greater understanding between parties, the improved mental health of individuals, and the **promise** of better relationships. If Janet and Roland want their relationship as co-parents to be more amiable, mediation may be more beneficial than litigation.

ACTIVITY 4.4: Preparing the Disputants for Mediation

In groups of three, role-play negotiating the time when Janet and Roland will meet with the mediator. How can the intake coordinator manage competing schedules? After the separate calls to Janet and Roland have set a time, brief each party and help them to prepare for the mediation. Be sure to work through some obstacles, such as competing obligations, desire to bring witnesses, and not knowing what to bring to the session. Place your chairs back to back to simulate the separate phone calls while you talk.

Explain the Clients' Responsibilities

In addition to educating parties about mediation, the initial communication with the disputants is an ideal time to set forth their role. In mediation, disputants present their stories in a quiet and private setting. Defining what will be expected helps create momentum for a successful mediation session. Failing to inform a disputant about who should attend can result in a disputant bringing young children to the session. In one instance, one individual in a neighborhood dispute arrived with three of her neighbors to speak as witnesses against the other disputant.

Mediators typically don't hear testimony from other parties because they prefer to have the individuals tell their stories from their own perspectives. Usually a disputant can provide all the information needed without bringing in others. If expert consultants are required, agreement on selection of the expert is a part of the negotiation process rather than chosen by one party. Ferreting out problems and educating disputants about their responsibilities and roles are part of the intake coordinator's job.

The intake coordinator should remind disputants if they make an appointment they are responsible for either appearing or canceling. When only one of the parties appears at a session, a higher level of tension is heaped onto an already strained relationship. Parties also should be apprised about what information they should bring to the table. In divorce mediation, for example, they should be able to produce a list of assets and liabilities, income statements, and other pertinent information. In the case of Roland and Janet, being prepared to discuss real numbers (not just projections) and real schedules (not just memory) may make the process flow more smoothly.

Discuss Billing and Charges

Most codes of mediator conduct are clear that clients should be informed of the mediator's rates and how they will be billed for the mediation service. For example, the Supreme Court of Texas *Ethical Standards for Mediators* (2011) states that, "As early as practical, and before the mediation session begins, a mediator should explain all fees and other expenses to be charged for the mediation. A mediator should not charge a contingent fee or a fee based upon the outcome of the mediation." A pricing structure should be easy to communicate and fair to the parties. Typically, fees contingent on settlement are considered unethical. Some mediators charge a set fee per hour or per mediation session. Others offer a sliding scale based on the income levels of the parties, or some other arrangement where the fee is divided fairly between the parties. Questions about the method of payments should be addressed. For example, are parties to bring payments to the mediation session or will they be billed? Will each party be responsible for part of the bill? If the mediation is billed hourly, is there a minimum and a maximum charge? Does the mediator charge for pre-mediation interviews or formalizing agreements? Some states have specific instructions for when and how rates and billing information are disclosed. Consult your state's codes of conduct for the rules that apply in your jurisdiction.

Discussion Question 4.2

VISIT SEVERAL mediation companies on the Internet. Find three different methods of establishing fees for a mediation. Could fee structures affect the perceived fairness of the mediation for the parties?

Make Necessary Referrals

Through the education process, disputants may find that mediation is not right for them. The intake coordinator also has an educational responsibility to explain other processes and resources available to the parties. Effective intake coordinators are informed about their community and service resources (legal aid, victim's advocacy groups, small claims court, homeless advocates, and so on) so they can help individuals select a next step.

Discussion Question 4.3

WHAT RESOURCES should the intake coordinator be aware of in the community? What circumstances may arise that would require the intake coordinator to explore options other than mediation?

Formalize the Agreement to Mediate

Once the parties agree to mediate, the intake coordinator may ask them to sign an **Agreement to Mediate** Form. One method is to mail or fax each party follow-up correspondence including: a congratulations on their decision to mediate, a brief statement about the nature of the process, the specifics for the meeting time and place, a reminder of materials to bring, the Agreement to Mediate Form, and contact information if there are any questions or concerns. In the case of Janet and Roland, Janet asked whether she could bring her attorney. In divorce cases, some mediators make room for attorneys in the mediation room, but they clearly outline the attorney's role as advisor. The intake coordinator explained these rules to Janet. She consented to proceed, so the intake coordinator then informed Roland that he also could bring an attorney, but that the mediation process would not use the attorneys directly in the discussions. If attorneys are not present, a mediator will encourage disputants to consult counsel if they have any legal questions or concerns. In larger value insurance claims, the attorney for the injured individual and the attorney for the insurance company may be the primary negotiators.

The *Agreement to Mediate Form* includes confidentiality policies, discloses fees, and may contain a statement that parties are welcome to seek legal counsel. In states adopting the Uniform Mediation Act or having other local rules, additional content may be required. In states without the Uniform Mediation Act or where **mediator privilege** is not assured, a **Subpoena Waiver** Form is prudent—a legal agreement that shields mediators from being subpoenaed to testify about the content of the mediation if the disputants carry their grievances forward into formal litigation. Many mediators will not proceed until both parties sign a Subpoena Waiver Form. Good practice dictates that disputants should have a copy of the Agreement to Mediate and Subpoena Waiver forms for their records.

Information-Gathering Role

While educating disputants, the intake coordinator simultaneously is gathering information about the nature of the dispute and the parties. Through the process of active listening, the intake coordinator builds a detailed picture of the conflict and determines the primary parties, level of emotionality, special needs of the disputants, obstacles to settlement, and suggestions for structuring the mediation session. The intake coordinator also elicits information on times each party is available for mediation and briefs the parties on how to prepare for the session.

Delve into Demographic Information

Basic questions about each disputant may reveal important **demographic information**. Are the disputants from the same **root culture**? What is their first language? Are the parties of the same gender? What ages are the disputants? What are their occupations? If the disputants and the mediator do not all speak the same language, a translator trained to be faithful to the mediator's comments must be scheduled. Gender or age differences can affect the dynamics of the session. A male–female **co-mediation** team may provide balance in some cases with female and male disputants. Juveniles require different skill applications than adults, and some models will employ youth trained in mediation as part of the process. The occupation of each disputant may give the mediator hints about power or status differences that could affect the session.

While it is not necessary to ascertain full demographic information in all cases, some information may be helpful in making decisions about the structure of the mediation.

For example, to reduce any appearance of gender bias, an employment dispute involving respect issues between male and female coworkers might proceed better with male and female co-mediators. Some college mediation programs balance student–teacher disputes by assigning a student and a professor as co-mediators. In cases where cultures differ, matching the demographics of the mediator to the disputing parties may be helpful.

Uncover the Clients' Expectations

In talking with Roland, the intake coordinator determined that he wanted his 11-year-old son, Rob, to come to the session so Rob could decide where he was going to live. Determining the primary parties who will attend the mediation is not up to the intake coordinator, but asking appropriate questions can assist disputants in choosing where the decision-making power should lie. Roland was adamant that Rob have a voice in the process. The intake coordinator and Roland discussed *when* in the process Rob should participate. They determined that a later session might be better than having the child attend the first session. Rob's presence was listed as a topic for discussion between Janet and Roland during the first mediation session.

Juggle Schedules

The intake coordinator asks detailed questions to gather information about the parties' schedules and general availability. Disputants often do not think of end times when scheduling a session. One mediator was surprised to learn on beginning a mediation session that a disputant needed to leave in 20 minutes to pick up her child from school. Many mediators prefer a two-hour session, but they do not tell the parties that the session will last exactly two hours. Disputants may feel like failures if they need more time or that they are not getting their money's worth if they finish in 45 minutes. Informing Janet and Roland "the room is scheduled until 3:00 for our mediation starting at 12:30" gives a deadline but a flexible one. The intake coordinator asks key questions to locate times when both parties are available and then searches for a match in the mediator's schedule. Finally, the intake coordinator notifies the parties and the mediator of the chosen time.

Determine Disputant Style and Degree of Freedom

Not all disputants come voluntarily to the mediation process. An intake coordinator should assess whether the disputants self-selected mediation or whether their participation was forced on them. Professional associations, divorce courts, and certain organizations may require mediation before moving to more formal grievances or appeals. Victim–offender mediation may be somewhat **coerced** from the perpetrator's perspective but voluntary from the victim's perspective. Mediators should know of any disputant resistance to the process. Intake coordinators must explain to mandated disputants that while attendance is required, coming to an agreement is not. Even if disputants did not volunteer to participate in mediation, the process of coming to *agreement* always is voluntary.

Developing a sense for the conflict style and emotional state of the disputants may be helpful in determining initial moves by the mediator. Disputants who are highly agitated and **verbally aggressive** may need clear and formal boundaries about appropriate venting. If disputants are highly competitive or rigid, coaching may be required in maintaining behaviors appropriate to **mutual gains** negotiation. Caseworkers share their observations about style with the mediator.

Assessment Role

Explore the Appropriateness of Mediation

While educating disputants and gathering necessary information, intake coordinators evaluate whether the case is appropriate for mediation. The intake coordinator looks for issues that can be mediated. In one situation, the intake coordinator determined that a young man was attempting to mediate with an ex-girlfriend in order to see her again. He claimed that she still owed him $28 on a past phone bill, but she told the intake coordinator that she "wasn't worried about the money since she didn't have a job." While he may have benefited from meeting with his ex, mediation was not the appropriate venue for such a reunion. In extreme cases, mediation could be a harassment tool used by stalkers. Bernard Mayer (2000) concludes that the "mediator's decision not to mediate or to suggest some other form of intervention is in itself an important contribution to a conflict resolution process" (pp. 202–203).

The *Standards of Ethics and Professional Responsibility for Certified Mediators* (Judicial Council of Virginia, 2011) articulates three criteria in assessing whether to take a case:

1. Mediation is appropriate for all parties.
2. Each party can participate effectively within the context of the mediation process.
3. Each party is willing to enter and participate in the process in good faith.

The role of the intake coordinator requires sensitivity to protecting parties from hidden agendas and being alert to possible misuse of the process by one party at the expense of the other.

Determine an Appropriate Structure

Decisions about the formality of the mediation process are shaped by the information garnered in the intake process. For example, if disputants have little trust and a history of high tension, the mediation may require more formality and **structure**. On the other hand, college roommate disputes may benefit from a more relaxed process and less formal structure. In a mediation program designed to handle disputes for a state medical association, the process may use rigid rules as a result of the professional and technical nature of the cases. However, for a neighborhood case, disputants may feel more comfortable in a less formal setting. Knowing about the disputants can help mediators tailor the structure to meet their needs.

Ensure Self-Determination and Informed Consent

Ascertaining whether mediation is appropriate is linked directly to the foundational principles of self-determination and **informed consent**. The Oregon Mediation Association's *Core Standards of Practice* (2005) is representative of how mediators define self-determination. "Self-determination is a fundamental principle of mediation that distinguishes it from other dispute resolution processes, including, but not limited to, litigation. Participants should be free to choose their own dispute resolution process, and mediators should encourage them to make their own decisions on all issues." *Self-determination* means the disputants are able and willing to make their own decisions and that the mediator will not decide for them.

Separate recommendations and rules for judging the capacity of persons who qualify under the Americans with Disabilities Act (ADA) have been created so mediators can modify their processes accordingly (ADA mediation, 2011). Self-determination is important because it affects the individuals' capacity to engage in the process. For example, individuals suffering from dementia may lack the capacity to understand the mediation process adequately and to participate effectively.

Informed consent means the disputants have the information needed to make decisions. The Oregon Standards (2005) comment on how the mediator disclosures before the session begins relate to informed consent and self-determination: "To fully support Self-Determination, mediators respect, value, and encourage participants to exercise Informed Consent throughout the mediation process. This involves making decisions about process, as well as substance, including possible options for resolution. Initially and throughout the mediation process, mediators further support Self-Determination by making appropriate disclosures about themselves and the specific mediation approaches they use." Ensuring informed consent to engage in mediation is a primary responsibility of the intake coordinator. The mediator has other obligations related to informed consent as the mediation session unfolds.

During mediation, the mediator asks questions to reveal information so the disputants make an *informed choice*. For mediation to work, the parties must be able to make decisions based on good information. Informed consent and self-determination only occur in safe environments. If the mediator cannot provide a safe environment, the mediation should not occur. Mediating a case where one party is impaired by alcohol or drugs generally is unworkable. Parties must be responsible for their decisions; disputants who are chemically impaired may have questionable capacity to follow through with agreements.

Assess Relationship History and Threats of Violence

The intake coordinator is a detective who assesses whether the relationship between the parties is appropriate for mediation. For example, if there has been abuse, violence, or a threat of abuse or violence, specialized training is essential before a mediator attempts the case. Most novice mediators are not equipped to navigate such delicate situations. However, determining the level of threat is something an intake coordinator must do. In a case over a barking dog, one neighbor held a black belt in Karate. He was so furious about a barking dog keeping him up all night that he kicked his neighbor's mailbox post, snapping the four-inch post in half. The violence frightened the owner of the mailbox. The intake coordinator evaluated the level of risk, discussed the situation with both parties, and made a judgment that the threat of violence to the neighbor was negligible. Nonetheless, the intake coordinator fulfilled a duty to provide a safe place for mediation by scheduling a volunteer, off-duty police officer to co-mediate that dispute.

Acts of abuse and violence themselves cannot be mediated. One cannot allow threats of violence as a **bargaining chip**. An offer to "not to hit the neighbor if he agrees to keep the dog inside" is not acceptable. While victim–offender mediation, for example, does engage in mediation in cases where violence may have occurred, the violence itself is not the negotiated issue. Victim–offender mediation is about restitution to the victim and society (Umbreit, Coates, & Roberts, 2000). A primary concern is ensuring that the victim is not re-victimized during the session. These sessions are a highly specialized form of mediation requiring extensive training far beyond a basic mediation course. Intake coordinators in victim–offender mediation receive training to distinguish cases appropriate for mediation from those that are not appropriate. Likewise, intake coordinators in family mediation should understand and screen for family and spousal abuse dynamics (Girdner, 1990).

Discussion Question 4.5

WHAT SHOULD an intake coordinator do if it is determined that Janet and Roland had an incident of physical abuse in their marriage? Is it appropriate to mediate this dispute?

Discover Advocacy Needs

When people are in conflict, they frequently seek support from friends and family. Intake coordinators balance the needs of disputants to feel supported and the mediator's need to have only decision makers at the table. In one case, the mediator chose to have a family advocate attend with a disputant as she negotiated with her ex-husband. The ex-wife felt intimidated because her husband was more educated and more confident than she, and all parties agreed that having the advocate present was desirable. Assessing the advocacy needs of disputants is a necessary requirement for the case manager.

If extreme power differences divide the parties, balancing power becomes a major concern. Inviting an advocate is one possibility to empower a disputant. The intake coordinator or mediator, however, should brief the advocate on the nature of mediation and on the advocate's role in the process. Disputants with communicative disabilities may require the assistance of an advocate in order to negotiate effectively.

Screen for Legal Issues

The intake coordinator will ask questions customized to the context of each case (divorce, neighbors, child custody, roommates, and environment). Questions to reveal past legal actions are prudent in some contexts. For example, in a divorce situation, mediators need to know, "Are there any restraining orders in place?" "Have there been any incidents involving police?" These questions can reveal how volatile or strained the relationship is between the parties. In one case involving unhappy neighbors, police had been called numerous times for various complaints by each neighbor. One call prompted the police to recommend mediation. One man, unhappy about the infringement on his parking place (even though he himself did not have a car), took a laser pointer and flashed his neighbor in the eyes through the windshield as he pulled into the disputed parking spot. A restraining order was issued against the laser-pointing neighbor and the case was forwarded to mediation. Because disputants with restraining orders cannot be near each other, the court issued special permission for the parties to be in the same room for the session. Mediators need to know these circumstances to provide safe and legally appropriate venues.

In Internal Revenue Service (IRS), agricultural loan, or foreclosure mediation, personal information is not as important as financial information, such as "What is the amount of the debt?" "Are taxes current on the property?" "Are there other outstanding state or federal suits regarding the property?" When children of divorced parents are involved, mediators need to know whether both parents have custodial, educational, or other designated rights.

Ascertain the Affected Parties and Decision Makers

Identifying the decision makers is another assessment step for the intake coordinator. For example, a group of students was living in a rented six-bedroom house. They agreed to divide the rent and utilities six ways. One roommate, Mia, was unable to meet her obligations for paying one sixth of the rent. The reason she couldn't make the rent was due to an extended illness. Mia's health also prevented her from coming to the mediation session with her five roommates. The mediation should not proceed if Mia, a key **stakeholder**, is not present. In another case, a mobile home park tenant's association was in conflict with the owners over landscaping issues. The tenant's association wanted to send eight members to mediate with the one owner. The mediator was concerned the power imbalance of having eight people on one side with only one on the other would be too difficult to overcome.

With the sick roommate case and the situation with the tenant's association, a similar solution was found: Each appointed a representative to attend the mediation. The sick roommate had her mother attend and negotiate on her behalf; the tenant's association elected one tenant to represent the entire group. It is critical, however, that the representative is delegated **bargaining** and decision-making power. Without the power to negotiate and make decisions, having a representative at the mediation table is meaningless. Intake coordinators ensure that the right people are at the table or have appropriate representation.

A strategy that may be attempted by disputants is sending someone who is not a decision maker to the mediation. Companies may send representatives who either do not have the power to negotiate or who are not able to accept negotiated offers. Intake coordinators should determine the level of decision-making power representatives have prior to the mediation session to avoid this classic manipulation strategy.

> ## Discussion Question 4.6
>
> WHAT PROBLEMS may occur if a party's representative does not have decision-making power?

Create a Preliminary Issue List

The final assessment task for the intake coordinator is creating a preliminary list of **procedural issues**, **psychological issues**, or substantive issues in the case. The preliminary issue list is used to build the mediation plan (discussed in Chapter 5).

Intake coordinators have the job of educating parties about the mediation process and gathering information from disputants to aid in structuring the session. They assess the issues, disputants, context, needs, power dynamics, and decision-making abilities of the parties to determine whether mediation is appropriate. The role of the intake coordinator should not be undervalued in the success of the mediation process.

SETTING THE STAGE

Once the intake coordinator has determined the appropriateness of mediation, the time, place, and environment of the session are chosen.

Time and Timing

At what point in a conflict is mediation appropriate? **Recency** (how current is the conflict?) and **ripeness** (how ready are disputants to work on problem solving?) are two variables used to analyze the timing of the intervention. Intake coordinators can assess recency by asking questions about when the dispute manifested. If a roommate contacts a mediation program and wants to mediate a dispute because his roommate moved out yesterday, the events are recent. Tension is high, trust probably is low, and feelings are freshly hurt. The recency of the event may make problem solving more difficult or easier—depending on the case. Some conflicts can be managed between the parties without intervention once the initial shock surrounding the incident has moderated; other conflicts where disputants have immediate needs should be scheduled quickly.

When the passage of time does not seem to be moving parties toward solution, the ripeness of the conflict may help gauge the readiness for mediation. Intake coordinators assess ripeness by determining if the parties have reached an **impasse**, deadlines are approaching, or other factors in the situation have changed. To establish whether the situation is ripe for mediation, the intake coordinator may ask the following query: "How long has this situation been going on?" "What steps, if any, have you taken to resolve this issue so far?" "What other alternatives have you tried to settle this dispute?" "Are there upcoming deadlines?"

When asked, "Describe the communication that has occurred between the two of you since he moved out," one roommate said, "Well, I can't talk to him without getting angry." The conflict was ripe because the disputants needed help in structuring their communication. If the roommates' communication remains cordial, but they haven't talked about the situation, the intake coordinator might encourage the caller to contact the ex-roommate and return to the mediation center if they had trouble working things out.

Place

Establishing the best place to mediate can influence the tone and safety of the process. Ideally, the location should be neutral and convenient for the parties. Two neighbors were having a dispute over the property line dividing their homes. One neighbor was elderly, didn't drive, and wasn't interested in coming into town for the mediation. Neither neighbor was interested in meeting in the other's home. The challenge for the mediator was to locate a space that was convenient and neutral to both parties. The mediator brought a folding table and set it up outside between the two properties, seating each disputant in his own yard. The neighbors not only negotiated an agreement, but they also established a neighborly tone (culminating in one bringing over fresh garden tomatoes to the other in exchange for a prized salsa recipe). The setting is important to establish a sense of fairness in the process.

Ideally, the disputants should feel equally comfortable (or equally uncomfortable) with the surroundings. They may each travel to a neutral setting where no one individual has the home court advantage. Hopefully, the mediation occurs in a convenient place for the disputants. Sometimes, however, a place convenient for one party is inconvenient for the other. In an estate case involving six heirs in different towns across a large geographical area, the mediator selected a central location that was equally inconvenient to everyone. The sessions were moved to accommodate different parties in an attempt to even out the travel distance between all of the participants over time.

Mediators can work to overcome the potential harm of mediating in non-neutral places. One strategy is to recreate the environment as the mediator's space. If a non-neutral location must be used, make it the mediator's space by formally inviting disputants into the room, moving furniture around, and directing where each individual sits.

ACTIVITY 4.5: Where to Hold the Session?

Are there difficulties with the following locations for a mediation session? If so, what alternatives might you suggest?

1. A manager mediates an employee dispute in his office.

2. A manager mediates an employee dispute in a glass-enclosed conference room on the same floor where the employee and colleagues work.

3. A neighborhood mediation occurs in one neighbor's home.

4. A school mediation takes place in the church the child's teacher attends.

5. An IRS mediation over back taxes takes place in a conference room in the federal building serving a five-state region.

6. A victim–offender mediation takes place in the victim's home.

Environment

The *mediation environment* includes all of the physical factors in the setting—size of the room, seating arrangements, temperature, noise levels, privacy, and distractions. Each decision about the environment affects the disputants and the overall tone of the session. For example, in a mediation about household obligations, chores, and appropriate communication, a 15-year-old male and his mother met in a room with a large window overlooking a park. The teenager could see people walking outside. Unfortunately, there were no blinds to be pulled or curtains to shut. In retrospect, changing the seating so the teen had his back to the window would have helped him to be more engaged in the process.

A quality mediation environment will have free parking, enough seating for all parties, and guaranteed privacy. Other items that may affect the mediation experience are the availability of water or vending machines, noise levels in the surroundings, restroom availability, and the formality of the furnishings.

While there is no one right way to seat disputants and mediators, space is a strategic element that the mediator can control. The mediator must consider the implication of who sits in *power chairs*. Chairs that are larger, more luxurious, or at the head of a table may be perceived as more powerful and create an advantage for the party who sits there. Some mediators choose not to have a table or to have parties sit side-by-side with the mediator working from behind a desk. Other mediators prefer a round table where all parties can see each other and there are no power positions available. Each choice creates a different dynamic. Some seating arrangements are designed to keep disputants physically apart; some are designed to keep them in close proximity. Some are arranged to encourage disputant eye contact with each other; some are designed to encourage disputant eye contact with the mediator. Regardless of the seating arrangement, mediators always should have both disputants within their gaze.

Discussion Question 4.7

WHAT FACTORS should affect the mediator's choice of seating arrangements?

Practical concerns for the mediator sometimes include accessibility of a computer, printer, flipcharts or white boards, or a copy machine. A place is needed for one party to go if the other is in a private meeting (caucus) with the mediator. Don't make the mistake of one mediator who scheduled only one small room for a session. When he needed to meet privately with one party, the other person was required to go outside on a cold, winter day.

Access to a phone can be valuable if disputants need to arrange for more time, secure additional information, or clear a schedule for a future meeting. However, cell phones generally should be turned completely off during a session to avoid the lure of incoming messages. In one session, having access to the Internet helped parties learn about current interest rates and make a decision about putting their home on the market. Each choice in designing the mediation environment is worthy of attention.

ACTIVITY 4.6: Where Does the Mediator Sit?

For the table shapes below, where would you seat the mediator and the two disputants? How might different seating arrangements affect conversation during the session?

ETHICAL ISSUES FOR PRE-MEDIATION CASEWORKERS

In the early days of professionalized mediation, M. Laurie Leitch (1987) made a compelling case that mediation is a dangerous place for those who are disenfranchised or underpowered in a society. Mediators may bring the biases of their culture to a session. For example, in a patriarchal society, many men are better equipped and socially trained to negotiate using power tactics than women. Those who have not learned rules for negotiating may find that without a mediator aware of possible cultural inequities, those same imbalances manifest during mediation. For this reason, mediation may not always be an appropriate place for those in low power to seek a fair settlement.

The appropriateness of some cases is hotly debated among mediation professionals. For example, mediators differ on whether spousal abuse divorce cases can be mediated fairly. Similarly, practitioners argue about whether workplace or school bullying is appropriate for mediation (Jenkins, 2011). Mediation requires the ability to assess a proposed solution and not be bulldozed into agreement by a higher power party. Individuals who have been in abusive situations may suffer from low self-esteem or a decreased sense of self-worth, and thus, they may not be in a good psychological position to practice self-determination. To create the most equitable mediation environment, mediators and intake coordinators must be aware of inherent cultural biases.

Some cases might not be mediated because of their social importance. In 1955, Ms. Rosa Parks refused to cede her bus seat to White passengers in segregated Montgomery, Alabama. Her action and the legal decision that followed was a turning point in the modern civil rights movement. The publicity of her case brought to the forefront the inherent inequities of segregation. Consider what might have happened if Ms. Parks had decided to mediate with the Montgomery transit authority. In a private context, the bus company may have agreed to let

Rosa sit where she wanted on a particular bus route, and one crucial spark that exposed segregation and ignited public protest might not have occurred. Similarly, cities with landlord–tenant mediation programs must be vigilant that unsavory landlords do not repeatedly use mediation as a tactic to avoid public scrutiny and legal obligations to improve substandard housing. Good mediators know that mediation is not appropriate for all cases. Ethical mediators are aware of the systematic, cultural factors that advantage some groups over others.

Summary

Pre-mediation casework or intake activities involve specialized skills. The intake coordinator may be an intake specialist or a mediator. There are advantages and disadvantages to separating the intake and mediator functions with two different people.

Intake coordinators fulfill three roles: educating the disputants, gathering information, and assessing the conflict. While educating the disputants, intake coordinators explain the process of mediation, establish neutral and impartiality boundaries, establish the credibility of the mediator and the mediation process, explain the clients' responsibilities, discuss billing and fees, make referrals to other services, and formalize the agreement to mediate. Information-gathering functions include active listening to gather demographic information, exploring clients' expectations, discovering whether bringing witnesses is contemplated by any of the parties, scheduling the session, and determining whether the disputants are mandated to attend or voluntarily chose mediation. Within their assessment role, intake coordinators explore whether mediation is appropriate for the disputants and whether the disputants are in a position to exert self-determination. Intake coordinators also screen for past violence, advocacy needs, and legal issues; establish that the key decision makers will be present or represented at the mediation; and check for power imbalances among the disputing parties.

The setting of the mediation includes timing, place, and the overall environment. Timing is judged by whether cases are appropriately recent and sufficiently ripe to motivate the disputants to work in good faith toward a mutually desirable outcome. The location of the mediation should be neutral, safe, and convenient. Other aspects of the environment that affect the mediation include the seating arrangement, size of the space, distractions, privacy, and the availability of private meeting rooms. The decision of which cases are appropriate involve unique questions of social equity and power.

Portfolio Assignments

Portfolio Assignment 4.1: The Referral Sourcebook

Create a list of resources available at your college and in your community. Where possible, include phone numbers and contact individuals. When clients express a need

(Continued)

(Continued)

for counseling, free legal advice, or other needs, the referral sourcebook includes information you can share.

Portfolio Assignment 4.2: Intake and Agreement to Mediate Forms

Create the forms listed below. You may find samples of many forms on the Internet (when using someone else's form, be sure to include full reference information). If you adapt someone else's form and personalize it for your use, include the words "Adapted from" followed by the full reference information about the original source. Unless otherwise specified by your instructor, create forms for on-campus disputes.

- *Intake form* (design a form with a client's name, address, contact information, needed demographics, case issues, or other information needed).

- *Agreement to Mediate Form* including a *Subpoena Waiver Clause.*

Ethical Considerations and Tactical Preparations

Mediator Roles	**80**
Ethical Considerations for Mediators	**82**
Neutrality and Impartiality	83
Competence	84
Dual-Role Relationships	85
Truthfulness	86
Informed Choice	86
Conclusions about Mediator Ethics	86
Disputant Roles	**88**
Analyzing Stakeholders	**89**
The Mediation Plan	**90**
Common Causes of Conflict	**91**
Conflict Causes and Mediator Moves	**93**
Cultural Awareness	**94**
Summary	**95**
Portfolio Assignment 5.1: Ethical Codes of Conduct	**96**
Portfolio Assignment 5.2: Mediator Supplies	**96**

CASE 5.1: The Roommates at Odds

Juanita and Julie are first-semester college students living in the dorm. Both were excited to be at college but sad to leave their families and friends back home. Both are from small towns about two hours from campus but in different parts of the state.

Juanita became distressed that Julie's many friends seemed to drop by the room at all hours of the day and night. Juanita doesn't mind studying down the hall or across campus at the library but not all the time! Julie's boyfriends also visit the room, and Juanita never knows whether it is "safe" to come in. Juanita is a little uncomfortable with all the boyfriends visiting late into the night—she's just not used to that type of "free" relationship and is a little embarrassed. Besides, when is she supposed to sleep and get her homework done?

Julie doesn't understand what the problem is with Juanita. She's always been nice to her and willing to share her clothes. Lately, Juanita has been borrowing things without asking, leaving snippy little notes taped to the mirror about Julie's boyfriends, and complaining that she can never study. Juanita goes home every weekend to see her family—Juanita should just study while she's home, in Julie's view.

Juanita approached the resident advisor for her floor and asked for a roommate change and told the advisor that her roommate was like a prostitute having a revolving door of men in the room at all hours. One of Julie's friends overheard the comment and told Julie. When Juanita got back to the room, Julie first yelled at Juanita and then started crying. Juanita left for the weekend without saying anything to Julie. The resident advisor asked the roommates to come to her office for mediation.

When pre-mediation activities are complete, the mediator plans the first session. Preparation involves psychological and tactical considerations. Psychologically, the mediator must review what is and is not the mediator's role, the roles the disputants play, and the ethical boundaries of professional conduct. Tactically, the mediator analyzes the stakeholders in the conflict, creates a plan to guide the session, compares the case to common causes of conflict, analyzes the conflict, and screens for cultural dissimilarities that might pose barriers to communication.

MEDIATOR ROLES

Mediators have numerous responsibilities. Awareness of the limits and boundaries of the mediator's role is central to professional conduct. Mediators must choose, develop, and maintain a strong sense of what is and is not their duty for three reasons. First, role boundaries guide the mediator in determining which skills need to be developed, what behaviors are to be embraced or avoided, and what one is to expect of the disputants. The role adopted by the mediator will align the mediator professionally with like-minded practitioners and potentially alienate the mediator from those who adopt an **incompatible** role.

"What should my role be as a mediator?" is the essential question guiding a mediator's strategies and behaviors. As discussed in Chapter 2, different philosophies bring different values to mediation. Transformative mediators believe their role primarily is to "transform" the participants—a perspective that is encapsulated in the book *Mediating Dangerously* (Cloke, 2001). Changing people is a more profound goal than assisting in problem solving. Some mediators contend they merely play the matchmaker role—scheduling the time and place where disputants meet and then passively sitting back unless a fight erupts and intervention is necessitated. Problem-solving mediators believe their role is to help the parties reach a resolution to their issues by facilitating their communicative process to explore options and determine outcomes.

The second reason that makes role awareness important surrounds the many contexts in which mediation is conducted (Moore, 2003). Typically mediators in the general European American model are impartial and neutral—having no connection to the disputants and no personal stake in the outcome. In the workplace, however, *supervisor mediation* embraces a role that is neither neutral nor impartial, as the mediator is the employees' direct supervisor and has a bias in favor of the organization's interests (Cohen, C. F., 1999). Likewise, mediation in several cultural contexts uses an elder or respected individual who knows the parties well and is invested in solving a breach in the social harmony of their community.

Finally, role awareness is important because mediators must ensure their preferred role matches the regulations of their state, province, or administrative district. For example, Hawaii's Supreme Court advisory for public and private mediators states that, "The role of the mediator includes but is not limited to assisting the parties in improving the definition of issues, reducing obstacles to communication, maximizing the exploration of alternatives, and helping them arrive at agreements" (*Standards*, 2002).

The balanced mediation model presented in this book acknowledges that mediators strategically select the role to be played depending on skill level, desired results, and context. We encourage beginning mediators to focus on the role of an independent mediator using the balanced model. Once basic skills are mastered, the mediator can consider more advanced options.

Numerous researchers discuss mediator roles (Domenici & Littlejohn, 2001; Isenhart & Spangle, 2000; Kheel, 2001; Ponte & Cavenagh, 1999). Typical mediator roles for beginners include:

- *Facilitator:* coordinates communication between the disputants

- *Impartial third party:* has no stake in the outcome

- *Neutral third party:* does not favor either disputant

- *Power balancer:* levels the playing field if one party has more power (see Chapter 7)

- *Face manager:* helps the parties settle without undue embarrassment (see Chapter 8)

- *Role model:* demonstrates constructive communication skills

- *Process controller:* manages the ebb and flow of the discussion within the mediation structure

- *Resource developer:* encourages the parties to consult outside expertise when necessary

- *Legitimizer:* validates the value of each party's perspective and maintains their rights

- *Catalyst:* spurs the parties to perceive the problem differently and move forward

- *Innovator:* builds a structure for creative thinking

- *Trainer:* educates the parties about effective communication strategies

- *Coach:* spurs the parties to talk directly and productively to each other

- *Agent of reality:* helps parties recognize unrealistic goals or unobtainable settlement options

Discussion Question 5.1
WHAT TYPICAL mediator roles apply most to Case 5.1?

ETHICAL CONSIDERATIONS FOR MEDIATORS

Mediator awareness of ethical responsibilities is part and parcel of being a professional. Unfortunately, different states and jurisdictions provide inconsistent messages. The 2003 Uniform Mediation Act approved by the National Conference of Commissioners on Uniform State Laws (2003) may provide message stability if it is adopted by individual states.

Currently, ethical standards vary widely across states. Some state codes cover mediator responsibilities, qualifications, formal certification, or all of the above. In other states, a professional mediator association sets specific ethical standards for members. However, many states provide little or no ethical guidance to mediators or consumers.

While the ethical codes within a state, judicial district, or professional association may differ on some specific points, common threads are woven among the many documents (McCorkle, 2005). When examining the mediator's ethical considerations, questions about neutrality, competence, **dual-role relationships**, and truthfulness are prominent. Mediator ethics include questions like the following:

1. Are there limits to mediator neutrality?

2. Do mediators always need to be impartial?

3. Can mediators be ethical practitioners if they lack particular skill competencies?

4. Should mediators be required to adhere to nondiscriminatory practice in acceptance of clients?

5. Should mediators be expected to do *pro bono* work?

6. Is it ethical for a mediator to have a bias toward settlement of the problem?

7. Does the mediator have responsibilities to people who are not at the mediation session?

8. Should mediation provider organizations have separate ethical responsibilities?

9. When should a mediator withdraw from a case?

10. Should different contexts of mediation require different standards of practice?

11. Are there limits to the concept of disputant informed consent?

12. Should there be limits to a mediator's promise of confidentiality?

13. Is dual-role mediation ethical?

14. Are mediators ethically responsible for the fairness of the disputants' decisions?

15. Are referral fees or fees based on settlement appropriate?

16. What ethical standards apply to caucuses or private meetings?

17. To what standard of truthfulness should a mediator be obligated?

Discussion Question 5.2

LOCATE THE code of mediator conduct for your state. If there is no state code, locate the Association for Conflict Resolution Code of Conduct. How does the ethical standard answer the 17 questions posed above?

Neutrality and Impartiality

Textbooks and most codes of conduct repeat the mantra that "ethical mediators should be neutral and impartial," but they do not always discuss the conundrums that simple directive creates. Frequently, a mediator keeps one party from dominating the session or helps the less verbally skilled disputant to express interests or makes offers (power balancing). Are these behaviors a breach of neutrality? Should impartiality extend to outcomes that the mediator believes to be unfair to one of the parties or that may harm others who are not at the negotiating table? If the disputants decide to take care of their mutual litter problem by dumping the garbage in a nearby gully, does the mediator have a responsibility to the unknown property owner whose land is about to be trashed?

Mediators also arrive at a session with past experiences, biases, worldviews, and opinions. While mediators strive to minimize visceral reactions to the stories disputants tell, we are all humans who cannot avoid being affected by information that strikes an emotional chord. Likewise, personal experience (or lack thereof) may be a source of unconscious bias. Some authors argue the term *equidistance* between the parties may be a more achievable goal than neutrality (Beck, 1999; Cohen, Dattner, & Luxenburg, 1999). A mediator applying the concept of equidistance maintains the same level of partiality and connection to each disputant. Mediators should consult the code of conduct in their jurisdictions for specific guidance on neutrality's limits.

Neutrality, impartiality, or equidistance are slippery, if not impossible, goals to achieve according to some scholars. Hilary Astor (2007) summarized, "research has not found Machiavellian mediators eager to impose their own world-view on unsuspecting parties. Rather it has shown that practitioners influence the content and outcomes of mediation despite asserting neutrality and consciously struggling to [practice] it. Mediators exert pressure in mediation towards outcomes they [favor] by selectively creating opportunities for the parties to pursue these outcomes" (p. 225). Only a deepening of self-awareness and a reflexive perspective can mitigate the dangers of unconscious biases.

Discussion Question 5.3

WHAT STRATEGIES can mediators employ to mitigate the tendency to sway disputants toward agreements the mediator personally prefers?

Competence

Competence is divided in some ethical codes into *mediator knowledge* and *skillfulness*. While some states have no technical requirements for mediator competence, the obligation to be knowledgeable about mediation theory and skillful in its practice is integral to professional behavior. William R. Cupach, Daniel J. Canary, and Brian H. Spitzberg (2010) and Kathy Domenici and Stephen W. Littlejohn (2001) maintain that keeping within the limits of personal competence is a challenge for everyone. While accepting any type of case may be tempting, a mediator unaware of the dynamics of child development and the effects of split-parenting on children probably should not be conducting child custody mediation. Some argue that child custody mediators must acquire enhanced information requirements about family law, child development, spousal abuse, and high-conflict situations (Irving & Benjamin, 1995). Marian Roberts (1997) argues that all mediators have the responsibility to become educated about, and respond to, cultural differences that might affect the outcome of a negotiation. For example, individuals from cultures where authority figures should be obeyed and respected might be disadvantaged in mediations where the other disputant is an attorney, teacher, police officer, or leader of a faith community.

In some jurisdictions or states, the competence issue is regulated by mediator certification. The Model Standards of Conduct for Mediators jointly adopted in 2005 by the American Arbitration Association, the American Bar Association, and the Association for Conflict Resolution states that, "A mediator shall mediate only when the mediator has the necessary competence to satisfy the reasonable expectations of the parties" (Standard IV). Mediators should consult their state or territory for guidance about training and competence in specialized areas of mediation.

Discussion Question 5.4

SOME CONTEND that a mediator is a "process expert," and thus, specific content knowledge is not a necessary requirement for competency. Others hold a mediator cannot claim competence without adequate content knowledge (e.g., special education law, environmental regulations, and so on). Must a mediator be a content expert to be competent as a mediator? Why or why not?

Dual-Role Relationships

Dual-role relationships occur when a mediator also represents one or both parties in another professional role, such as an attorney or a counselor. Codes of conduct that address dual-role relationships universally state they are not appropriate. Some codes further clarify that recruiting or accepting a disputant as a counseling or legal client, after first meeting him or her in a mediation session, is not appropriate.

A View from the Field: One Mediator's Ethical Dilemma

I mediated a case about a barking dog. The disputant who complained about the barking professed to hate all dogs. The other party, a husband and wife, had a 10-year-old golden retriever who meant the world to them. I have two retrievers of my own, and I felt some kinship with the owners of the dog. The issue was that the dog was barking, and the plaintiff in this small claims court case was a writer who demanded absolute quiet in the neighborhood during the day while he worked at home. He had filed suits against four other dog owners in the same neighborhood. This case was the first to come to mediation through the court.

Through the emotional disclosures in the storytelling phase, I learned that the dog owners had made several attempts previously to appease the neighbor. They brought the dog inside during the day. Their efforts were not enough for the writer who could still hear the dog barking at the mail carrier and kids who passed by. The dog owners then agreed to put the dog in the bathroom of the house, where there were no windows or walls to the outside, while they worked during the day. Over the course of two months, the dog gained considerable weight and this worried the owners.

These efforts were not enough for the writer. During the mediation, the writer expressed a demand that the dog wear a shock collar that would shock the dog each time he barked. The owners were opposed to this in principle, but they decided that keeping peace with the neighbors and avoiding court was more important, citing their religious belief that people were more important than pets.

(Continued)

(Continued)

I brought the dog owners into caucus and shared my concerns that they seemed very distraught over their agreement to use a shock collar. They said they were, but they wanted the conflict to end. The woman cried throughout the caucus. I informed them of their options: that they didn't have to make a decision today and that we could postpone or they could go to court. They said, "No. Getting this over with and not dealing with this jerk anymore was more important." I asked questions about the workability of the decision for them and their dog. I laid out their alternatives if the case didn't settle in mediation. Truth be told, I hated this agreement.

My unspoken bias was that they should take this guy to court, as I believed they would prevail. I felt badly for the dog. I felt badly for the couple. I really disliked the plaintiff's bullying behaviors. But ultimately, I wrote the agreement for their signatures. Of all the mediations I've done—including divorce and child custody—this was the one that caused me the most angst and had me question my ethical responsibilities.

Truthfulness

As you consider your role as a mediator, how truthful must you be with disputants? Most codes of conduct are clear that the mediator must disclose any potential conflicts of interest, prior relationships with one of the parties, connection to some stake in the outcome, and fees to be charged. Other areas remain murky. How truthful must the mediator be in talking with the disputants about facts or in representing offers made in caucus? Is it appropriate to try to motivate the parties by saying they are very close to coming together during a monetary negotiation when the parties actually are quite far apart? Attorney-mediators are trained to accept a level of deception in their role as advocates for their clients (Cooley, 2000). Should attorney-mediators or judge-mediators who run settlement conferences be held to the same standards as non-attorney-mediators? If deception is a part of the "game" in some types of mediation, should that fact be disclosed to the disputants? Mediators must confront these questions and mentally prepare to remain within boundaries accepted in the profession.

Informed Choice

A common feature of codes of mediator ethics is *informed choice*. The mediator has some obligation to ensure that parties have enough data so their choices are well founded, rather than permitting the disputants to make decisions based on partial or erroneous information. If one party discloses information to the mediator in caucus and asks that the mediator keep it secret from the other person, the mediator has an ethical dilemma stemming from the concept of informed choice.

Conclusions about Mediator Ethics

While the landscape of mediation ethics remains uneven across states, beginning mediators can be guided by eight basic principles:

1. *Do no harm.* It is better not to mediate than to make the situation worse.

2. *Uphold the parties' right to self-determination by creating a situation where they can make informed choices.* Roberts (1997) summarizes this viewpoint by saying, "The mediator's first responsibility is to protect the right of the parties to be the architects of their own agreement" (p. 104). The mediator is responsible to respect and maintain the disputants' rights to determine their own solutions and decisions, as well as to be sure they have the information and capacity to make informed choices.

3. *Work within your level of competence.* Withdraw from cases for which you do not have the specialized training needed or cannot ask the right questions due to lack of content knowledge.

4. *Disclose any limits to your neutrality or impartiality.* Any past associations with the parties, their businesses, or interest in potential outcomes must be disclosed.

5. *Disclose your limits to confidentiality and then maintain that confidentiality.* Many states' laws require mediators to report child abuse and threats of physical harm to self or others. You must know what is required in your state or territory. Confidentiality applies to casework, private meetings, and the mediation sessions. Mediators should not divulge the names or details of cases in ways that **compromise** the disputants' anonymity, except as required by law.

6. *Avoid professional dual-role relationships.* Do not act as the counselor, attorney, or in other professional capacities for a client during, or for a reasonable amount of time after, a mediation. Do not solicit mediation clients for other professional relationships. Any exceptions to the dual-role relationship principle must be disclosed. For example, manager mediation involves direct supervisors mediating with their subordinates. In Case 5.1, Julie and Juanita's resident advisor might mediate their case if the college has provided specialized training to take advantage of the advisor's relationship with both roommates.

7. *Withdraw from the case when you cannot maintain your professional role or when withdrawal is best for the disputants.* While mediation is appropriate for many cases, it is not always the right choice. Likewise, continuing a mediation that is outside one's comfort zone is unwise. The Kansas Supreme Court Dispute Resolution Advisory Council (2002) standards make the following comment: "Mediation is an appropriate method to use when parties wish to preserve their ongoing relationships or terminate an existing relationship in the least adversarial and most cooperative way. Solutions arrived at in mediation tend to last over time because the people affected by the decisions are the ones making them. Because the parties are responsible for making their own decisions, mediation may not be appropriate if a party is unable to negotiate due to substance abuse, psychological impairment, physical or emotional abuse by the other party, or ignorance." In the latter cases, the mediator should withdraw from the case.

8. *Know the law and any mediator codes of conduct binding on those who practice in your state or territory.*

DISPUTANT ROLES

Cupach, Canary, and Spitzberg (2010) argue that disputant knowledge and competence also affect how a mediation proceeds. Preparing the disputants to hold up their part of the mediation is an important task for the mediator. Sometimes, preparation begins during pre-mediation interviews. Sometimes, individuals learn about their role on a website. The mediator also coaches disputants on their role during the opening statement.

Disputants have a responsibility to know and convey their interests, be knowledgeable about their issues, negotiate in good faith, and be open to creative solutions. Some individuals who come to mediation have responsibilities to the constituencies they represent. In general, disputants should be able to:

- Communicate well enough to explain their interests and tell their stories

- Follow the instructions of the mediator

- Listen to the other party and the mediator

- Negotiate and consider creative solutions to problems

- Seek or share the facts and information necessary to make informed choices

John M. Haynes (1994) commented that a mediator who enters a dispute faces clients who are invested in their side and are motivated to convince the mediator that their perspective is right. An emotional investment in "being right" is a barrier to settlement. Disputants need to be guided to see more than one side of an issue—to move from advocate to negotiator and from opponent to participant in mutual problem solving.

In the case of Juanita and Julie, the mediator explained the disputants' roles during the opening statement. When Julie repeatedly interrupted Juanita while she was relating her view of their roommate situation, the mediator reminded Julie of her role as a listener while Juanita was speaking and assured her that she would have an opportunity to speak in a moment. A part of mediator preparation is reviewing the roles that disputants should play and to communicate those roles to disputants.

CASE 5.2: Reverend MacDonald's Mediation

Mason MacDonald has been counseling one of his parishioners, Olivia Smythe, who was unhappy with her marriage and family. Mason sat through a four-hour mediation workshop and is eager to put his new skills to work. He persuades Olivia that family mediation is a good idea and to bring her husband and 13-year-old daughter together to discuss some issues that might help the family. Olivia agrees and brings the family to mediation. Mason acts as their mediator. He is glad to finally meet Dan and the daughter, Marquerida, who do not attend services with Olivia. During the session, Olivia and Dan discuss how their marriage has been unhappy and how stressful it is for the whole family. Marquerida is withdrawn and hardly speaks. The parents decide to send Marquerida to live with a cousin in Nevada

> (Continued)
>
> over the summer so they can work on their marriage. They haven't talked to the cousin for a while, but he is family. Olivia, Dan, and Reverend MacDonald all are pleased with the outcome of the session.
>
> *Are there mediator ethics issues with any of Reverend MacDonald's choices?*

ANALYZING STAKEHOLDERS

A *stakeholder* is any person who holds a substantial and direct interest in the outcome of the mediation. Typically, beginning mediators work with cases where only two disputants come to the table. Mediation cases, however, may include any number of potential stakeholders who could be disputants. For example, in a juvenile victim–offender mediation case where a swimming pool was damaged and taken out of service during a hot August week, an entire family might be the victims. If the pool were owned by the city, an entire community may have a stake in the situation. There also may have been more than one offender who committed the crime. While it is possible to **fractionate**, or break the case down into one person representing a family or the community and one offender, the mediator must realize that there are other stakeholders who are not at the table.

In mediations involving spouses or business partners, the mediator analyzes who has a stake in the outcome and whether the person who comes to the table has the authority to negotiate on behalf of a larger group. If the swimming pool case involving damage to a city pool were mediated within the *community circle model,* representatives of each group having a stake in the child's future may attend the session: the offender's teacher, parents, the pool manager, someone representing others who use the pool, and perhaps a person from the faith community.

In one case, two juveniles broke 30 car windows in their neighborhood. Imagine having 30 car owners lined up on one side of the table and 2 adolescent boys on the other. Because a combined session was not workable, the program coordinator scheduled each boy separately with each car owner who was willing to mediate—resulting in 60 potential sessions, each with its own personal dynamics and resulting restitution plan. In another example, all relevant parties to a large-scale environmental issue were brought together at once to negotiate a creative solution to what should become of a rusting, abandoned factory site labeled as Brownfields by the Environmental Protection Agency (Brownfields and Land Revitalization, 2012). Parties might include the city, county, state, federal agencies, nearby businesses, neighbors, tribes, *ad infinitum.*

Those who come to the mediation table should either be the direct stakeholder in the case or have authority to make binding decisions on behalf of the stakeholder. A common frustration in small claims court mediation is discovering partway through the session that the person who came to court representing a business does not have authority to negotiate an outcome. Establishing whether the party who comes to the mediation table has authority to make a decision is necessary. Disputants who are ordered to small claims court mediation by a judge commonly obey the command to appear at the designated time or send a representative. All too often, however, the representative will know nothing about the case or and does not feel authorized to negotiate.

Determining who should *not* come to the mediation table also is important. While friends, attorneys, or other support networks sometimes are allowed in the mediation room, they may or may not sit at the table where negotiations occur and typically are not allowed to speak as a party to the negotiation. When a parent comes to support a child who is an adult defendant during a small claims case, it is rare for the defendant to admit any wrongdoing. For example, if a landlord is suing for damages to an apartment, the defendant is unlikely to admit any responsibility in front of a parent. The individual disputants, of course, always will be permitted to speak privately with an attorney or a support person.

Just as it may be ill-advised to have people who are only loosely connected to the conflict sitting at the table, it is problematic to exclude someone who has a direct stake in the outcome. When three neighbors have a conflict about their shared responsibility for maintaining a rural road, it is wrong to have only two of the individuals negotiate a decision that is binding on the third. Analyzing the conflict and the potential issues will help the mediator determine who the stakeholders are and who should be involved in the session.

THE MEDIATION PLAN

Numerous mediations are conducted with the benefit and insights gained through pre-mediation. The mediator analyzes that information and deduces probable interests, issues, commonalities, and stumbling blocks. Christopher W. Moore (2003) lists ten critical questions to use when creating the mediation plan:

1. Who should be involved in the mediation effort?

2. What is the best location for mediation?

3. What physical arrangements need to be made?

4. What procedures will be used?

5. What issues, interests, and settlement options are important to the parties?

6. What are the psychological conditions of the parties?

7. How will rules or behavioral guidelines be established?

8. What is the general plan for the first joint negotiations in the mediator's presence? How will specific agenda items be identified and ordered?

9. How will parties be educated about the process, and how will they arrive at agreement to proceed with negotiations?

10. What possible deadlocks could occur, and how will they be overcome? (pp. 146–147)

Based on the analysis of the case information, the mediator strategically creates a preliminary plan of how, when, and where the mediation will unfold. Like most good plans in flexible situations, it is only a starting point. As new information emerges during the session, it could seem like the mediation plan is unraveling. We prefer to think that the mediation plan is fluid and changeable.

Having the opportunity to talk to the disputants in advance and research the case offers several advantages. The mediator can create a theory about the case, prepare for predictable outbursts if emotions are high, stockpile questions to elicit information, and make other strategic preparations. The disadvantages occur when the mediator begins to believe the theory too much. The result of the case analysis is tentative and speculative. When the mediator sticks to the plan, despite new information provided by the disputants, the session is sure to go awry.

Cold-mediation sessions, where the mediator has no prior knowledge of the case or the disputants, have the advantage of permitting the mediator to "fish" for very general stories at the beginning of the session and to model positive communication behaviors as each party's story unfolds. The disadvantage is that the mediator must be able to analyze the situation quickly and have a deep mental storehouse of tactics to respond to unexpected situations. A mediator's portfolio containing forms, lists of tactical options, and other help is particularly useful as a reference for cold-mediation sessions.

COMMON CAUSES OF CONFLICT

Knowledge of common causes of conflict assists in the preparation of a mediation plan. Each conflict cause requires a different initial strategy.

Conflict causes can be analyzed in many ways (see Mayer, 2000; McCorkle & Reese, 2010). Issues of power and emotion may manifest as overlapping issues in any conflict. Broadly envisioned, conflict causes can be categorized into the following types:

- *Communication/Communication Style:* Humans are not always skilled at communication and often misperceive each other's intentions or behaviors. In addition, individual **personality style** and communication preferences can exacerbate conflict.

- *Emotions:* Fear, hurt feelings, anger, and other emotions drive and sustain some conflicts.

- *Values:* Values are deeply rooted concepts tied to core beliefs and are defended vigorously when threatened. Sometimes generational issues manifest in value-laden ways.

- *Structures:* External rules and frameworks can precipitate or sustain conflicts, such as resource distribution, how to make decisions, scheduling, or how to arrange physical space.

- *Information:* Sometimes conflict emerges because individuals unknowingly have different information, believe only their information is correct, argue about criteria, or are withholding information.

- *Culture:* Each culture carries a template of how to express conflict and whether to be direct or indirect in use of tactics.

By locating what is sustaining a conflict, mediators can plan where to begin their work. If the conflict between Julie and Juanita seems to center around hurt feelings, the mediator would choose different strategic options than if the conflict were about mistaken information. Chapter 7 will detail how conflict cause analysis can be used strategically during the storytelling and issue identification phase.

One pattern mediators see is labeled by Roxane S. Lulofs and Dudley D. Cahn (2000) as the *competitive conflict escalation cycle.* A problem emerges and the parties try, unsuccessfully, to work it out. A conflict ensues. The conflict escalates, and one or both parties have emotional reactions. Feelings are hurt. Now there is an emotional issue layered on top of the original substantive issue. If trust is lost, a relationship issue also may emerge. The individuals become polarized around specific positions, which may have little connection to the original problem. One or both parties feel they have "lost" in the exchange, leaving an unresolved conflict that sets the stage for the next conflict episode. What began as a conflict over a tangible interest became a relationship problem dominated by emotional hurt. In general, when emotions dominate a situation, mediators try to moderate the level of emotional sensitivity before moving to negotiation of the substantive issues.

Suzanne McCorkle and Melanie J. Reese (2010) claim that a perception of differing *goals* can lead one party to resist the other and be the flashpoint that starts a conflict. The roommates Juanita and Julie may have different goals about their relationship or about how to use their mutual space. If Juanita's goal is to have Julie as her best friend and Julie just wants to share a room for financial reasons, they may be trying to pull each other in different directions. Likewise, an overt or subtle use of power to restrict the other's choices may lead to resistance and escalated conflict. If Julie is using the room as a space for socializing with friends, her presence precludes Juanita's ability to use the room as a place to study or rest. Mediators attempt to deduce where disputants perceive the other party is interfering with goal attainment.

Style differences also can be a contributing cause of conflict. Joseph P. Folger, Marshall Scott Poole, and Randall K. Stutman (2013) define *style* as a "consistent, specific orientation toward the conflict, an orientation that unifies specific tactics into a coherent whole" (p. 108). The classic and oft cited rubric offered by Robert R. Blake and Jane Mouton (1964) identified five primary management approaches to conflict that provide useful labels when thinking about conflict styles:

- *Withdraw:* ignoring the existence of the conflict

- *Accommodate:* agreeing to whatever the other party wishes

- *Compete:* opposing the other's goals from a desire to win

- *Compromise:* splitting the difference on issues to achieve a settlement

- *Collaborate:* working until a solution is reached that meets the interests of all parties

Style differences cause conflict when they inhibit productive dialogue about the problem. Two competitors may become stuck in a destructive win–lose pattern of interaction as both escalate their behavior to win. Any conflict with a withdrawer may need a third party to persuade the avoider to participate in solving the problem. Over-reliance on compromise can lead to a temporary resolution that satisfies no one and does not really address the core issues. Accommodators faced with competitors may need the power balancing assistance of a mediator to have a fair chance to have their needs met during negotiations.

If you have ever worked with someone whose communication style clashes with yours, you know how style differences can infuriate people or create the illusion of insults where none really exist. While we do not concur entirely with the popular literature that suggests that men and women have completely different communication styles, we do agree with Leda M. Cooks and Claudia L. Hale's (1992) observation that some men and women exhibit differences that exacerbate conflict. Mediators should be aware of gender dynamics, cultural influences, and other factors that may impact communicative style.

Discussion Question 5.5

WHAT "STYLE" differences in how people communicate create barriers to conflict management? Hint: Think about the ways that others communicate that are different from how you communicate or that you find irritating.

CONFLICT CAUSES AND MEDIATOR MOVES

Discovering which general causes are driving the conflict helps the mediator to plan first moves during the early phases of the session, identify skills that might be useful, and speculate about barriers to settlement. A mediator can assess a cause and determine a beneficial plan for how to address the concern. For example, if the parties share deeply rooted, mutually exclusive value systems, resolution by transforming one or both parties' value structure is unlikely, so the mediator knows to frame the agenda phase around how the parties can work together even though they have strong value differences. Or, if the conflict arises because one party has information that the other party does not have (an information conflict), planning questions that elicit information early in the process is a natural first step. In all cases, the mediator must remember that the cause of a conflict and barriers to settlement will be a combination of actual events and the disputants' *perceptions* of those events. Uncovering and managing different perceptions is an important mediator skill. Erik J. Van Slyke (1999) comments:

> Constructive conflict management depends significantly on our emotional awareness and social interaction skills, and less on our cognitive capabilities. A high IQ may, in fact, interfere with positive interaction because conflict is not always rational, and an analytical approach may overlook significant emotional needs. While we can break

every conflict down into its structural components, isolate the variables, identify the problem, and develop systematic solutions, we are still dealing with humans. And no matter how "right" our answer may be, if we have not satisfied the other party's temperamental, peculiar, exacerbating personal issues, we have not resolved the conflict. (p. 32)

ACTIVITY 5.1: The Preplanned Question

Mediators often preplan several questions for use during storytelling. The examples below illustrate preplanned questions. Select a case from the first four chapters of this book, and then create your own preplanned questions by substituting details from the case for the [bracketed] content.

1. When [you saw the message taped on your car door], how did you feel?

2. What is it about [where you park your car] that is important to you?

3. How did you reach the decision to [tape a note on Jen's car]?

4. Did you talk with [Jen] about [the parking situation] in the past? How did that conversation go? What was your intention when you started that conversation?

5. Did the two of you know each other before the event? How did you first meet?

6. Was there a time when your relationship was better?

7. If you were back home in [Taiwan], how would [a neighbor issue] be settled?

8. I'm curious, what were you thinking when you used the word ["tidy"]?

9. What is it about [your neighborhood] that you like? If you had an [ideal workplace,] what would that be like?

10. What do you do in an average day [at work]?

Discussion Question 5.6

ANALYZE CASE 5.1 and create a list of preplanned questions.

CULTURAL AWARENESS

We return to the discussion of culture throughout the book because of its pervasive importance. When contemplating the mediation plan, culture must be considered. Mediators determine whether the disputants are from dissimilar cultures. Is there a juxtaposition of race, ethnicity, background, socioeconomic status, family of origin, environment, or gender that might affect how the disputants perceive the world? If the disputants' cultures have different norms about authority figures, public loss of face, how to express conflict, or appropriate non-verbal behaviors, the mediator will need to prepare to manage these differences—perhaps applying power balancing techniques, finding ways to inform each participant about the other's cultural preferences, or finding a co-mediator who better understands the cultures. While there is a risk of stereotyping all persons from a general geographic area as being essentially the same, an awareness of cultural variability is essential for mediators.

When separate immigrant families are referred to mediation by the police and one is from Bosnia and the other is from China, the mediator should consider the probable cultural differences that might affect the session. Bosnian culture encourages more vocal and emotional expression of conflict than Chinese culture. Both cultures, however, share values in work and sacrifice for the good of the greater group. In Case 5.1, if Juanita comes from a first-generation, traditional, Mexican American family, her values toward premarital relations *may* be quite dissimilar to Julie's more free-spirited upbringing.

A mediator should not assume that a particular ethnicity automatically means a disputant will share the dominant culture and values of their homeland. There are general techniques a mediator can apply during a session to discover cultural traditions and values. The mediator might ask each disputant, "When you were growing up, what did you learn about how neighbors should interact with each other?" "What would an ideal roommate situation be like for you?" "How were problems settled back home before you moved here?" Advanced training in intercultural conflict management should be on every mediator's continuing education list.

Discussion Question 5.7

WHAT CULTURAL groups dominate your geographic area? What values and communication patterns might they bring to a mediation session? How can you learn more about each cultural group? What are the dangers in making assumptions about cultural groups?

Summary

Preparation for a mediation session involves both psychological and tactical aspects. Psychologically, the mediator must review role boundaries, impartiality, neutrality, and state- or province-specific regulations. Beginners can assume the role of an independent, balanced model mediator. Psychologically, the mediator must review the standards of practice in her or his state or province and personal considerations of neutrality, impartiality, competence, dual-role relationships, and truthfulness. Eight ethical guidelines for beginning mediators were suggested. The mediator psychologically reviews the disputants' roles and is prepared to explain those roles to disputants, as well as to guide disputants in staying within acceptable boundaries during the session.

Tactically, the mediator must analyze the stakeholders and establish that the correct parties come to the table, as well as ensuring that superfluous parties are not present.

Those who come to the mediation table as representatives must have the authority to negotiate outcomes. The mediator creates a tentative mediation plan, keeping in mind the advantages and disadvantages of prior knowledge of the case. A mediator compares the most common causes of conflict to the case to determine probable barriers to settlement. Common causes of conflict include communication, emotions, information, values, structure, and culture. Other common causes of conflict are competitive conflict escalation cycles, perceived goal differences, and style differences. Each potential cause of conflict suggests a different opening move by the mediator.

Cultural awareness must be integrated into the mediator's psychological and tactical preparations. Mediators should be aware of the communication patterns and cultural assumptions of the groups with whom they work.

Portfolio Assignments

Portfolio Assignment 5.1: Ethical Codes of Conduct

What are the rules and regulations for mediation in your state? Discover whether your state has a *professional mediation association* with a code of conduct. Individual states or provinces also may have codes of conduct provided by the courts or laws/codes passed by a state legislature. Print out the relevant codes and requirements concerning mediation. If your state has no regulations or codes, go to the national Association for Conflict Resolution website (http://acresolution.org/) and print out their code of conduct.

Portfolio Assignment 5.2: Mediator Supplies

Create a checklist of needed supplies you could bring to each mediation session. For example, the checklist might include:

- Paper/notepads (for mediators as well as disputants)
- Writing utensils (for all parties)
- Calculator
- Calendar (two year)
- Schedule of room availability for future mediations
- Tissues
- Watch or clock
- Receipt book
- Mediator's portfolio

The Mediator's Opening Statement

Opening Statement Functions   **98**
Opening Statement Styles   **99**
   Monologue Style   99
   Interactive Style   100
Opening Statement Dynamics   **100**
   Length   101
   Order   101
Key Components of the Opening Statement   **103**
   Welcoming   103
   Introductions   103
   Building Credibility   103
   Establishing Stakeholders   104
   Explaining the Nature and Scope of Mediation   104
   Explaining the Mediator's Role   105
   Explaining the Caucus   105
   Explaining Impartiality and Neutrality   105
   Giving a Confidentiality Pledge   106
   Disclosing Notetaking   106
   Establishing Ground Rules   107
   Discovering Time Constraints   108
   Explaining the Role of Outside Experts   109
   Securing the Commitment to Begin   109
   Transitioning to Storytelling   110
Building Credibility and Rapport   **110**
The Relationship between Opening Statements and Mediator Control   **111**
Notetaking for Mediators   **111**
Summary   **113**
Portfolio Assignment 6.1: Creating Your Personal Opening Statement   **114**
Portfolio Assignment 6.2: Creating Your Personal Notetaking Form   **114**

The words that begin a mediation establish the tone and protocol for the session. A good opening statement builds trust and puts the mediator in control of the process. A poor opening statement erodes disputant confidence and permits the eruption of power struggles between the mediator and the parties. Kathy Domenici and Stephen W. Littlejohn (2001) established three purposes for the mediator's opening statement: Introduce the disputants to the mediator and to each other, explain the mediation process, and establish trust (p. 40). The symbolic nature of the opening statement should not be undervalued. The opening statement creates the first visible commonality for the parties: Both are conceding process control to the mediator. This chapter presents the functions and practical realities of the first phase of mediation—the mediator's opening statement.

OPENING STATEMENT FUNCTIONS

The mediator's opening statement must accomplish several functions:

- Introduce the parties and the mediator to each other
- Model a positive tone
- Build trust between the mediator and each party
- Establish the mediator's control of the process
- Educate parties about mediation as a process and preview the stages
- Reduce anxiety about what will occur during the session
- Discuss the role of the mediator
- Discuss the role of the disputants
- Transition to the phase where the disputants tell their stories

Christopher W. Moore (2003) recommends that the mediator's opening remarks "should set a positive tone and meet the basic needs of the parties for comfort and safety. To establish a safe environment, the mediator should consider both emotional and physical safety" (p. 212). Physical safety concerns are accomplished nonverbally "through the physical arrangement of the parties in the room and verbally with his or her opening statement" (Moore, 2003, p. 212). In Chapter 4, we discussed the importance of seating arrangements. Establishing an emotionally safe environment equally is important. Effective mediation requires that parties feel secure enough to share information about themselves and their issues. The mediator creates the right psychological environment by appearing fair, consistent, and inclusive of each party.

> ### Discussion Question 6.1
>
> CHOOSE ONE of the mediation cases presented in the previous chapters. Identify any safety issues to be considered by the mediator. How can the mediator's opening statement address those safety concerns?

The opening statement also fulfills the need of educating disputants to make informed choices. To have *informed choice,* disputants must be able to anticipate what will occur during the process, what the mediator will and will not do, and how decisions might affect their rights. Informed choice is so critical that some states specifically identify the topics to be covered in the mediator's opening statement. The Arkansas Alternative Dispute Resolution Commission (2011) *Requirements for the Conduct of Mediation and Mediators* requires mediators to discuss:

- The role the mediator plays to assist the parties in voluntary decision making
- The difference between a mediator's role and the role of a legal authority
- The procedures to be followed
- The mediator's pledge of confidentiality
- The mediator's commitment to neutrality
- The mediator's responsibility to foster a reasonable negotiating atmosphere
- The mediator's ability to stop the process for a variety of reasons
- How parties not represented by an attorney may consult legal counsel at any time
- The binding nature of mediated agreements once signed

Roxane S. Lulofs and Dudley D. Cahn (2000) believe that if disputants doubt the process or the credibility of the mediator, the information and tone of the opening statement may help to build trust (p. 351). The opening statement fulfills many functions for the mediator.

OPENING STATEMENT STYLES

Monologue Style

Mediators have choices about how to deliver the opening statement. As the term *monologue* suggests, the mediator can be the one who does most, or even all, of the talking. In sessions that are highly structured, and where consistency is paramount, an opening monologue may be scripted. For example, in state agencies dealing with discrimination issues, a pure monologue where only the mediator speaks may be prudent. Implementing a one-sided monologue sets a formal atmosphere where the mediator is communicating that he or she is in strict control of the mediation process.

In the monologue style, the mediator prepares a short speech that is presented in a **conversational style**. The monologue can be read from a script, memorized, or extemporized from a list of key words. In monologue style, the disputants do not speak, except at carefully chosen points. The disputants become accustomed to listening to and heeding the mediator's control of the process. The mediator might only permit the disputants to speak when answering how each one wishes to be addressed, to agree to the **ground rules**, and (at the end of the speech) to ask any questions about the process. A monologue style helps beginner mediators maintain control of the process.

Interactive Style

In an interactive approach, the mediator includes the disputants in a conversation. After providing information about the mediator's role, confidentiality, and some other elements of the opening statement, the mediator asks questions, such as "Is the goal of the mediation clear?" or "Do you have any questions about my role?" An interactive opening statement encourages the parties to take part in the creation of the process. Mediators may explain mediation in segments and invite the disputants to "buy in" to the process by soliciting their approval. In sales, this process of gaining agreement early and often is called the *yes response*. The interactive style is less rigid and allows the mediator to convey the information and functions of the opening statement through a dialogue with the disputants. For example, after explaining why ground rules are necessary, the mediator might ask the disputants what ground rules they would find useful. Creating a dialogue with the disputants has the additional benefit of checking understanding and keeping disputants focused on the main points of the opening statement. In a mediation where an informal tone is desired, more interaction between mediators and disputants may occur.

Discussion Question 6.2

WHEN WOULD a strict monologue approach be most appropriate? When would a more interactive approach be appropriate? How would a mediator decide which style would be best?

OPENING STATEMENT DYNAMICS

Every opening statement will address several key issues. While opening statements are modified in specialized contexts, such as juvenile victim–offender mediation, a general opening statement will include many of these elements:

Welcome

Introductions

Mediator's credibility statement

Establish stakeholders are present

Overview of mediation

Voluntary

Parties create solution

Caucus/private meetings

Role of outside experts (if necessary)

Phases/steps in the process that will be followed

Explanations of mediator role

Not attorney or judge

Impartial and neutral

Confidentiality pledge

Notetaking procedures

Ground rules

Respect

Honesty

Speak one at a time

Agreement to ground rules

Breaks and facilities

Time constraints

Commitment to begin

Transition to storytelling

Length

While the list of basic components may seem long, most elements are described quite briefly. A mediator's opening statement should be long enough to cover all points, and yet short enough not to bog the disputants down in unnecessary details. Opening statements typically run one to three minutes in length and rarely more than five minutes. Opening statements will be longer if many questions are asked or if the function of the opening statement must also fulfill goals of educating the disputants about some aspect of mediation.

Order

The order of the topics in the opening statement is flexible. For example, in a mediation where there is high tension between disputants, a mediator may decide to address ground rules early in the opening statement. If mediator credibility must be established, more time may be spent to build confidence in the mediator. The sample opening statement in Figure 6.1 is a compact presentation of the basic elements.

FIGURE 6.1 Sample Opening Statement

Hello. My name is Carol Hutchison. Please call me Carol.	*Introduces self, builds*
First, Welcome to the campus mediation center. I commend you both for	*rapport, and establishes*
choosing to work out a solution to your issues together. I've been mediating	*credibility*
cases for this center for two years now, and I am confident that this process	
will be helpful.	*Briefly explains process*

Hello. My name is Carol Hutchison. Please call me Carol.
First, Welcome to the campus mediation center. I commend you both for choosing to work out a solution to your issues together. I've been mediating cases for this center for two years now, and I am confident that this process will be helpful. — *Introduces self, builds rapport, and establishes credibility* / *Briefly explains process*

As a mediator, I am going to walk us through a process that will ask each of you to help me understand what brought us here today, and then see whether we can come up with a resolution that meets your needs. I'm not here to make decisions for you or offer you legal counsel. My job is to help the two of you come up with a solution that works for you both. In that role, I strive to be neutral and impartial, meaning that I will not favor either one of you or champion any particular solution. If you have any concerns about how the process is going or what I am doing, please let me know so we can discuss it. — *Establishes roles* / *Explains neutrality and impartiality*

You have each been sent a copy of the Agreement to Mediate and Subpoena Waiver forms. Are there any questions? I would like to draw your attention to the confidentiality clause and remind you the only reason I would break confidentiality is if one of you threatened harm to yourself or others. I also want to inform you that in the event we don't resolve your dispute here and this case proceeds to court, I cannot be subpoenaed by either side. I will take notes through the course of this mediation just to keep my thoughts in order, but I will destroy those notes after this session. — *Explains confidentiality issues* / *Explains subpoena waiver* / *Explains notetaking procedures*

At some point I may find it necessary to meet with you individually. If so, what is said in those meetings also is confidential, unless you choose to share it with the other person. — *Explains caucus*

I've reserved this room until 4:30 today. Are there any time constraints? Good. If you need a break, let me know. Bathrooms are just across the hall. — *Discovers time constraints, explains facilities and breaks* / *Sets ground rules*

Just a couple of items about ground rules before we get started. I expect that you will speak honestly and bargain in good faith. I've found it easier to hear if only one person talks at a time. I may ask you to write down concerns you have while the other person is talking. I promise to make sure you have an opportunity to share your concerns. Also, if we could promise to be respectful to each other, even if we don't agree, this would be very helpful. Do either of you have anything to add? Okay. Are you both willing to following these guidelines? Great. — *Gains agreement to rules*

Are there any questions before we get started? Okay, let's begin with Aaron since he called the center first, if that is OK with you, Selena? Aaron, what has brought you here today? — *Asks for questions before beginning, Transition to next phase*

KEY COMPONENTS OF THE OPENING STATEMENT

Welcoming

Mediators begin by welcoming the parties to the session. A simple statement such as "I'd like to welcome the two of you to our center" can suffice. A common addition to welcoming the parties is to praise them for coming to the mediation table. These "welcoming" comments add a positive tone at a time when the individuals probably are feeling uncertain. The mediator might say, "I'd like to commend you for coming here today in an effort to work on your concerns together." The first words should be delivered conversationally, with the mediator's attention and eye contact split evenly between the two disputants. Speaking only to one disputant might imply favoritism or lack of neutrality. What the mediator does at the outset has a large effect on the overall tone of the session. An approachable mediator with a friendly tone can set the stage for positive interactions.

Introductions

The next task in the opening statement is to ensure that all parties are introduced to each other and to the mediator. Several factors are considered as an introduction strategy is devised. When high tension abounds or the context requires more formality, the mediator might use a title or honorific. For example, the mediator may name herself Dr. Hutchison and address each party formally as Mrs. Marin and Mr. Randall (or Ms. or Miss, depending on the wishes of the disputants). If you choose to use a title for yourself, then referring to your disputants as Ms. or Mr. also is advised.

If an informal tone is desired, only the mediator's first name might be used. Informality opens the door to having the parties call each other by their first names as well. For example, "Hello, my name is Sean O'Reilly. Please call me Sean. And you must be Ms. Davidson. May I call you Chloe?" Another approach could be, "My name is Sean O'Reilly. Please call me Sean. Which of you is Katherine Bradshaw? Is it okay if I call you Kathy or would you prefer Katherine? And you must be Camilla Wilson. May I call you Camilla?" If you would prefer, you can avoid the guesswork by simply stating, "Hello, I'm Sean O'Reilly. Please call me Sean. And you are?" Then wait for the parties to introduce themselves.

Formality of address also has cultural implications. For parties who are older, issues of respect and being addressed by title may be important. Elderly disputants may perceive being called by their first name without permission as rude. Not using formal titles may be considered to be disrespectful in a cross-cultural mediation. If you are unsure about decorum, we recommend erring on the side of formality.

Once the mediator has determined the names of the disputants, recording the names is a good idea. The mediator can place the names on the mediator's notetaking form, which will be discussed later in this chapter.

Building Credibility

Letting the disputants know the mediator is competent and experienced builds trust. Referring to the program or center through which you mediate may be one way to establish credibility. For example, a campus mediator might say, "Thank you for choosing the Campus Mediation Center. We've been helping university students like yourselves resolve disputes for over a decade."

Another means to build credibility is to refer to one's credentials. The mediator may make a statement about certifications or titles held, by saying, "Hello, my name is Madison Smith. I'm a certified mediator in the Commonwealth of Massachusetts and member of the Massachusetts Council on Family Mediation." Beginning mediators might say, "Hello, my name is Madison Smith. I'm a mediator trained by the University Dispute Resolution Program and an intern for the university in the Small Claims Court Mediation Program."

Establishing Stakeholders

If pre-mediation has not established the relevant stakeholders, the mediator will check to be sure the right parties are at the table and that they have the authority to negotiate a settlement. The decision makers and those affected by the decisions are called *stakeholders.* In small claims court, a mediator will ask, "Ms. Bradshaw, are you authorized to negotiate the issues of the case today and do you have the ability to make decisions? Great. Ms. Finnegan, are you authorized to negotiate the issues of the case today and do you have the ability to make decisions?" Using precisely the same phrasing with each party demonstrates the mediator's equal treatment of each disputant.

Explaining the Nature and Scope of Mediation

Part of upholding the disputants' informed choice and self-determination is ensuring that they understand their rights in the process. Even if the disputants are required to appear by a judge or other authority, they are not required to reach an agreement. The mediator explains that the negotiation process is voluntary. If the mediation was self-selected by the parties, the mediator might say, "I commend both of you for choosing to come to mediation today to try to work out your differences. As you probably know, the negotiations today are entirely voluntary and you are not compelled to come to any settlement if you do not wish." If the mediation was mandated, the mediator could state, "Today's mediation involves a process where you can choose to work out the issues between you, and you may or may not reach an agreement. Participating in mediation does not deter you (or the courts) from pursuing other actions if you don't reach agreement in this session."

In addition to describing the basic premise of mediation, many mediators also give the disputants a brief overview of the process. As mentioned in previous chapters, different mediation models are used in various contexts. A mediator using the balanced mediation model might relate that, "What will happen is that each of you will have a chance to tell me what brought you here today and the issues that are important to you. Once we've identified issues that need to be worked out, we'll set an agenda of the items that the two of you need to negotiate. I will then help you through the negotiation process and document any agreements you may make." An explanation of how the mediation will unfold manages the disputants' expectations and reduces anxiety about time spent initially on one person's story—the other party knows that each person will have a chance to speak.

Explaining the Mediator's Role

Explaining what the mediator will and will not do helps the disputants understand the difference between the role of mediator and the roles of judges or others who make decisions for the parties. Mediators must be very clear in communicating their facilitative role to the disputants. If mediators are not attorneys, they must be vigilant to avoid presenting themselves as such by giving legal advice. Even when mediators are attorneys, separating the role of attorney and the role of mediator is advised. Nonattorneys who dispense legal advice may be guilty of the unauthorized practice of law (Association for Conflict Resolution, 2002). Make sure your clients know your role. "My role here today is to assist you in discussing the issues that brought you here and in helping you formulate any decisions the two of you might reach. I am not a judge or attorney, and I will not make any decisions for you. Any decisions that you make are your own. Additionally, I will not offer you any legal advice."

Explaining the Caucus

If the model permits or requires a caucus, disputants need to understand what a caucus is and what might happen during a private meeting with the mediator. The terms *caucus* and *private meeting* are interchangeable. "There may come a point in this process where I'll want to meet privately with each of you." The mediator also should explain the rules of confidentiality during caucus. For instance, the mediator may relate that, "The same rules of confidentiality apply to the caucus, and I won't tell the other party what you say without your permission."

Explaining Impartiality and Neutrality

Disputants should be made aware of the mediator's commitment to fairness in the process. The mediator explains: "During the mediation, I am impartial—meaning I don't have any stake in the outcome of the issues you decide here today—and neutral—meaning I have no bias toward either of you personally." The explanation of impartiality and neutrality should be accompanied with a disclosure of any factors that might limit neutrality or impartiality. If the mediator has seen one of the disputants before in a professional capacity or has some stake in the issue of the case, he or she must disclose those factors. "Now that I see Ms. Bradshaw, I recollect that I have mediated a case before when she also was representing the QuickRent Management Company. I don't feel that this impacts my neutrality. Ms. Wilson, do you feel comfortable proceeding with me as your mediator?" If there is a connection between the mediator and the issue, the mediator might disclose that, "I see that this case is regarding a rental in the Summer Winds subdivision. I have a home in that subdivision. In the nature of this case, I don't perceive any conflict that would cause me to recuse myself. Are both of you comfortable with me proceeding as your mediator?"

In some cases, the mediator may not be neutral or impartial. For example, when the mediator is a first-level supervisor mediating employees or a college dormitory resident advisor mediating for two roommates, the mediator has both personal knowledge of the disputants and a stake in an amiable solution to the conflict. Under these conditions, the neutrality and impartiality statement must be altered. "As you know, the university wants difficulties between roommates to be resolved, when possible, by the people who are closest to the issues. In this mediation, I'll be fair and equal in my treatment of each of you as you work toward a possible solution that is agreeable to you both and makes our dormitory a better place to live for everyone."

The field of mediation continues to engage in a spirited debate about the words *neutrality* and *impartiality*—recognizing that human biases may make absolute neutrality or impartiality impossible. The laws or codes of conduct in the state where a mediator practices provide insight into that region's preferred terminology. For example, some codes of conduct prefer the promise to approach the parties with *impartial regard.* Mediators who also are licensed in another field may vary their descriptions of neutrality and impartiality as required by legal, social work, or other professional codes of conduct.

Giving a Confidentiality Pledge

As discussed in Chapter 5, mediators must consider what they are willing or able to keep secret. What is and is not confidential is detailed in the mediator's *confidentiality pledge.* Most state laws require any person with knowledge about harm or threat of harm to another person to alert proper authorities. Mediators must know what limits to confidentiality are required by state, province, or local laws. Parties must be informed about the mediator's confidentiality policy and the limitations to the pledge of confidentiality. For example, the mediator may make the following promise: "Anything you say to me today I will hold confidential. The exceptions to my confidentiality are [insert the exceptions in state, local, or province law]. In addition, as a Resident Advisor for this dormitory, I am also under obligation to report underage drinking and illegal drug use."

ACTIVITY 6.1: The Confidentiality Pledge

What is your state's legal reporting requirement, and how might that affect the mediator's confidentiality pledge in the opening statement?

Disclosing Notetaking Purposes

Disputants will be curious about why the mediator is writing while they are speaking and interested in what will become of the notes. A campus mediator could make the following comment: "I'll be taking personal notes during the session just to keep things straight in my mind. I'll destroy the notes at the end of our mediation. The only information I will report to the Dormitory Grievance Board is that the two of you did meet and whether you came to an agreement."

Destroying notes offers further protection for mediators in the unlikely event that they and their records are subpoenaed. While it is unlawful to destroy records once the courts have requested them, many mediators make a habit of destroying notes of the mediation once it is completed. Some mediators even collect the personal notes of the parties to be destroyed. On some college campuses and in many government agencies, documents may be considered part of public records available for disclosure. Once notes are classified as a public record, it may be illegal to destroy them. Therefore, a court subpoena may not be the only threat to the confidentiality of the mediation session. Unless otherwise required, mediators generally only retain a permanent copy of the agreement to mediate and memorandum of understanding forms. Mediators are encouraged to research the rules in their jurisdictions to ensure that record keeping and destroying practices are legal.

Establishing Ground Rules

Ground rules create expectations for courtesy and inform the disputants of what is and is not appropriate behavior. Most mediators have a list of ground rules in mind before they begin the session. Myra Warren Isenhart and Michael L. Spangle (2000) identify four typical ground rules:

- Only one person speaks at a time

- No interruptions while someone else is speaking

- No personal attacks will be allowed

- Information shared during the session will be treated as confidential (p. 79)

We recommend modifying the phrasing of these general ground rules. Saying that there will be "no interruptions while someone else is speaking" is not entirely true, as the mediator may interrupt the parties frequently to guide and control the flow of the session. A more accurate ground rule is that the disputants should allow each other to speak uninterrupted. Likewise, saying that information shared during the mediation session will be treated as confidential may not be accurate. Mediators must differentiate between their confidentiality (and its limits under state or territorial law) and confidentiality expected of disputants or others in the room. Unless the disputants and others at the session sign a confidentiality agreement, there is no reason to expect them to keep what has occurred secret. To be more accurate, mediators can say that they will keep information shared in the session confidential, except as required by law. As many of the cases in this text stem from real-life mediations, we have changed enough of the details and all names to protect the anonymity and confidentiality of the disputants. Each mediator should understand and be able to explain what confidentiality means.

We further recommend that mediators refrain from sounding punitive in their establishment of ground rules. Stating desired behavior instead of unacceptable behavior seems less parental. For instance, instead of saying, "Do not interrupt when the other is speaking," say, "When one of you is speaking, it is important that she is allowed to finish. If you have something you want to add when someone is talking, please write it down and I promise we will get to your concerns." Maintaining **civility** is an important goal for the mediation. A ground rule about respecting each other may be presented as, "In my experience, these sessions work best when we are respectful and courteous to one another, even when we don't agree." Using the term "we" here includes the mediator in the rules and sounds less dogmatic.

As a ground rule, some mediators (particularly novices) ask that disputants begin the session by talking only to the mediator and not to each other. Once emotions are moderated, the mediator seeks a congenial turning point where the disputants are asked to begin speaking directly to each other.

Another area for discussion in the ground rules section of the opening statement is a brief description of the surroundings such as the location of the restrooms or water fountains. A mediator may say, "If you need a break, please let me know. Bathrooms are down the hall to the left, and soda machines are across the foyer."

Having each party agree to the ground rules is critical and can be accomplished by asking a direct question, such as "Can we agree to these ground rules before we begin?" The mediator will look at each person to confirm that individual's agreement. If a party becomes unruly later in the session, one response strategy is to take some of the blame for the need to adhere to the rules. For example, the mediator could say, "I'm finding it very difficult to follow this conversation when more than one person is talking. Could we go back to one person speaking at a time? Jessie, please continue with your explanation." Asking for compliance to rules should be handled graciously as the "scolded" party may perceive bias in the mediator (Fraser, 2007). Major infractions may be handled most effectively one-on-one during a caucus.

An optional strategy for establishing ground rules allows the disputants to set the rules. The mediator would tell the disputants that the sessions work better when the parties agree on how they will treat each other in advance, and then ask each party what rules of behavior would be important to them. The mediator helps the parties negotiate the rules they will adopt. Once the parties agree on their rules, the mediator can add any other ground rules critical to the model being applied and praise the disputants for working together to reach their first agreement. John W. Keltner (1987) relates that in some instances rules are written and signed by all parties.

Discovering Time Constraints

Mediators must ensure that there will be sufficient time to explore issues and negotiate effectively. In one instance, a disputant was feeling that the negotiations were not going in her favor and informed the mediator that she had to leave to pick up her daughter. This tactic caused the negotiations to stall on the spot, and the mediation ended abruptly.

During pre-mediation, the disputants may have been informed of a typical range of time for the session, but reminding them of their time commitment is helpful during the opening statement. Be cautious, however, not to create a false expectation about *exactly* how much time the mediation will take. We advise not giving disputants cause to worry that they are taking too long or, if they are fast, not doing it right. Commenting, "We have scheduled the room until 4:00, so we can take the time we need to work on your concerns," will give disputants an idea of their time commitment for the session. Do ask directly about their time constraints. "Are both of you alright with that time frame?" You also may wish to address avoiding distractions: "If you'll turn off your phones, I think we're ready to begin." Occasionally, disputants cannot turn off their phones for emergency purposes, but typically it is best to reduce distractions by having communication devices turned completely off.

ACTIVITY 6.2: Practicing the Opening Statement

Practice your opening statement aloud until you are comfortable with the words and phrasing. Find two partners in the class with whom to practice your opening statement. Deliver the opening statement to your partners, striving for a personable and conversational tone that will build trust and confidence in you as a mediator. While speaking, divide your attention and eye contact equally between both parties. Arrange the chairs as you would during a mediation session.

Explaining the Role of Outside Experts

At the onset of a session, disputants may believe that they have all the information and advice that they need to negotiate. However, during the mediation, they may find that access to more resources is necessary to make informed decisions. Mediators can include a statement that addresses their right to seek counsel, such as "Each of you should know that any agreements you reach today may be binding and that agreements may restrict your rights in later actions. You may seek legal counsel before finalizing any agreements if you have any doubts or need legal advice." This statement may be repeated during the agreement writing stage.

If the issue is complex enough to require impartial experts to establish facts in the case or provide criteria for decisions, the disputants should be briefed on how experts would be used. For instance, the mediator may relate that, "Should there be a dispute about facts in the case that both of you decide needs to be resolved, we may bring in an impartial outside expert to assist the two of you. If that time comes, I'll assist you in choosing an expert that you both feel will give fair and impartial facts, as well as lead a discussion to negotiate how you will pay the expert." The desire of the mediator is for disputants to be well informed and comfortable in the decision-making process.

Securing the Commitment to Begin

By this point, the disputants have received considerable information that may or may not be new to them. Asking about their readiness to move to the next phase of the mediation elicits a verbal agreement to move forward. The commitment to begin a statement should be simple, such as "Now that we've covered the basics, are there any questions? (pause) Are we ready to begin?"

Transitioning to Storytelling

In transitioning to the storytelling and issue identification phase, the mediator must decide who will talk first and present some rationale to the disputants for the choice. If one disputant is visibly agitated, sometimes it is best to start with the more emotional person, as those who are agitated rarely can listen to the other party before their fears and emotions have been moderated. Other strategies for deciding who will speak first include selecting:

- The person who first contacted the mediator

- The plaintiff in a court case

- The individual with less power

The mediator may or may not reveal a motivation for selecting who speaks first. In a session with a professor and a student, the mediator may wish to power balance by having the student speak first. The explanation given to the disputants, however, might be that, "You were both referred to the Mediation Center by the Academic Grievance Board, so I'll have the person on my right [where the student is sitting] go first. Anthony, could you tell us what brought you here today?" Jennifer E. Beer and Eileen Stief (1997) suggest two other basic opening prompts: "Please explain to us what has been happening" and "Can you give us some background?—tell us your view of the situation?" (p. 106). More details about storytelling and issue identification are presented in Chapter 7.

BUILDING CREDIBILITY AND RAPPORT

Throughout the opening statement, the mediator strives to build **rapport** with each disputant and a perception of personal competence. William A. Donohue, Mary E. Diez, and Deborah W. Weider-Hatfield (1984) contend, "the mediator must encourage each of the disputants to attribute trust to him or her so that both parties will comply with the mediator's requests" (p. 230). The mediator may need to interrupt the parties, encourage changes in how the parties perceive the facts in the situation, coach the parties in how to hear each other's concerns, or ask the disputants to make difficult choices to transform the pattern of an intractable conflict. All of these actions require trust between the parties and the mediator. Disputants must believe that the mediator will be fair and keep the session under control.

Dominici and Littlejohn (2001) also view the opening moments of the mediation as key to the building of trust: "If a trust relationship is created, the disputants can participate openly while seeing the mediator as competent. All components of the opening statement are designed to establish trust. If a trusting environment is evident from the start, it will facilitate the entire process. People often have misconceptions about mediation, and this is the time to get everyone on the same track" (pp. 65–66). The mediator's demeanor during the opening statement cues the disputants that the mediator is trustworthy and competent.

THE RELATIONSHIP BETWEEN OPENING STATEMENTS AND MEDIATOR CONTROL

By definition, mediators control the process of the session. The balanced mediation model recommends a fairly active role for the mediator to guide the disputants through the phases in the model and to intervene to keep the session on-task and moving in productive directions. Donohue, Diez, and Weider-Hatfield (1984) define relational control as the "right to direct, delimit, and define the action of the relationship" (p. 229). They continue, "in mediation, control of the interaction is a key objective for the mediator to increase his or her flexibility in pursuing some particular pattern of questioning or topic development. The opposing parties may also be trying to compete with the mediator for control depending upon their objectives. Nevertheless, negotiating control is one of the relational parameters that the mediator must be able to manage" (p. 229).

The mediator establishes control during the opening statement through the creation of ground rules and by building confidence in the minds of the disputants. Isenhart and Spangle (2000) see the function of ground rules as creating a safe and predictable space for the disputants to negotiate their differences. A composed and confident presentation of the opening statement implicitly says to the disputants, "I will keep your conflict under control and create a safe space for you to work things out."

NOTETAKING FOR MEDIATORS

During the session, the disputants will disclose many facts, fears, solutions, or other information. While some mediators can retain all the information mentally, most people need to take notes. A mediator's notes are strategic and sparse rather than a comprehensive transcript. Mediators do not try to capture every word and every detail mentioned by the disputants. Any fact missed by the mediator is not lost forever, as the disputants will bring up information important to them again if it has been overlooked. Experienced mediators can attest that disputants will continue to say the same thing over and over until the mediator notices the importance of a comment.

A mediator's notes also are more than just facts—they also contain analysis. Donohue, Diez, and Weider-Hatfield (1984) explain that the mediator "uses his or her skills to listen for potential links, to sort and analyze elements of the discourse, synthesizing or structuring the information to delete the 'hidden' principles clouding the assessment of potential solutions. This is a critical interpretation skill, requiring the ability to analyze and synthesize on the spot" (p. 235).

FIGURE 6.2   Sample Notetaking Form

Party A's Name	Party B's Name

Party A's Interests/Needs:	Party B's Interests/Needs:

Misc. Notes:

As the mediator progresses in skill and confidence, each will develop a unique method of taking notes. Beginning mediators can profit from a simple structure. Figure 6.2 illustrates a sample notetaking form for beginning mediators. This general format can help keep notes organized.

When the disputants are introduced, the mediator fills in each party's preferred name at the top of the page, typically with the name of the person on one's left in the left column and the person on one's right in the right column. As the storytelling and issue identification phase proceeds, the mediator will note a word or short phrase in the "interest" section whenever a need is disclosed by one of the disputants. Issues will be recorded in the center of the page. Issues are common to both parties and hence are recorded in a space that represents both disputants. The issues section of the notes will contain the information the mediator uses to create the agenda for negotiation. The key to effective notetaking is not writing too much. Additional observations the mediator wishes to remember (such as settlement offers made early in the process that the mediator tabled at that time but may wish to bring back into the discussion later) can be recorded at the bottom of the page.

Mediators highlight commonalities in their notes. These very important revelations are simple but profound. *Commonalities* are practices, values, traits, goals, or other discernible facts shared by both parties. Commonalities can be indicated in the mediator's notes by connecting two interests or facts with lines across the page or by writing them separately somewhere else on the page (either in the center with issues or at the lower section of the page). Mediators treasure commonalities and will insert them strategically into the conversation, as we will discuss in later chapters.

Summary

The mediator's opening statement begins by informing the disputants about the mediator's role and the process that will be followed for the session. Opening statements may be a monologue or interactive. The opening statement serves to introduce parties, set the tone, and establish the mediator as the process facilitator for the session. Informing disputants about their rights and responsibilities is accomplished in the opening statement. Disputants should know what is expected of their behavior and how much time a mediation may take. Disputants also should be made aware of the role attorneys or outside experts may play in the mediation. One important area that deserves careful attention is the issue of confidentiality. Mediators share with the parties a confidentiality promise and its limitations.

The opening statement establishes the mediator's credibility and control of the process. Making sure that disputants are on board with ground rules and are educated about the process enables mediators to create a safe and productive negotiation environment.

The notes that mediators take during a session function as a reminder of facts and a storehouse of the mediator's insights about the case. Typically, the mediator's notes are destroyed after the session.

Portfolio Assignments

Portfolio Assignment 6.1: Creating Your Personal Opening Statement

Examine the opening statement elements in this chapter and the sample in Figure 6.1. Create a version of the monologue that covers the required elements but is adapted to your personal vocabulary and way of speaking. Use your opening statement during class practice mediation sessions.

Portfolio Assignment 6.2: Creating Your Personal Notetaking Form

Create your own notetaking form based on the sample in Figure 6.2. Place several copies of the blank form in your portfolio. Use the form during practice mediation sessions. Revise the form as you discover personal preferences for notetaking.

Storytelling and Issue Identification

Theories of Storytelling   117
   Symbolic Interaction   117
   Attribution Theory   118
   Emotional Intelligence   119
Functions of Storytelling   120
   The Individual   120
   The Mediator   122
Mediator Strategies in Storytelling   126
   One Storyteller at a Time   126
   Co-Constructing Stories   127
   General Inquiry Approach   127
   Whole Picture Questions   128
   Being Columbo   128
   Specific Inquiry   129
   Establishing Agreed-on "Facts"   129
   Weighing the Importance of Disagreements   129
   Perspective Taking   130
   Humor   130
Conflict Causes and Mediator Moves   131
Overcoming Common Pitfalls during Storytelling   132
   Pitfall 1: Unchecked Power Differences   132
   Pitfall 2: Allowing Blaming and Attacking   133
   Pitfall 3: Acting on Overstatements or Generalizations   133
   Pitfall 4: Taking Sides   134

Pitfall 5: Permitting Interrupting and Bickering 134

Pitfall 6: Mismanaging Emotional Outbursts 134

Pitfall 7: Letting One Party Monopolize Time or Control the Process 136

Pitfall 8: Being Overwhelmed with Evidence 137

Summary **138**

Portfolio Assignment 7.1: The Vision Quest **138**

Portfolio Assignment 7.2: Reframes **138**

CASE 7.1: The Privacy Fence

The Holleys and the Wallaces have been next-door neighbors for more than 20 years. Each had two children, and over the years several incidents had occurred that caused tensions between the families. When the children were small, the neighbors' sons were playing with matches behind the Holleys' shed. In fact, they burned it down. Each boy blamed the other, and their respective families believed their own child's version of events. Since that time, the children were not allowed to play together. The kids have grown and moved away, but tensions still exist between the two neighbors. Mrs. Wallace grows prize roses, and the rose garden is on the line between the two properties, currently marked by a three-foot-high chain-link fence.

Mr. and Mrs. Holley are planning to build a new, solid fence between the properties and are irritated that the Wallaces refused to pay for half of the new fence. Mrs. Wallace doesn't want the fence, as the shade will destroy her garden that currently receives lots of sun. The Holleys have wanted a fence for 20 years, so they can have additional privacy for their yard and, now, a new hot tub.

The time and energy spent discovering the individual stories of the participants is the heart of the mediation process. While listening to how each party has experienced the conflict, the mediator validates where needed, explores when more clarification is required, and identifies key issues or interests that must be highlighted throughout the rest of the process. New mediators have a tendency to rush through this pivotal step. What usually results from a rush to problem solving, however, is an unraveling of the process when disputants discuss solutions. Parties who do not have an adequate chance to explain their concerns are not ready to negotiate. Thus, effort in storytelling is time well spent, making the rest of the mediation flow more smoothly.

In many mediations, a large percentage of the total session time is spent in the storytelling and issue identification phase. In contexts such as victim–offender mediation, the interest and issue identification can occur in extended pre-mediation sessions (where the mediator meets individually with parties before bringing them together). However, in the balanced model of mediation, the mediator strives to complete this crucial phase in the presence of both parties.

According to the Pepperdine University Institute for Dispute Resolution (1995), the parties' initial statements in a formal mediation offer valuable psychological benefits for the disputants as well as vital information for the mediator. Specifically, the storytelling offers insights about the parties personalities, a chance to hear the other disputant's ideas, a place to find areas in common, and a time when parties have their day in court.

This chapter presents theories useful for understanding storytelling. Additionally, it presents the basic functions of storytelling, the importance of separating interests from positions, strategies for encouraging parties to tell their stories, and how to avoid common pitfalls in this phase of mediation.

THEORIES OF STORYTELLING

Theories of human communication enhance our understanding of what happens during storytelling. When looking through the lens of a particular theory, certain elements of the event are revealed. Theories help mediators see the process from a different perspective. Understanding several theories offers options for making sense of human behavior. Three theories that inform the storytelling phase are *symbolic interaction, attribution theories,* and *emotional intelligence.*

Symbolic Interaction

Symbolic interaction is a broad-based theory of how humans create meaning. Although more complex than will be explained here, symbolic interaction provides mediators with a core understanding of the importance of the storytelling event. Three tenets of symbolic interaction are of particular interest to mediators:

1. Individuals act according to how they understand the world based on their subjective interpretations of the circumstances

2. People understand and interpret their world through language (symbols)

3. Through social interaction we construct (and reconstruct) meaning (Ballis Lal, 1995)

Disputants come to mediation with personal views of the conflict, usually two different views. Subjective interpretations of experience are a primary focus of mediators. Disputants see the world independently and uniquely. Mediators attempt to understand how each disputant has constructed reality and how each has created meaning.

Disputants enter the mediation with stories that have been constructed independently. In the storytelling phase, the mediator draws out the individuals' stories and weaves them into one story (co-construction). The goal through the lens of symbolic interaction is to create a *shared meaning* (or story) from which both parties enter negotiation. Changing how the past is perceived is one way that a mediator transforms the conflict situation. Sometimes, parties will refuse to give up their feelings of "rightness" about personal interpretations of past events. In these cases, the mediator can help the disputants move beyond the past by agreeing that they will never agree on what actually happened, but they can accede to a need for different standards of future behavior.

Discussion Question 7.1

WHAT IS a probable outcome of a negotiation where parties continue to operate from their individual perspectives without being able to see the other's view?

Attribution Theory

Humans naturally try to understand what motivates behavior. When we are not certain of why someone acted a certain way, we have a tendency to guess. Fritz Heider's (1958) **attribution theory** provides insights into how disputants may create meaning using personality and situational attributions. A **personality attribution** manifests when we assume that an element of someone's personality, something *inside* of that person, is responsible for a behavior. A **situational attribution** assumes that a person's behavior is a result of *outside* circumstance.

Personality and situational attributions provide clues to how each party perceives the other. For example, a professor notices that a student, Gerald, is sleeping in her class. A natural human tendency is for the professor to assign a motive to the behavior. A possible attribution by the professor would be that Gerald is lazy or disinterested, both personality attributions. From his perspective, however, a situational attribution may be more accurate. Due to a friend's car breaking down on the freeway (a situation), he had to go help out his buddy at 3:00 A.M., drive an hour and a half to rescue him, and tow his car back to town—barely making it to class on time.

Humans also subconsciously weigh two other variables when attributing motives: *consistency* and *uniqueness*. Consistency describes the stability of a behavior over time. For instance, if Gerald has taken two other courses from the professor and never snoozed before in class, the behavior is inconsistent. In that scenario, the professor is more likely to make a situational attribution. Uniqueness refers to the idiosyncratic nature of a behavior. If the same professor observed that all of her students are nodding off during a lecture, Gerald's behavior is not unique and might not be attributed to his personality. The cause is affecting all students; therefore, the heat in the room must be the reason for the sleepiness (or, perhaps, the content of the lecture).

Fundamental attribution errors are mistaken assumptions about people's motives (they are lazy, rude, insensitive, uncaring, and irresponsible). A **self-serving bias** occurs when an individual accounts for personal mistakes. Generally, we do not blame our own personalities, but instead we provide a situational attribution.

Discussion Question 7.2

PROVIDE AN example where two competing attributions were operating in a conflict in which you were involved. What happened? Do you think the effect occurred because the individuals were not aware of the differing attributions? How would (or did) the conflict end?

Knowing the human tendency to favor oneself in attributing motive to situation and in blaming other people's personalities when their motives are called into question helps mediators recognize and deal with attributions. For example, Janelle sees Mac using new office supplies. When she goes to the supply closet to get some markers, pens, and tape, there is little there. She sees Mac has new supplies all over his desk. Janelle may see Mac as selfish and inconsiderate (personality attributions). However, Mac, unbeknownst to Janelle, has taken over a sick colleague's account and is working overtime doing his work and his colleague's. He has taken most of his old supplies home so he can work on the project and has restocked his desk with new supplies. He sees his use of supplies as part of his situation, not as part of his personality. The mediator, on hearing Janelle's personality attribution, "Mac is being so piggish with the supplies!" could ask Mac to explain from his perspective, thus, revealing the situational circumstances. The mediator could say to Mac, "Janelle has noticed a change in the use of supplies. Could you tell me about what changed?"

Mediators should have an understanding of how disputants subjectively frame their experiences. With the insights gained from theory in mind, the mediator can better understand the functions of storytelling. Likewise, mediators should become self-aware of attribution errors they might make due to bias, stereotyping, or personal experiences.

Emotional Intelligence

Scholars have added a companion concept to intellectual intelligence (IQ) called emotional intelligence (EQ). Emotional intelligence encompasses how sensitive an individual is to others' feelings (see McCorkle & Reese, 2010). Low EQ individuals literally may miss the boat in sensing distress in others and have razor-focus only for substantive issues. These individuals need the mediator's help in understanding how their actions affect others.

Individuals low in emotional intelligence may exhibit insensitivity or have poor communication skills. For example, they might behave in ways that use aggressiveness more than in ways that show **assertiveness**. Insights into a disputant's emotional intelligence are evidenced in the absence or presence of the 16 characteristics identified by Marcia Hughes and James Bradford Terrell (2012) itemized in Table 7.1. **Reality testing** is a feature of emotional intelligence that is of particular interest to mediators. A disputant low in emotional intelligence may need the mediator's help in seeing the consequences of their negotiation offers.

TABLE 7.1   Sixteen Key Emotional Intelligence Competencies
1. Self-regard
2. Emotional self-awareness
3. Expression of emotion
4. Assertiveness
5. Independence
6. Self-actualization
7. Empathy
8. Social responsibility
9. Interpersonal relationships
10. Stress tolerance
11. Impulse control
12. Reality testing
13. Flexibility
14. Problem solving
15. Optimism
16. Happiness

FUNCTIONS OF STORYTELLING

The storytelling and issue identification phase offers important benefits for the disputants. It also provides information to guide the mediator in strategy selection.

The Individual

The needs of the disputants in mediation can vary, but generally they fall into three categories: to be safe, to be heard, and to be acknowledged.

The Need to Be Safe

Through the mediator's opening statement, disputants should be aware that the process fosters a fair, equitable, and safe forum for the exchange of ideas. Mediators encourage, display empathy, maintain a neutral and impartial demeanor, and keep control of the process.

Disputants need to feel confident that the mediator can handle any changes in dynamics that may result if they make themselves vulnerable to attack or share information that may be difficult for the other party to hear.

The Need to Be Heard

Parties may also need to be heard and to vent their frustrations with the current situation. The disputants' initial remarks during storytelling may be their first chance to tell their stories in full. The mediator creates the atmosphere where feelings can be vented safely, while stopping the other party's attempts to interrupt. The mediator uses reframing or other listening skills to prevent restimulation of defensiveness through trigger words. Research indicates trigger words have negative impact on clear thinking and the ability to engage in fair negotiation (Schroth, Ban-Chekal, & Caldwell, 2005). For example, the mediator will avoid questions that start with the word "why" as it asks for justification rather than for elaboration. The mediator reframes trigger words such as "stupid" into more neutral language:

Disputant: "He was just stupid."
Reframe: "You were concerned about the project."

Disputant: "She ought to help me more with my work and not be so lazy."
Reframe: "You'd appreciate more help."

The need to be heard relates to another important need for some disputants—the need to overcome fear. Disputants sometimes come to mediation because their fear about the situation has made it difficult to work with the other person. By using the listening skills highlighted in Chapter 3 during storytelling, the mediator helps disputants moderate their fear enough to move forward in negotiation with the other party. When the work is not done during storytelling to moderate emotions, negotiation is very difficult.

The Need to Be Acknowledged

Parties have a need to be acknowledged and to feel validated about their concerns. They yearn to have their story recognized as having value and being important. They may worry their ideas will be perceived as inconsequential or trivial and need the mediator to acknowledge the worth of their feelings by listening to them.

Mediators should adapt to the cues from disputants about what is important to them. In one session, a new mediator, equipped with a toolbox of listening skills, entered the session eager to validate. The disputants were not friends, did not have an ongoing relationship, and were only in disagreement about how much money should be returned for a defective piece of construction equipment that was rented to dig a trench. The mediator, with the best of intentions, continued to validate the parties' emotions and attempted to create a shared relationship where none existed. When the disputants grew tired of the mediator focusing on feelings while they wanted to focus on the money, they both became mad at the mediator. One exasperated party said, "Look. I don't care about how she felt, and it's none of her business how I felt. I just want my money back!" Storytelling offers the individual disputants the chance to highlight what is important to them. It should not be a showcase for the mediator's skills or focus on what is important to the mediator.

CASE 7.2: The Catering Dilemma

Andrea works for a state agency as an administrative assistant. She is exceptionally efficient, thorough, and takes pride in doing a good job. The agency, always under public scrutiny, asks everyone to share cost-saving ideas that can be implemented throughout the agency. Andrea has been charged with organizing several large group meetings and training events for her manager. These meetings usually involve providing lunch to participants. Through her research, she's found that the average cost of catering lunches through local restaurants is $10.50. The agency has a cafeteria attached to the building used by many state employees. Because there is no overhead for the space, the prices are low, and the food is varied and good. The cafeteria will provide vouchers for meetings where individuals can come down and order what they want from the menu, up to $10. What happens is that most people end up spending about $6.50 per meal in the cafeteria. Andrea presented her cost-savings plan to the higher administration who sent out a mandate to the agency to stop using catering and to use the cafeteria instead. The other administrative assistants are getting negative feedback from their bosses about the change and wish Andrea would have brought the suggestion to them first before going to administration. They claim that there are other reasons to use local businesses, including networking, and that the quality of food and service is much better than the cafeteria. Andrea has begun to notice that she's not included in as many conversations and after hours invitations for social time. Some people are openly hostile to any idea she brings up now.

The Mediator

The storytelling phase allows mediators to determine underlying interests, to identify issues to be negotiated, and to establish common ground, if possible. These three elements form a springboard for the negotiation phase.

Separating Interests from Positions

As discussed in Chapter 1, mediation is an interest-based conflict management process. Unfortunately for mediators, disputants do not automatically come to the mediation table ready to list their interests. Most people in conflict approach negotiations from a *positional base* focused on personal advantage. Working to change positions into interests during negotiations is discussed in Chapter 9. However, at this point, knowing that parties see the conflict differently is important. There are three parts to their typical complaint: their version of events, their complaint about the other, and their definition of the problem. John M. Haynes (1994) points out that "each person defines the problem in such a way that the problem can be solved only by a change in the behavior or position of the *other*" (p. 8). For example, a disputant may come to the mediation table believing that the only way to be satisfied is if the other party apologizes. This position often is verbalized in the form of a demand: "She should apologize to me." Parties are adept in making demands for particular solutions. Examples of other positional statements are as follows:

- "We won't sign a contract that does not include a dental and vision plan."

- "Clean up your room or you're grounded!"

- "I won't take a dime less than $800.00 for the damage she did to that carpet."

- "He can see the kids every other weekend and two weeks in the summer."

- "Emma should move out of the dorm."

- "She needs to move that wreck of a car from in front of my house."

- "Fire that lazy clerk or I'll quit."

Behind every positional statement is an interest waiting for the mediator's discovery. Interests are what drive positions—the needs that underlie the demands. Skilled mediators listen for positional statements so they can explore the interests that brought the parties to those conclusions.

The listening skills presented in Chapter 3 come into play for the mediator during the storytelling phase. When a position is stated, the mediator considers which tools would best draw out the interest and shift the focus away from the position. Mediators may ask questions to clarify or explore substantive interests. Mediators validate, emotionally paraphrase, or reframe the speaker to identify **psychological interests** (such as respect, safety, inclusion, or self-determination). In all cases, mediators strive to change the focus of the discussion to interests, without hardening a disputant's position. For instance:

Wrong
DISPUTANT: "I won't pay her a dime for those calls. They're not all mine."
MEDIATOR: "So you don't want to pay her for the calls." [A content paraphrase restating the position.]

In the previous example, the mediator repeated the position of the disputant—he didn't want to pay for any calls. By restating the position using a content paraphrase, the mediator adds power to that position, making it more difficult for the disputant to consider other options. Instead, the mediator could reframe the statement into an *interest* and work to clarify more of the story:

Correct
DISPUTANT: "I won't pay her a dime for those calls. They're not all mine."
MEDIATOR: "You're looking to be treated fairly and have a concern with the request for payment. Tell me, when did you first find out about the phone bill?"

Interests become criteria in the evaluation of possible solutions later in the negotiation stage. "Fair treatment" is an interest that can be explored by the mediator. For example, if one party, fearful of being robbed again, bought a big dog for protection, the underlying interest may be feeling safe in his home. If, through negotiations, the same party agrees to give up the dog because the neighbor is afraid of it, the home security interest may re-emerge. Consequently, establishing criteria may be useful in this mediation: Any solution would need to meet the safety issues of both parties. More about establishing criteria and evaluating options will be discussed in Chapter 10.

ACTIVITY 7.1: Issue or Interest?

The *Interest* is the Underlying Need
　　The *Issue* is the Problem to be Negotiated
　　In Case 7.2, if a mediation occurred between the person who suggested the change to use the cafeteria for meeting lunches and one of the administrative assistants who did not like the change, what are the possible interests of each party? What are the probable issues that would be negotiated? How do mediators discover interests? How do mediators discover issues?

Identifying Issues

In addition to addressing the emotions that the parties may bring to the table, the mediator also must determine the issues to be negotiated. *Issues* are the topics of the mediation, those items that will be negotiated. Mediators constantly are identifying issues important to the parties and further separating them into categories of what can and cannot be negotiated. The mediator tracks these issues and uses them to frame the agenda (discussed in Chapter 8). In the storytelling and issue identification phase, the mediator locates and explores the topics to be negotiated so all parties understand the basic facts, interests, and considerations connected to the issues.

Not all issues are negotiable. Negotiable issues include those where the parties at the table have the power to effect change. A buyer and seller of a small business who want to change the reporting requirements to the state about the details of their purchasing agreement really have no control over that issue. However, the two at the table could negotiate their own responsibilities about which party reports to the state.

Christopher W. Moore (2003) identifies three types of issues that can be negotiated: substantive, procedural, and emotional (p. 75). According to Moore, most mediators begin with the *substantive issues,* focusing on the cause and desired outcomes of the dispute. In the case of a divorcing couple, the substantive issues may include the division of property. However, focusing too early on this substantive issue may create problems if the parties are not in a psychological space conducive to listening to each other. Mediators must evaluate the needs of the disputants to attend to other nonsubstantive issues. Consequently, the mediator fully explores the terrain of the case during storytelling rather than immediately moving to negotiation once an issue is discovered.

Procedural issues evolve around how things are done: how agendas will be created, when and where events occur, how information is shared, how a process is governed by rules, or how records are kept. According to Moore, when procedural issues are identified during storytelling and placed early on the negotiation agenda, a history of successful negotiation is created and trust in the mediation is built. Examples of procedural issues include discussing who else, besides the parties, will be privy to the mediation agreement; determining the amount of time available for the mediation session; and developing rules about how parties will communicate with each other. By exploring the nature of any procedural issues during storytelling and issue identification, the mediator is prepared to decide where to place procedural issues on the negotiation agenda.

Psychological (emotional) issues emerge from paying particular attention to the relationship of the parties and creating a safe environment where the mediation can unfold. Hurt feelings often impede the parties' abilities to talk together. In neighborhood disputes, mediators may highlight the ongoing neighbor relationship that the parties share and determine the importance of this relationship for each neighbor. The focus on linkages provides a superordinate, or umbrella, issue under which the other issues can be framed.

Discussion Question 7.3

USING CASE 7.1, identify the substantive, procedural, and psychological issues that may need to be addressed. Which of these would you address first? Explain.

A second function of focusing on the emotional issues is helping the disputants create a space where they can communicate effectively. Mediators may take time early in the session to coach disputants in civil communication or to establish behavioral codes. The mediator may teach disputants to exhibit ownership through **"I" statements**, such as "This is how I see it" or "From my perspective." Mediators can encourage validation and active listening behaviors from each individual. In this way, the mediator aids the parties in creating a communication environment where their emotional issues can be heard. When one or both disputants are low in emotional intelligence, they may be oblivious to how their behavior affects others. They may not know how to behave in more socially smoothing ways. During storytelling, the mediator may discover the disputants have challenges in expressing themselves in ways that don't create defensiveness in others.

According to Kenneth Cloke (2001), "the poses" the parties take, or the public face they show, affect the entire mediation process. Cloke writes, "As long as parties hold on to their poses, whether of injured virtue, anger, or self-righteousness, honest communication will be blocked and conflicts left unresolved. The mediator's role is to assist parties in dropping their poses, communicating honestly and empathetically, and taking responsibility—not only for their intentions, but their words, actions, and effects they have on others, regardless of intention" (p. 35). The mediator must create a productive communication environment where the disputants can hear, and be heard by, all participants. Whether or not emotional issues appear on the agenda for negotiation, the mediator must work through these issues during storytelling for the mediation to proceed.

Establishing Common Ground

Common ground encompasses any area where the disputants are in agreement or have similar interests, such as a desire to have a good relationship with each other, to have a successful business, or to be treated fairly. Common ground is considered by many mediators to be the "golden nugget" of mediation. By framing issues and interests as common problems, the mediator is moving the problem psychologically to the "other side of the table." Initially, party A believes that party B is the "problem" and that the way for the problem to be fixed is to fix party B. Party B, however, sees party A as the source of the problem, and both are looking to change the other instead of focusing on the problem itself. What the mediator is attempting to do—metaphorically—is put both parties on the same side of the table facing the problem. If the mediator can identify a common concern or interest, problem solving in the negotiation phase becomes easier. According to Haynes (1994), "Neither A nor B will change unilaterally, and neither will change to conform with the other's definition of the problem, since both have their own definition. Therefore, the mediator's task is to help the participants discard their individual problem definitions and adopt a mutual and common definition of the problem. Only then can problem solving begin." (p. 9)

Discussion Question 7.4

USING CASE 7.1, identify how each party sees the other as the "problem." What would be each party's solution to the fence situation? How would you move the problem to the other side of the table? How would you frame the problem to include both parties?

MEDIATOR STRATEGIES IN STORYTELLING

Mediators must consider the consequence of any strategy employed to begin and continue the storytelling phase. For example, the simple act of choosing one party to speak first allows that individual to frame the discussion. The other disputant is placed in the position of responding to the first speaker. As with any technique, mediators make choices about the use, effectiveness, and possible consequences of adopting one strategy over another.

This section presents several strategies for eliciting stories and uncovering information from the disputants. No single strategy will be useful all of the time. Donald T. Saposnek (1998) presents an aikido metaphor for his approach to mediation, calling it the strategic approach. Saposnek claims that if something isn't working, don't do more of the same. Instead, think strategically by "maintaining an organized and goal-directed but flexible thought process that allows the mediator, in the face of obstacles, to shift gears, change tactics, and continue moving toward a preplanned goal" (p. 58). Thinking strategically means that mediators do not use a technique for its own sake; mediators must have an idea where the strategy will go and how it will move the parties forward. Having a toolbox containing many strategies and communication tools is a part of mediator competence. The portfolio assignments at the end of each chapter help novices collect a variety of tactical options.

One Storyteller at a Time

The one-storyteller-at-a-time strategy gives the floor to one disputant to express a personal view of the current situation. After the opening statement, the mediator may say to one party, "Martin, you were the one who contacted the mediation center, would you please tell me what led to your call and what has been the situation as you see it?" The mediator then prompts and validates as needed, taking notes on issues and identifying interests as the speaker relays the story. Some follow-up questions can be included, but the mediator should not let one party monopolize a great deal of time. The other party is waiting for a turn to speak and refute. The mediator would then use the same prompt ("Tell me what the situation is as you see it") and give the floor to the second party. Using the identical opening prompt with each person is important to begin the mediation in a balanced way.

The benefit of the one-storyteller-at-a-time approach is that individuals tell their stories with relatively few interruptions. Each has a chance to vent and receive the attention of the mediator, which, in turn, may create more trust in the process.

The disadvantages, however, also should be considered; one person may attempt to monopolize the session. If one disputant is more articulate or prepared than the other, he or she will have more to say and can create an imbalance of power. The other party may become frustrated by not being allowed to interrupt. A disputant suffering from communication anxiety may speak very little in contrast to the other party. Additionally, the first person to speak establishes the frame of the story that the other party must work from rather than having a chance to develop a separate story.

Co-Constructing Stories

An alternative to the strict one-at-a-time strategy is to let the parties present their perceptions of their stories incrementally. This strategy works best if there is a history of cooperation between the disputants and tension is reasonably low. In this approach, one party begins sharing and then the mediator interrupts and moves to the second party. The switching back and forth between the disputants ensures that each party adds details to the story as it unfolds. The strategy of switching back and forth between the parties may have the added benefit of creating opportunities for the mediator to ask questions that clear up simple misunderstandings as the details emerge. Another advantage is that since the story is created together, both parties can participate directly and are not relegated to a passive listener role. The goal of creating shared meaning is easier when co-constructing stories.

However, co-construction is not an easy approach to manage, particularly when disputants disagree about key issues during the story construction. New mediators may have difficulty tracking the issues and interests of both parties at the same time. Another risk is that parties may bicker about the details because they are not ready—yet—to agree about anything.

Once the storytelling process begins, the mediator must employ strategies to uncover hidden agendas, reveal important elements of the situation, and gain a sense of the issues to be mediated. The following strategies help the mediator get the underlying story into the open.

General Inquiry Approach

The **general inquiry questions** are designed to build a sense of the "big picture." Ask disputants to express their views with broad strokes. "What is the situation that brought you here today?" or "I understand that you are having concerns over the upkeep of the employee lunchroom. Could you tell me a little bit about that?" In the initial storytelling, it is effective to create a general picture from each party and to delve into the specific details later. The mediator avoids having one disputant sitting silently for a considerably long time while the other spins out the details of the story. In general inquiry, the mediator attempts to discover the general issues. In the specific inquiry (discussed later), the mediator probes the facts distinct to the issues.

Whole Picture Questions

Disputants may bog down a session with details. As the mediator works to get a sense of the bigger picture, **whole picture questions** may be helpful. Every story has a past, a present, and a future. In the initial storytelling, the mediator attempts to understand what led up to the point when the mediation was scheduled. Disputants can be directed to focus on the past with direct questions, such as "What was the past situation with your boss like, prior to this incident?" or "Has there ever been a time when this wasn't a problem?"

Questions that focus the disputants on their current situation also shed light onto how they are experiencing the event now. Asking, "How is this currently affecting your business relationship?" or "What are the consequences to you now?" may present the mediator with the party's interests. Having the disputants answer vision questions is another strategy. The mediator may ask, "What is your idea of a good neighbor?" Portfolio assignment 7.1 helps build vision questions to get big picture answers.

Future-focused questions typically are saved for the option-generating part of the mediation (see Chapter 10). However, a well-placed future question may provide insight into how this affects the disputants. For example, asking, "Can you see a time when you will have more flexibility in your schedule?" may provide everyone with information about one party's personal situation.

Being Columbo

In a retro television drama series, the criminal detective Columbo's trademark was getting criminals to answer apparently silly questions and, in doing so, inadvertently disclosing key evidence. Columbo adopted a naïve perspective to solving cases. He asked questions that seemed elementary but were relevant. "Do these windows lock?" "How long did you know Ms. Gray?" "So you drive to work every day and come home for lunch?" Asking questions about things where the answer seemed obvious allowed Columbo to uncover information that others would deem irrelevant but ultimately cracked the case at hand.

As mediators, we have the same latitude to ask seemingly irrelevant or elementary questions to gain a good understanding of the disputant's situation. More importantly, we ask questions of one person that reveal unknown information to the other party. In a dispute about a night-light shining in a neighbor's window, the mediator can ask one neighbor, "What is it about the light that bothers you?" The mediator can then query the other neighbor, "What was your thinking when you decided to leave that light on all night?" Mediators can request the disputants to draw a diagram of their neighborhood or to explain what they mean by "being uncomfortable around that equipment." When disputants differ about rules or processes, a mediator can say, "Does anyone have a copy of that rule?" Answers to this seemingly ordinary question can uncover that the disputants are talking about different rules or neither one actually knows what the rule really requires. Mediators are in a position not to take anything for granted. Nothing is obvious during the early stages of storytelling. Using the Columbo technique can uncover facts that transform how the disputants see the situation.

Specific Inquiry

As the storytelling phase progresses, the mediator elicits more details from the disputants. **Specific inquiry questions** ask for **concrete** information, such as "How much?" "When?" and "Where?" For example, the mediator may ask about a past assertion: "You said that the automobile does run, but you say there are still areas where it is having problems. Could you tell me about those?" or "How did you arrive at that amount?" or "Would you discuss your normal billing procedures?" Other information may be gleaned from specific inquiry as the mediator attempts to discern how the disputant experienced the situation, such as "When you weren't paid for your carpentry project, how did that affect you personally?" and "How has this tension affected your work?"

Establishing Agreed-on "Facts"

If parties are having a difficult time hearing each other's perspectives, one strategy is to establish clear places where they do agree and use these "facts" as springboards for discussion. For example, the mediator may state, "So there was a $300 deposit paid on July 14. What was the understanding about this deposit?" Stating a fact and then asking for interpretations allows the disputants to see how the other party may view the same situation differently. A mediator might say, "From what I can tell, the original payment amount was to be $55 a month for the medical bills. There were ten payments made last year and no payments made since October. What changed in October?" Parties are focused on the month of October instead of solely attending to the total amount in dispute.

Discussion Question 7.5

DISCUSS HOW at least five of the techniques in this section could be applied to Case 7.2

Weighing the Importance of Disagreements

People disagree; otherwise mediators would not be needed. Determining the importance and relevance of disagreements is instrumental to deciding when a "difference makes a difference." In one consumer mediation, a woman took a precious heirloom doll to a restorer to have the doll's eyelashes reconstructed. The woman claimed that not only did the eyelashes fall out again but also that the restorer switched the entire eyes, which were brown when she brought them in, and now were blue. The restorer adamantly denied switching the original eyes. The mediation quickly dissolved into name-calling where both called the other a liar. The mediator deftly stepped into the fray and reframed the discussion, stating, "We are not here to determine what color the original eyes were. Obviously there is disagreement and no way to resolve this issue. Can we move past this area of disagreement and determine where we go from here?" The mediator must ascertain whether areas of disagreement are tangential or paramount to problem resolution. In this case, the disputants agreed to disagree.

Another strategy for working through impasse is unpacking the disagreement over specifics by asking questions about how a "fact" was established. "How did you learn about the extent of the damage?" or "You estimate the damage at $4,000. How did you arrive at that figure?" When the onus of responsibility is placed on the disputant to elaborate, more information emerges that will help the mediator decide how to move the process forward.

Perspective Taking

Perspective taking requires the disputants to see the world from the other's view. Saposnek (1998) identified *interactional* questions as a means to achieve perspective taking. The question, "What do you see the other parent as doing?" requires the disputant to see the world through the eyes of the other. Another more direct strategy involves one party reacting from the perspective of the other party. For example, the mediator may ask, "Let's say for a moment that you are the boss. Sales are down and you are required to make changes in the sales force. How do you go about making these decisions?" Some mediators will require disputants to speak as if they were the other person: "Let's say you are Jenny. As Jenny, what would be a fair settlement from your perspective?"

Caution is required when employing perspective-taking tactics. If the parties aren't willing to go along with the strategy, it can backfire. In one instance, a disputant responded to this strategy with anger saying, "Look, I don't have the foggiest idea why he thinks the way he does. A normal person wouldn't have gotten us in this situation in the first place." Cooperation and trust by the disputants are prerequisite for employing perspective-taking strategies.

Humor

The disputants or the mediator may attempt humor during storytelling. Some humor is productive, and some is not. Four types of humor commonly are identified: self-enhancing humor (a positive coping mechanism during stress), affiliative humor (nonhostile connecting among people), aggressive humor (negative ridicule), or self-defeating humor (negative humor directed at oneself) (Cruthirds, 2006). In mediation, humor can relieve stress or be a stealthy attack. The mediator should divert or reframe negative humor while allowing/encouraging positive humor that connects individuals against a common situation or relieves tension. Shared laughter is life enhancing and relaxing.

CONFLICT CAUSES AND MEDIATOR MOVES

As the storytelling and issue identification phase progresses, the mediator may discover that the conflict is based in one of the primary causes of interpersonal conflict discussed in Chapter 5. Through identification of the cause of the conflict, the mediator can determine a strategy to move the mediation process forward. Conflicts stemming from different causal clusters require different skill applications from the mediator. Table 7.2 suggests moves to respond to each type of conflict.

Mediators experience many bumps on the path toward peaceful settlements. Even with a tool chest full of strategies, problems can arise at any point in the session. New mediators find it helpful to collect a set of tools to employ when faced with these common errors. The following section addresses some of these sticky situations.

TABLE 7.2 Mediator Moves and Causes of Conflict

Conflict Cause	Indicators	Mediator Move
Communication or style	Parties have difficulty listening to each other, misunderstand each other, exhibit communication apprehension, or have different personal communication styles.	• Validate and emotionally paraphrase • Suggest parties reverse paraphrase each other • Coach parties in how to make comments more productively • Comment on their style and communication differences as an unrecognized, common source of mutual annoyance
Emotion	Parties blame or attack the other, express high feelings, or exhibit anger or sadness.	• Validate and emotionally paraphrase • Adopt a future focus • Highlight positive remarks made about the other party • Work for acknowledgment or apologies • Coach parties in "I" language
Structure	Parties agree on goals but not on methods; parties are fighting about how decisions should be made.	• Validate common goals • Set criteria for good decisions • Assist the parties in selecting a procedure that is mutually beneficial • Make differences in criteria transparent to both parties
Value	Parties denigrate each other's background or assume that the other should think and feel exactly the same. Parties may be from different age, ethnic, political, religious, or national groups.	• Make value differences transparent • Validate both perspectives • Emphasize commonalities • Focus on a larger, common goal

(Continued)

TABLE 7.2 (Continued)		
Conflict Cause	**Indicators**	**Mediator Move**
Culture	Individuals are from different root cultures.	• Make observations about possible cultural style differences • Help parties establish a common way they can communicate during conflict
Information	Parties have information differences, lack criteria, or argue about criteria.	• Establish how each is interpreting information differently • Help parties establish criteria

OVERCOMING COMMON PITFALLS DURING STORYTELLING

Pitfall 1: Unchecked Power Differences

Parties do not necessarily enter the mediation process with the same power resources. One party may be a stronger communicator and have greater negotiation skills. A supervisor usually has more power when in conflict with an employee. A member of the dominant culture in an area may feel more comfortable than one who is part of a minority population or a new immigrant. Additionally, cultural power may be unevenly matched when one party is like the mediator in gender, race, age, or social background. Left unchecked, these power differences detract from building fair agreements.

Mediators must be acutely aware of the place and construction of power in any relationship and make critical decisions based on power differences. In mediating workplace conflict among supervisors and employees, spending more pre-mediation time with the subordinate explaining the process may mitigate the anxiety that subordinates feel when facing their supervisors (Bollen, Euwema, & Miller, 2010). Another strategy in balancing power is to let the lower power party speak first. According to Sally Engle Merry (1990), the first person to frame the story has more power. Another strategy, however, is to do the opposite. In some instances, letting one party lay out her or his argument allows the other party to contemplate a response, thus, creating less pressure. A third strategy is to co-construct the story, so that neither side is advantaged by the "first to go" phenomenon. As you can see, no one strategy is a panacea for overcoming power differences. Mediators must ascertain the root of the power imbalance and consider the consequences, risks, and advantages to any course of action (Gewurz, 2001).

Being neutral does not necessarily require treating people the same or spending the same amount of time with each person. To balance power and create a fair environment, the mediator may spend more time helping one party identify areas of concerns, articulate ideas, express emotions, and identify interests. If one individual is adept at communicating, the extra time spent with the less skilled individual may seem lopsided. The mediator can overcome perceptions of bias by making sure that each party's interests and concerns are kept in the forefront while working with the less communicative party. Fair does not necessarily mean equal.

Pitfall 2: Allowing Blaming and Attacking

Earlier in the chapter the ways in which individuals attribute motive to the other party's behavior were discussed. Because of this natural tendency to blame and use **internal attributions**, the mediator must develop strategies for overcoming defensiveness. Often, the disputants see the other as the sole cause of the problem, taking no responsibility for their own feelings or perceptions. As Cloke (2001) comments, "A desire for revenge is present in every conflict, though it is more significant in divorce, sexual harassment, wrongful termination, discrimination, victim and offender, and neighbor disputes" (p. 74). Dealing with such raw emotions and the destructive behaviors that accompany them is a necessary skill for all mediators.

Some coaching may be helpful in cases where parties are not accepting responsibility for their emotions or are using considerable "attack" language (typically in the form of "you" statements). The mediator might teach parties to use an "I" statement. Another less direct method is to help the individual give voice to a feeling. For instance, when a disputant says, "Erin is so lazy. She comes into work late every day and sits around instead of finding work to do," the mediator can respond with a question about how the situation affects the speaker. "How does it affect you when Erin is not there?"

Another strategy is to reframe attacks and blaming into interests. A loaded statement such as "He's a sexual harasser and should be fired," can be reframed as "You want to be respected and to have a fair outcome to this mediation. Let's discuss how you were affected by his comments."

In a related pitfall, called the **second party paraphrase**, the mediator miscasts a paraphrase to include a blaming statement. Paraphrases that begin "You feel that he . . ." repeat one party's perspective about the other party. Paraphrases should focus on the feelings of the person speaking, not on their opinions of the other disputant.

Disputant: "My roommate Rhonda is a slovenly pig."
Wrong: "You think Rhonda is messy."
Wrong: "You wish Rhonda were neater."
Right: "You like a tidy room."

Pitfall 3: Acting on Overstatements or Generalizations

Disputants habitually use absolute terms like "never" or "always" to paint the other party's behaviors with the broadest brush possible. If absolute statements are not addressed, resentment and lack of trust in the mediator's ability to facilitate the process fairly can result.

The primary strategy for dealing with overstatements and gross generalizations is asking for examples. The mediator then can prompt disputants to focus on the consequences of the behavior. For example:

PARTY A: "Geoff never picks up the kids on time and they're always left waiting for him. He's so inconsiderate."
MEDIATOR: "Could you tell me a time when the kids were left waiting and what happened as a result?"

In this situation, the mediator focuses the parties on the problem behavior and the consequence without addressing Geoff's overall past record. Geoff is more likely to hear the consequences of his actions if it is no longer framed in a global attack on his personality.

Pitfall 4: Taking Sides

As disputants tell their story, they may become more and more convinced that their actions and feelings are justified and want the mediator to agree. A disputant might say, "Do you see my point?" or "You can tell that this is a problem, can't you?" The disputant is attempting to get the mediator to take a side. The danger for the mediator is appearing (or being) partial to one party. The mediator cannot take sides, even when asked.

When a disputant attempts to elicit an agreement or opinion, the mediator can validate the interest and redirect the query back to the party. For example, the mediator could say, "I can see that this has been a frustrating time for you. How have you handled the situation up until now?" Another strategy is to reassert your neutrality by saying, "My opinion is not really relevant. How did you feel about your choice?" Should a disputant become insistent, the mediator can repeat the mediator's roles and responsibilities, clarifying the purpose of the session.

Pitfall 5: Permitting Interrupting and Bickering

Sometimes parties have a difficult time listening without responding or correcting the other's perceptions. These interruptions can poison an environment so ideas cannot be expressed freely and open dialogue about issues cannot occur. If bickering or arguing becomes a fixed feature of the mediation, negotiation around possible solutions becomes very difficult.

As mentioned in earlier chapters, one strategy is to blame yourself as the mediator for the disputant's inability to follow certain procedures. You can explain that you have trouble following the conversation when two people are talking at once and reassure the interrupters that you will get to their concerns. Ask them to write down their concerns so they can be sure to express them later. If continual bickering is a problem, the mediator can add more structure by establishing ground rules to counter the effects of the negative behavior. Mediators can validate concerns by writing down the topic and reminding the disputant that "everything can't be discussed at the same time and we'll get to every concern before we are done." If interrupting and bickering becomes a block to moving the mediation process forward, the mediator may caucus (meet privately) with the individuals to help them move beyond their disruptive behaviors.

Pitfall 6: Mismanaging Emotional Outbursts

In a particularly difficult divorce and child custody mediation, the husband had enough of listening to his soon-to-be ex-wife disparaging his parenting skills. Spurred by fear of losing his kids and feelings of being painted unfairly, he jumped up suddenly from the table, forcefully pushed his papers onto the floor, and yelled, "I'm done with this crap! I'm leaving!" He began walking toward the door. The mediator, thinking quickly, said, "You know, you're right. I think we could all use a break. Let's take a breather and meet back here in ten minutes." Much to the surprise of the other party and the mediator, the man returned in ten minutes ready to negotiate calmly.

Maintaining control in the face of emotional outbursts can be taxing and tricky. According to Georgia J. Kosmoski and Dennis R. Pollock (2000), "Anger is about power. The angry individual who is acting inappropriately does not feel that his or her opinions or feelings are being recognized, adequately considered, given any weight, or accepted" (p. 4). Kosmoski and Pollock agree that anger has a tendency to beget more anger and that irate individuals often precipitate escalating behaviors in the other party. Behind expressions of anger is an unvoiced fear. Mediators respond by uncovering and mitigating fears while managing anger.

When considering options to respond to emotional outbursts, the safety of all parties must be maintained. A mediator who believes anger may turn to violence should immediately end the session and reassess how to ensure safety if the mediation resumes. Other safety measures include keeping a barrier between you and the agitated individual and maneuvering yourself and the other party toward a doorway.

If safety is not a pressing concern, effective strategies for managing emotional outbursts include:

- Show calm in the face of emotional displays

- Be aware of mediator language choices that may provoke defensiveness

- Use inclusive language

- Postpone

- Develop awareness of personal emotional triggers

- Practice calming techniques

- Create psychological distance

- Collect tools and phrases to moderate emotion

- Take strategic breaks

- Educate parties in effective communication

One strategy for dealing with emotional displays is de-escalating emotions by not getting pulled into the fray. Often the disputant will feel embarrassed after the incident, but he or she will be more likely to return to the table if it seems a safe place. A calm mediator encourages calmness in others.

Mediators should be hyper-aware of their language choices in the face of emotional outbursts. One client, who was feeling attacked, stood up with such force he tipped over his chair. The mediator looked at him and said, "You seem really upset." This understatement elicited a violent retort of "Don't try your mediator BS on me!" This mediator, turned the table back on herself, and said, "I'm sorry. I'm really confused. I am trying to understand what just happened, and I see you are really upset right now." The new phrasing of the same emotion was easier for the disputant to hear, allowing for some **metacommunication** about what had just occurred.

Using inclusive language such as "we" and "us" can help reassure the emotionally charged individual. For example, the mediator may say, "This topic is pretty tense for us right now. Let's move to another issue and come back to this one in a bit." This example illustrates another strategy of postponing discussions when emotions are high. In some cases, coming back to the issue at some future meeting is appropriate. When **postponement** is tied to a break, give the disputants positive "homework" to deter negative **mulling**. "We seem to be in a tense place right now and could use a little breathing space. Let's take a five-minute break. During that time, I'd like you to think about what your real underlying need is in this situation and how you might be able to tell me about that need in a positive way."

Mediators must be aware of how they react personally to emotional outbursts in others, know their own triggers, and how they react when attacked. Disputants often cry. A mediator who finds crying unsettling should develop a response strategy. Mediators can practice calming techniques like breathing exercises or collect phrases to handle difficult situations. Mediators should develop phraseology to postpone or end sessions. Finally, if disputants cannot engage each other civilly, the mediator can attempt to educate the parties in effective communication skills in caucus.

Pitfall 7: Letting One Party Monopolize Time or Control the Process

Occasionally mediators encounter an individual who attempts to "out talk" the other party or to control the flow of the process. Both of these actions usually are the result of one disputant trying to establish power. Mediators must assert themselves into the process with authority when disputants try to take control. Mediator control can be established immediately at the start of the storytelling by asking the identical first question to each party—and by not letting the first to answer speak at length.

The primary mediator strategy for parties who monopolize time is to interrupt, summarize, and redirect conversation. Sometimes individuals repeat the same issues or tell more stories on the same subject. This could be a hint to the mediator that the party needs to be validated or that there is an undiscovered layer to the problem. **Probing questions** can determine whether the disputant needed a prompt to give new information or whether the answer is just more of the same information. If validating does not work to stem the flow, the mediator can attempt to get the other party to acknowledge the concerns (keeping in mind that there is no requirement for agreement, just acknowledgment of one party by the other). However, if after validating, a party continues to belabor the topic, mediators can summarize to break the pattern of complaint. A numbered list is one means of accomplishing this task. The mediator can jump into the conversation and say, "So you are concerned about four items: (1) the plumbing bill, (2) the damage to the drywall in the basement, (3) the process of having your complaint heard, and (4) the treatment you received by the office manager. Is there anything else?" When the party goes into another story included within the list, the mediator can interrupt, saying, "Okay, so you're wanting to make sure your bill is accurate. The other items to cover are the damage to the basement, the complaint process, and the interaction with the office manager. So does this list cover your primary concerns?" Generally, this summarization process is an effective means to stop repetitive stories.

Haynes (1994) warns, "the mediator is constantly faced with choices as to what to summarize and what to ignore. Whatever the mediator focuses on becomes important in the eyes of the participants" (p. 14). The mediator must be aware of the power of summarizing. Mediators can unobtrusively shape the issues by ignoring some information and focusing on other information. The mediator must be diligent in keeping the disputants involved in the verification of the summary statements.

Pitfall 8: Being Overwhelmed with Evidence

Occasionally disputants will come to the mediation table with an excessive amount of material that they will try to present as evidence to support their case. This behavior may be motivated by the desire to intimidate the other party, may be designed to convince the mediator to see things "their way," or may be because the disputant is acting on a mistaken assumption of what is expected in mediation. Depending on the type of mediation, documentary evidence may or may not be helpful.

When overwhelmed with unhelpful evidence, the mediator must ensure that his or her role as a neutral third party, not as a judge or an evaluator, is clearly established. The mediator can be forthright that his or her interpretation of evidence and data is not germane due to the nature of mediation. Another important strategy is to require that information shared during mediation be made available to all parties. If the disputant hands the mediator a photograph, the mediator may say, "Can we share this with the other party?" Sometimes a single document can shed light on the circumstances for both individuals. Once disputants are certain that the mediator is not going to judge their evidence, usually the impetus to present reams of paper to the mediator quickly dissipates.

TABLE 7.3 Novice Mediator Primary Skills During the Storytelling Phase

Early Storytelling	Middle Storytelling	Late Storytelling
Open-ended questions	Open-ended questions	Open-ended questions
Emotional paraphrases	Emotional paraphrases	Emotional paraphrases
Reframing	Reframing	Reframing
	Probing questions	Probing questions
	Being Columbo	Asking seemingly naïve questions
		Probing questions
		Being Columbo
		Future focus questions

Summary

The storytelling and issue identification phase of mediation usually comprises a large block of time during the session. Recognizing how disputants will frame similar events differently through their attributions of others' behaviors helps in developing strategies for creating a story shared by both parties. Symbolic interaction theory, attribution theory, and emotional intelligence help explain some disputants' actions. Effective storytelling meets the safety, recognition, and acknowledgment needs of the disputants, while allowing mediators the opportunity to identify issues, interests, and establish common ground. Mediators work to separate *interests* from *positions* during the storytelling and issue identification phase.

Mediators can choose to have disputants take turns telling their stories or to have them co-construct stories. Basic strategies for storytelling include beginning with general inquiries, asking whole picture questions, using specific inquiry questions, being Columbo, establishing agreed-on facts, weighing disagreements, and developing perspective-taking tools to aid the parties in seeing each other's side.

This chapter concludes by identifying eight common pitfalls and offering communication strategies for working past those problems. Storytelling, issue identification, and detecting common ground provide the necessary groundwork for later agenda setting and negotiations between the parties.

Portfolio Assignments

Portfolio Assignment 7.1: The Vision Quest

Questions that ask disputants for their vision of an ideal may be useful during late storytelling or negotiation. For example, in a workplace setting, a mediator might ask, "What would your ideal work setting look like?" Create a list with one vision question appropriate to each of the following contexts:

Workplace Vision Questions

Neighborhood Vision Questions

Roommate Vision Questions

Group Projects Vision Questions

Portfolio Assignment 7.2: Reframes

Create a preplanning list of common reframes to match predictable situations in mediation. For example, in business conflicts, it is not unusual for one disputant to accuse the other of not working hard enough or being lazy. Preparing an appropriate reframe in advance helps the mediator respond to negativity or attacks.

(Continued)

Reframes for a Business Context ("You don't respect me.")

Reframes for Roommate Conflict ("You never clean the room.")

Reframes for Neighbor Disputes ("Your yard is trashy.")

CHAPTER 8

Setting the Agenda for Negotiation

The Mediator's Notes Are the Building Blocks of the Agenda	**143**
When to Shift to the Agenda Step	**143**
Components of the Agenda	**144**
The Commonality Statement	144
The Agenda List	146
Sequencing the Agenda	**146**
Who Decides the Order of the Agenda?	146
Methods of Choosing the Sequence	147
Adding an Issue for Continuing Relationships	149
The Language of the Agenda	**150**
Framing the Agenda Mutually	150
Framing the Agenda Neutrally	151
Summary	**151**
Portfolio Assignment 8.1: Methods of Ordering the Agenda	**152**
Portfolio Assignment 8.2: Transitioning to the Agenda	**152**

CASE 8.1: The Estate Settlement

After the issue identification and storytelling phase, your notes indicate that there are several potential issues to be settled in the estate of Sophia and Rashid's mother. Sophia is mad at her brother, Rashid, for not being around very much while their mother was ill and thinks that Rashid should get less of the estate because she carried all the burden of their mother's end-of-life care. Rashid was going through an unpleasant divorce at the time and was battling for full custody of his twin sons. Rashid feels badly that he wasn't around when his mother was ill. Rashid and Sophia haven't been talking much, which is why the case finally came to mediation. Rashid and Sophia each seem to have emotional connections to particular items in the estate. For example, Sophia has fond memories of working with her grandfather in the woodworking shop and wants some items as a remembrance of her grandfather; Rashid hopes to travel with his sons in the motor home. Rashid lost his own house and furniture in his divorce and needs furniture. Some positional statements were made during the opening phases of the mediation. Each party made demands about which items of the property they wanted to receive.

Sophia Wants	Rashid Wants
Table valued at $4,000	Table valued at $4,000
All the $100,000 cash	Half the $100,000 cash
All the jewelry ($10,000)	The gold watch ($800)
All of the photographs	The diamond ring ($4,000)
Three quarters of the total value of the estate	One half of the total value of the estate
The antique mirror ($1,000)	Refrigerator/freezer ($1,000)
The car ($15,000)	The car ($15,000)
The table saw and shop equipment ($8,000)	The motor home ($70,000)
The entertainment system ($4,000)	Most of the furniture ($15,000)

The agenda phase is shortest in duration, but it is as important as any part of a session. When setting the agenda, the mediator presents the issues that will dominate the negotiation. How the mediator frames the agenda can restrict the disputants' thinking about potential outcomes or expand opportunities to approach their difficulties in new ways. The phrasing of an agenda should continue the mediator's role as an impartial and neutral third party. If worded improperly, an agenda can bias the negotiation toward one side or subtly move the disputants toward solutions the mediator prefers.

This chapter examines when to shift to the agenda phase and presents the techniques mediators use when framing the agenda. The agenda itself is composed of two parts: a commonality statement and a list of issues to be negotiated. Before discussing the components of the agenda, we present strategies for mediator notetaking to assist in remembering issues raised by disputants during storytelling and issue identification.

THE MEDIATOR'S NOTES ARE THE BUILDING BLOCKS OF THE AGENDA

The mediator listens to each disputant during storytelling while simultaneously searching for negotiable issues. *Negotiable issues* are within the disputants' control and can be framed to be behavioral, concrete, and observable. "Respect" is not a negotiable issue. One party cannot be forced to feel respect. However, a mediator may reframe a respect issue into questions about *behaviors* perceived to demonstrate respect. For example, in Case 8.1, Sophia and Rashid describe their past relationship as acrimonious and unsatisfactory. If Sophia repeatedly states that Rashid doesn't value and respect her care of their mother, "showing respect" might appear in the mediator's notes. If reviving a previously warm relationship is an important issue for the two parties, the mediator might record "improve relationship" as a potential issue. When the mediator realizes that "what is a fair distribution" of the estate is a concern for one or both parties, the words "criteria of a fair settlement" might be noted.

The issues recorded in a mediator's notes are the building blocks of the agenda. Fortunately, mediators have an easy way to verify that they captured the issues—asking the disputants. Mediators always check with the disputants that all of the important issues are contained in the agenda. If something is missed or forgotten, the disputants will know.

WHEN TO SHIFT TO THE AGENDA STEP

Spending insufficient time in the storytelling phase can be a problem. Disputants who are moved to negotiation too soon are less prepared to be cooperative and may bring up new issues in the final moments of a session. Several indicators cue the mediator to move to the next phase. Susan T. Wildau (1987) identified five signs that the time for the agenda step has arrived:

1. Parties begin to repeat themselves

2. The mediator has enough material to work with and the main issues appear to be on the table

3. Parties state they feel they have been heard

4. Parties allow the mediator to define the issue as a joint problem

5. Parties indicate, either verbally or nonverbally, that they are ready to proceed to problem solving (p. 8)

Disputants may indicate their readiness nonverbally by conversing congenially or turning toward each other in their chairs. Generally, transition to the agenda occurs when the parties have told their stories enough to be prepared to negotiate and when the mediator assesses that the basic issues have been discovered.

> ### Discussion Question 8.1
>
> WHAT ARE the probable consequences if the mediator moves to the agenda step too quickly? Discuss how a premature agenda could affect the parties, the process, and perceptions of the mediator.

COMPONENTS OF THE AGENDA

When the issues have emerged and a general understanding of each party's needs is accomplished, the mediator begins the agenda step. The mediator employs a transitional statement, such as "I think I have a general understanding of the issues that brought you here today. Let me see whether we can summarize what you've expressed in the shape of an agenda." Novice mediators may take a short break at this point to prepare the exact phrasing of the agenda.

Based on the issues identified during storytelling, the mediator sets the agenda using a two-step process. First, the mediator presents either a general or a **two-way commonality statement.** Second, the mediator itemizes the issues to be negotiated.

The Commonality Statement

A commonality statement is the mediator's summary of characteristics, attitudes, or context shared by the parties. Neighbors share a common boundary line; disputants may share a desire to resolve the difficulty; employees may want to excel in their work. The mediator may state either a two-way or a general commonality statement.

The General Commonality Statement

The mediator might simply list one or two things the disputants have in common. For example, "I see that both of you want to finish this issue today so you can get it behind you" or "Both of you want to do your jobs well and need each other in order to get your jobs done." General commonality statements highlight mutual interests and increase the probability of cooperation during the negotiation phase. The primary goal of the general commonality statement is to move the parties metaphorically to the same side of the table against a mutual problem rather than against each other.

The Two-Way Commonality Statement

A second way to begin the agenda phase is with a two-way commonality statement. The *two-way commonality statement* links a specific goal or interest of each party. It is a method of expressing the general goals of the negotiation in mutual terms. Advantages of a two-way commonality statement include conceptually interweaving the needs of the parties and encouraging cooperative problem solving. It creates a common anchor for both parties.

For example, the mediator may observe that Jake and Carl want to remain roommates, but they have incompatible goals—Jake wants to party and Carl wants to study. The mediator might phrase the two-way commonality by saying, "It seems like the basic issue is how can Jake have social time with his friends and Carl have quiet time to study. Does that get at the heart of the matter?" An appropriate two-way commonality statement encompasses the goals and interests of the parties without implying a particular solution. If the mediator said, "The main issue seems to be how can the two of you split your time in the room so you can both pursue your individual interests," the mediator intruded into the dispute by suggesting a solution. While the roommates may choose to divide the hours spent in the room, they may also discover more creative options such as socializing together or studying together either in the room or at different locations. Creative solutions are preempted if the mediator suggests a specific outcome. Mediators using the balanced model are prohibited from suggesting solutions.

The formula for a two-way commonality is:

How can Party A meet the goal of _____ while at the same time Party B meets the goal of _____?

Hopefully, both parties will nod or say, "Yes," to the two-way commonality statement. If not, the mediator may return to storytelling by asking, "What have I missed?" By laying the goals side-by-side with equal priority, the mediator validates each party, encourages creativity, and fosters mutual-gains thinking.

ACTIVITY 8.1: What's the Commonality?

Examine Case 8.1 and offer a two-way commonality statement for Sophia and Rashid. For additional practice, create a two-way or general commonality statement for the following cases.

1. During storytelling and issue identification, Bob repeats several times that he just wants to know where the property line is so he can build a fence and have some privacy in his backyard. Celia is very concerned that a fence would block her majestic view of the lake and hillside. What two-way commonality statement can the mediator make?

2. During storytelling and issue identification, Naomi bluntly states that she wants $500 from Ty because Ty won't give her a receipt for the work. Naomi can't get reimbursed for the $500 from her supplier if she doesn't have a valid receipt. Ty won't give her a receipt because he could not get back into the house to finish the inspection and can't give a receipt for work he never finished. What two-way commonality statement can the mediator use?

3. Ramon and Henry each complain bitterly about the other's unkind remarks and slovenly work habits. Both like their jobs and feel they are good at what they do. What general commonality statement could open the agenda phase?

The Agenda List

The second task during the agenda phase is creating a list of issues to be negotiated. The list might be an exhaustive itemization of every small matter to be negotiated or grouped in some way. For example, in Case 8.1, if every disputed item appeared on the agenda, it would be a lengthy but exhaustive list. Typically, the mediator clusters similar items together as one agenda item. For example, two roommates may be in a dispute about the upkeep of their rented apartment. If the roommates had no arrangement for care of the apartment when they moved in, the mediator may frame the agenda as two issues for negotiation: How they will make decisions (procedural issue) and how to accomplish the list of housekeeping chores (substantive issue).

The agenda list is created from the mediator's notes about the negotiable issues raised by the disputants—not the mediator's personal ideas. The exception is that the mediator may add an item to the agenda if the parties have a probability of communicating with each other in the future. In those cases, even if the disputants do not discuss the need for better communication, it is appropriate for the mediator to add that item to the agenda: "Since you are neighbors, I'm going to add an agenda item of how the two of you could communicate better in the future."

The mediator ensures that the items on the agenda are phrased positively and are negotiable. For example, "Cece's bad attitude" would never appear on an agenda. It is negatively phrased and attitudes are not negotiable. The better phrasing might be an agenda item: "How the two of you can communicate in a way that will fit the needs of the workplace."

SEQUENCING THE AGENDA LIST

Who Decides the Order of the Agenda?

Once the items on the agenda are set forth, a strategy must be adopted to sequence the order in which the items will be negotiated. The mediator's first choice in the negotiation and problem-solving phase is whether to decide the order of issue discussion for the disputants or to let them decide. The advantages of mediator choice are threefold. First, the mediator maintains control of the process. Second, the mediator strategically can choose an issue to be first for many reasons: It might be critical to the rest of the negotiation (a linchpin); it might seem the logical place to start because it is important to the disputants; or it might be an easy issue to settle and build momentum. Ultimately, the difficulty of any agenda item is a judgment call by the mediator. If the disputants are acrimonious, some mediators will start with small, easy items to build a pattern of negotiation success. For example, in Case 8.1, Sophia and Rashid have large differences on the amount of cash they request in the settlement, but they may have fewer differences about items like the entertainment center or the refrigerator. Starting with less-contested items may lead to more cooperative negotiation. Thirdly, mediator control of the agenda order prevents either disputant from manipulating the agenda to personal advantage.

If the mediator determines that the disputants should choose the agenda order, the mediator assists the disputants in negotiating the sequence of topics. Disputants might negotiate the order of all of the items to be negotiated, or they might alternate who selects the next negotiation topic. There are two advantages to the disputants choosing the agenda order. First, the disputants are involved in the decision, so they have ownership of the process. Second, working together on the agenda order is a cooperative achievement. The mediator can praise their success and leverage this success into a more cooperative negotiation experience. In both the mediator choice and the disputant choice strategies, it is the mediator's job to ensure that all agenda items receive attention.

Methods of Choosing the Sequence

The mediator considers several variables in deciding how to order the agenda:

- Have criteria been established that will assist the disputants in their decisions?

- How divisive has the past relationship been?

- Have the disputants exhibited greater understanding for each other's needs?

- Is one party more adamant on particular issues than the other person?

- Is one issue a linchpin that will affect all of the other items on the agenda?

- Is there an issue that is a Pandora's box that might explode if opened too soon?

After the mediator considers the strategic elements that affect the choice of which issue is first, the mediator selects a method of ordering the agenda.

Discussion Question 8.2

HOW COULD a non-negotiable issue such as "respect" be incorporated into the agenda?

Some mediators habitually begin the negotiation phase with specifying criteria that any decision must meet for both parties to be satisfied (discussed more in Chapter 9). The decision criteria should match the party's interests expressed during the storytelling phase. The mediator ensures that the criteria are goal-centered rather than restatements of individual positions. For example, criteria might include that the decision must be fair to both parties or a decision must settle the issue so it doesn't continue.

How a mediator sequences the agenda is a strategic decision. For example, in cases where the disputants are congenial and emotions are low, starting with specific issues may be more desirable than beginning with more **abstract** ideas. Some methods include:

- Criteria as the first issue
- In the order they were identified during the storytelling phase
- In the order in which they will be implemented, if adopted
- Alternating choice of the next issue to each disputant
- Most important to least important
- Least important to most important
- Linchpin items first
- From the most abstract to the most concrete
- From the most concrete to most abstract
- Packaging similar items together

The various methods of ordering the agenda can be illustrated using Case 8.1. If the mediator asks what would characterize a fair decision, *criteria* are addressed as the first issue. The mediator might list the agenda in the order discussed during storytelling *(order of identification)* or in two sections called estate settlement and future communication *(order of implementation).* The *alternating selection method* would be used if the disputants decide who has the first choice and then Rashid and Sophia alternate in picking the next item. A mediator might ask each disputant what issue is most important and mark the items that are common. Next, the mediator would move through the list from *most to least important.* If settlement of the criteria of a fair outcome is so important to Sophia and Rashid that it overshadows the negotiation on all of the specific issues, the mediator may suggest it be negotiated first and use the *linchpin* method. If all of the actual furnishings and items are negotiated before the more intangible issues of fairness and future relationship are addressed, then the *most concrete to most abstract method* is used. If all of the furniture is disposed as one group rather than breaking it down into each separate object, then the specific items to be negotiated are *packaged.*

The strategy of packing and unpacking may carry over into the negotiation phase. As the negotiation proceeds, the mediator may connect agenda items together if settlement of one issue is linked to settlement of another issue. Sometimes, items are linked to provide room for tradeoffs. **Competitive worldview** negotiators may need to swap **concessions** on different agenda items to feel as if they are not giving in to their "opponent." For example, in Case 8.1, Sophia might be willing to settle for half the value of the estate, but only if that concession is traded for the right to select the first five items of property. **Cooperative worldview** negotiators may need to link issues to spur creative thinking and mutual gains options. For example, Sophia and Rashid might link all the items together that have sentimental value and negotiate their disposition as one decision; then they will deal with the rest of the estate.

Larger issues may need to be *unpacked* or unlinked. After listening to Sophia and Rashid's demands during storytelling, the mediator may lump their concerns together during the agenda under the general headings of cash, vehicles, and furnishings. During the negotiation, the three large agenda items would be unpacked. For example, the large package of furnishings might be considered item by item.

Regardless of which method of ordering the agenda is selected, the mediator must verify that all issues are on the list. Before transitioning to the negotiation phase, the mediator will summarize the agenda list and inquire, "Are there other issues that need to be added to the agenda?"

Discussion Question 8.3

WHAT MIGHT cause the mediator to change the order in which the issues are addressed during the negotiation phase?

Adding an Issue for Continuing Relationships

As mentioned previously, in cases where the parties have a continuing relationship, we recommend an agenda item about future communication. As discussed in Chapter 7, disputants with a continuing relationship who come to mediation have experienced some breach of trust or lapse in effective communication. In cases where both parties have lamented the toll this situation had on their relationship, the mediator can pursue a discussion about how to improve communication. The mediator leads the parties in a discussion of what they would prefer their communication to be like in the future, how they wish to have future communication, or what they will do if another difficulty arises in the future.

After listing the other issues to be negotiated, the mediator might say, "The two of you seem dissatisfied with your past interactions, should we put a discussion for how to interact in the future on the agenda?" At other times, the mediator will not list the item on the regular agenda but may prompt future communication as a point of discussion after the parties have experienced some negotiation success.

Discussion Question 8.4

WHAT ARE the probable consequences if a mediator repeats negative phrasing as part of an agenda item? For example, what might happen if the mediator said, "Part of the solution is finding a way to balance Rashid's lack of help against Sophia's care for your mother?"

CASE 8.2: What a Bad Dog

Evan is a graduate student finishing his Master's in engineering. He rents a house that belongs to his brother who is stationed overseas. Evan had a roommate, Rico, for a couple of years. Rico was quiet, cleaned up after himself, and his dog was well behaved. When Rico moved out, Evan decided he needed another roommate and Shannon moved in. Shannon is a 19-year-old airman stationed at the local airbase. This was her first experience living off the base, and she was excited to be able to bring her family dog to her new home. Evan believed her when she said she was a neat freak, quiet, and that her dog was a "good" dog.

Winnie, a large boxer mix, lived on a farm since birth. When Shannon's orders came to go overseas to Afghanistan, she really didn't have a chance to train the new puppy. At the farm, Winnie spent most of the time outside in a five-acre fenced area. While house trained, Winnie is energetic and a bit high strung.

Within a week of moving into Evan's house, Winnie chewed a window frame and pushed through the screen to get outside. Winnie urinated in Evan's closet—after eating a pair of new hiking boots. Most of the sprinkler heads in the back yard have been chewed into an unworkable state, and the yard is full of holes now.

After 10 days, Evan asked Shannon and the dog to leave immediately. Shannon knows he didn't evict her according to a law requiring a 7-day written eviction notice. Evan filed in small claims court for $2,325 in damages ($200 for the boots, $125 for new sprinkler heads he can install, $1000 for a landscaper to even out the holes in the yard and replant the grass, $500 for carpet cleaning to remove the dog urine, and $500 for the repair of the window). Shannon thinks the $300 pet deposit should count against the damages; Evan says it was just a general nonrefundable deposit. Shannon also thinks she should be credited for the days she prepaid rent from the time Evan asked her to move out (a proration of $210.00).

ACTIVITY 8.2: Creating an Agenda

In Case 8.2, the former roommates are disputing issues around the dissolution of their rooming arrangement. Create an agenda list for this case. Pay careful attention to framing issues neutrally and mutually.

THE LANGUAGE OF THE AGENDA

Framing the Agenda Mutually

It is tempting for mediators to keep separate lists of which issues are important to each disputant and then present the two lists as part of the agenda. The agenda, however, must be phrased as one set of common issues rather than as a list of competing demands. By *mutually framing* the issues, both parties are advantaged equally and a win–lose frame is avoided.

Framing the Agenda Neutrally

The commonality statement and the items on an agenda list should be phrased neutrally and impartially. Failing to do so can create feelings of mediator bias and erode trust in the mediation process. Lela P. Love (2000) commented as follows: "Practice in extracting and neutrally labeling issues is one of the challenging and important aspects of a training program, particularly because the exercise is unique to the role of mediator and hence foreign to most newcomers to mediation" (p. 32).

Three common mediator errors occur when framing the agenda:

Error #1: The agenda is framed using one disputant's suggestions. When two siblings are arguing about the estate of a relative, the negotiation could be slanted toward one party or the other if the mediator repeats one person's words when framing the agenda. If the mediator labels one item on the agenda as "What to do about the table that Sophia wants," the issue is advantaged toward Sophia. Instead, the mediator could deliver a more generalized statement, such as "How will the two of you dispose of the remaining furniture items?"

Error #2: A mediator slants the negotiation by putting personal ideas into the agenda. If the mediator assumes that daughters should inherit jewelry and sons should inherit tools, the mediator might jump to conclusions that the disputants have not made. For example, the mediator might say, "One of the issues is what to balance against Sophia's receipt of the jewelry." A better agenda statement might be "What to do about the jewelry."

Error #3: Mediators may exclude some avenues of creativity when they presume issues must be resolved in particular ways. Assuming that the parties can only find an equitable solution by dividing the furniture between them excludes potential outcomes. Instead of framing the agenda item as "Who will get which piece of furniture?" the mediator might frame the agenda item by saying, "What will the two of you do with the remaining furniture?" For instance, the parties may decide to each pick pieces of furniture in alternating turns, or one party could buy items of furniture from the other, or furniture could be traded for other items in the settlement, or they could sell all the items and divide the proceeds, or they could decide to donate all of the furniture to charity.

The phrasing of agenda items matters. Mediators must label agenda items carefully.

Summary

The agenda phase is short but important. The shift to the agenda occurs after the parties feel they have been heard and the mediator determines all the issues have been uncovered. From the notes taken during the storytelling and issue identification phase, the mediator forms either a two-way or general commonality statement that links the goals of the parties together and a compressed list of the issues to be negotiated.

The mediator chooses whether to state the agenda for the parties or involve them in the decision. The three advantages to mediator selection are as follows: (1) The mediator maintains control; (2) the mediator strategically can select which item is addressed first; and (3) it prevents disputants from manipulating the order to personal advantage. Two advantages of the disputant choice method are that (1) the disputants have more ownership of the process and (2) negotiating the agenda order creates their first cooperative success.

Several variables assist the mediator in analyzing how to sequence the agenda. When the agenda is created, similar items initially are grouped together. The mediator may package or unpack items as seems beneficial. Three common errors in phrasing the agenda are slanting an agenda item in one party's favor, suggesting outcomes, and deterring creative thinking.

Portfolio Assignments

Portfolio Assignment 8.1: Methods of Ordering the Agenda

Create a one-page summary of the methods for sequencing the agenda to place in your portfolio as a reference.

Portfolio Assignment 8.2: Transitioning to the Agenda

Consider what you will say as a mediator to move the disputants from the storytelling and issue identification phase to the agenda phase. Write at least one transitional sentence to tell disputants that you are moving to the next step.

Problem Solving and Negotiation

The Two Worlds of Negotiation 154

Directiveness vs. Intrusiveness 157

Mediator Techniques to Foster Disputant Problem Solving 158

    Starting the Negotiation 158

    Techniques for Cooperative Negotiation 158

    Techniques for Traditional Negotiation 162

Using the Caucus to Respond to Common Problems 167

    Not Bargaining in Good Faith 168

    Hidden Agendas 168

    Reality Check 168

    Lying or Withholding Information 169

    Shuttle 169

Breaking Deadlocks 170

    Analyze the Impasse 170

    Techniques to Break through Impasse 170

Face-Saving 171

Ending the Negotiation Phase 172

Mediator Ethics and the Negotiation Phase 173

Summary 174

Portfolio Assignment 9.1: Questions to Start Negotiation 175

Portfolio Assignment 9.2: Going into Caucus 175

Be patient. Some negotiators dance fast. Some negotiators dance more slowly.

—Eric R. Galton, 1996, p. 374

Once the emotional and other barriers to settlement have moderated and the issue agenda is formulated, the mediator assists the disputants with problem solving and negotiation. If hurt feelings have waned, negotiation over the remaining substantive issues may flow easily for the disputants. Most conflicts, however, contain enduring thorny problems that are difficult for the disputants to manage. This chapter discusses the mediator's role in creating structures for problem solving, bringing specialized techniques to the table, and—when feasible—fostering a cooperative approach to bargaining. Because disputants bring assumptions about negotiation with them to the mediation session, the mediator needs a basic understanding of negotiation theory and strategy.

CASE 9.1: Not if He Wins

Jim Mallard and John Dillard were roommates in a house off-campus for two years. They both moved out of the house to room with different people and have been embroiled in an acrimonious dispute ever since. Through the storytelling phase, the mediator determined that their mutual goal was to settle their differences so the two former roommates could clear their debts from the house without being taken to court or hurting either party's credit record. Both Jim and John agreed with the mediator's analysis that there were three primary issues to be negotiated: (1) How the landlord will be approached regarding the damages to the house; (2) what to do about an outstanding balance on the cable bill; and (3) the disposition of several items that the two of them purchased together while they were roommates.

The mediator opened the negotiation and problem-solving phase by selecting the cable bill as the first item to be addressed and asked, "Do either of you have an idea on how we can approach the cable bill in a way that is objective and fair?" John immediately replied, "I'm not paying any of it. I never watched any cable programs." Jim retorted, "But you used the computer to go online and that was part of the cable package!" The mediator asked John, "Did you use the cable for the high-speed Internet connection?" John did. The mediator then reframed, "It sounds like you both had some interest in having a cable line into the house. Given that fact, how can the two of you approach the outstanding bill in a way that is objective and fair?" John stuck to his position that he wouldn't pay any of the bill because it didn't cost Jim anything when he used the computer, since it was already there. Jim asserted that John should pay half of the entire bill.

THE TWO WORLDS OF NEGOTIATION

An array of terms label the two opposite worldviews about negotiation: competitive and mutual gains, competitive and cooperative, adversarial and problem solving, hard and soft, principled and competitive, or distributive and integrative (Erickson & Johnson, 2012; McCorkle & Reese, 2010; Murray, 1996). In this book, the terms "competitive" and "cooperative" represent the two primary approaches to negotiation. Most cases are **mixed motive** conflicts that contain both competitive and cooperative dimensions.

Competitive bargaining involves a give and take of concessions to reach an agreement. Bargaining frequently includes compromise (a loss of a personal goal) in order to reach an agreement satisfactory to both parties. Traditional competitive bargaining is *distributive,* meaning the available resources are divided among the parties at the table. Competitive bargaining assumes there is a limited number of resources and that it is impossible for each person to achieve every goal. For example, a couple who unexpectedly inherits $20,000 may hold different opinions about what to do with the money. One may want to put the money toward a new car, and the other may wish to save half of the money and remodel the bathroom with the other half. In traditional bargaining, one of two results typically will occur—the most powerful person will control the decision, or both parties will compromise and split the difference. If the most powerful person wanted to buy a car, she might spend all the money on that purchase. Compromise might mean deciding to allocate $10,000 apiece, and neither individual can achieve their original goals.

Competitive negotiations inherently are *positional*—disputants open with hard, inflexible, outcome-centered demands. Tactics in competitive negotiation include:

- Making concessions only when some principled rationale justifies the change
- Focusing solely on personal outcomes
- Blaming the other
- Arguing and debating
- Hiding interests to maintain power
- Threatening and promising
- Real or feigned aggressive behavior
- Offering tit-for-tat (this-for-that) trades
- Fabricating information
- Withholding information

In Case 9.1, both disputants argue their side of the issue competitively and forge hard, positional stances.

Cooperative negotiation takes a different approach. The cooperative approach was popularized by Roger Fisher and William L. Ury of the Harvard Negotiation Project in their 1980s best-selling book (revised in 2011), *Getting to Yes.* The mediator who prefers a cooperative approach begins with the *interests* of each party that were discovered during the storytelling phase rather than with the positions. The negotiators are encouraged to search for solutions that maximize the outcome for *each* party, called *mutual gains.* For example, a cooperative-oriented couple who receives a $20,000 inheritance will discuss each individual's underlying needs that might be met with the money. They discover his desire to buy a condo and her impulse to save money share the same underlying need—providing a means to spend their retirement years in a warmer climate. When approached creatively, they may choose to put $15,000 aside for a down payment on a condo, spend $1,000 on a vacation/condo shopping trip, and allocate $2,000 to each individual for discretionary spending.

Kathy Domenici and Stephen W. Littlejohn (2001) illustrate one mutual gains strategy to open negotiation and cooperative bargaining:

> "I see that John needs _____ and Manuel needs _____. If we are able to achieve a solution that meets those interests, would you be satisfied?" (p. 91).

In Case 9.1, the mediator might apply this formula by saying, "I see Jim needs to have a clean credit record going into the future and John needs a settlement of the property so he can plan to furnish his new apartment. If you are able to negotiate a solution that meets both your needs in these areas, will that settle the issue for both of you?"

By beginning with the interests, the mediator frames the negotiation as a search for creative solutions that might satisfy the underlying needs of *each* party—to integrate their interests into an outcome that is mutually beneficial. Tactics of cooperative bargaining include:

- Focusing on the problem as a mutual issue

- Striving to meet each person's needs

- Continuing to moderate emotional displays

- Disclosing interests and needs

- Having more than one item on the table at a time so agreements can be packaged

- Generating several options for settlement

- Remaining provisional about solutions until all items are negotiated

- Bargaining in good faith

Roger Fisher and Scott Brown (1988) assert that substantive issues must be separated from relationship issues. For example, the issues surrounding money or household possessions are separated from the issue of whether former roommates will remain friends. Furthermore, they assert that the cooperative negotiator is unconditionally positive, eschews negative tactics, and listens to understand the other's perspective.

David A. Lax and James K. Sebenius (1986) explain the three primary actions that characterize mutual gains: (1) Reaching agreements that are better for both parties than each individual's alternatives if there is no settlement (BATNA); (2) discovering an outcome that is agreeable to each party; and (3) discovering potential value by finding commonality and reducing differences. In a successful mutual gains settlements, each party gets the most they can from the agreement. The cooperative approach is less likely to work when one or both parties are focused on personal revenge or seek to establish precedents.

Research points to the importance of continuing to moderate emotion if it is present during negotiation. In particular, expressions of anger have been found to give individuals an advantage during negotiation—angry people elicit more concessions (Van Kleef, De Drue, Pietroni, & Manstead, 2006). The mediator moderates advantage-grabbing tactics to keep the negotiation fair and to give the cooperative approach a chance to work.

Discussion Question 9.1

ARE YOU equally comfortable with competitive and cooperative negotiation approaches in your personal life? If you prefer one perspective, what do you like about that way of negotiating? If you dislike one of the approaches, what is it about that approach that you dislike?

DIRECTIVENESS VS. INTRUSIVENESS

The mediator may be highly involved in leading the process during the negotiation phase or speak very little. As we stated earlier, if the conflict primarily was spurred by emotional issues that have been moderated during the storytelling and issue identification phase, the mediator may be able to lean back and observe as the disputants conduct their negotiation. The parties might amiably work through their problem solving and reach agreement. In many sessions, however, bad feelings continue, intractable issues persist, and the disputants have low communication or negotiation skills. In these cases, a more hands-on approach is required.

Directiveness is the degree of control the mediator exerts over the process. A high-directive mediator might lead the disputants through several problem-solving exercises to help them assess their options and to generate possible solutions. A high-directive mediator continues to reframe and paraphrase offers throughout the negotiation phase. A low-directive mediator will sit back and observe as the disputants talk their way through the negotiation—acting only when the disputants become too emotional or are deadlocked. Most mediators begin the negotiation and problem-solving phase somewhat directive and lessen that control as the disputants are able to work together successfully. The mediator listens for the moment when a rule that disputants talk only to the mediator can be loosened by asking the parties to speak directly with each other.

Mediator directiveness is different from mediator intrusiveness. An *intrusive* mediator inserts personal opinions into the substance of the settlement. When disputants are deadlocked, the intrusive mediator will suggest settlement options rather than lead the parties through a process to help them break their deadlock. If Jim and John in Case 9.1 can't find a compromise, the intrusive mediator might suggest they just split the basic cable bill but have each party pay for his personal long-distance calls. In the law profession, some advocate a pure facilitative role and others adopt an *evaluative mediation model* where the attorney-mediator gives advice about the legal merit of a case or suggests settlement options (da Silveira, 2007). In the balanced mediation model for general practice, mediators may be *directive*—but not *intrusive*—and are prohibited from inserting ideas about possible solutions.

Discussion Question 9.2

WHAT HAPPENS when the mediator is overly intrusive? Do you think intrusiveness affects the probability that the disputants will carry through with their agreements? Do you think an intrusive mediator can work from the transformative perspective discussed in Chapter 1?

MEDIATOR TECHNIQUES TO FOSTER DISPUTANT PROBLEM SOLVING

Starting the Negotiation

As stated in Chapter 8, sometimes the order of the agenda is the first item to be negotiated. Once the order is determined, the mediator opens the session for negotiation. Angela Cora Garcia (2000) labels a general request for solutions directed at both parties a *collective solicit*. A collective solicit may be effective in eliciting offers, for example: "What ideas do either of you have that might work for both of you?" At other times, one or both parties will avoid the mediator's solicit or not wish to be the first to make a concession. In these instances, disputants will repeat prior demands. If one party repeats a position, "I have to have $5,000," the mediator might reframe by saying, "You're looking for an amount that meets your needs." The mediator could probe for the needs underlying positions by asking, "How did you arrive at that figure?" or "What will a monetary settlement do for you?"

When the disputants remain fixed in positions and demure from techniques to elicit productive negotiation, the mediator may need to return to the skills and functions of the storytelling phase to work through emotional or relationship issues and/or create face-saving opportunities. Later in this chapter, we discuss the potential of empathy and face-saving to transform conflicts.

ACTIVITY 9.1: Starting Negotiation

Role-play the beginning of the negotiation phase in Case 9.1. Begin by asking Jim and John a question that will elicit some criteria for fairness.

Techniques for Cooperative Negotiation

When disputants are not progressing on their own, the mediator intervenes to assist the parties in discovering options. The competent mediator is adept at multiple strategies to help disputants create ideas for settlement. Because each session and every disputant is unique, the technique that functions well in one mediation may be ineffective in the next. We discuss nine common techniques used to foster cooperative negotiation.

Creating a Mutual Frame

The mediator's opening question during the negotiation phase sets the tone for cooperation or competition. A mediator who asks for "ideas that either of you might have that would work for both of you" is more likely to get a cooperative response than one who asks: "What ideas do you have?" The answer to the latter question frequently is one person's favorite position, which may start the negotiation phase with polarization.

Establishing Criteria

Establishing criteria is useful in both competitive and cooperative bargaining, but it may be essential to foster cooperation. Criteria connect directly to the interests that were uncovered during the storytelling and issue identification phase. In Case 9.1, the mediator might state: "I have found that disputants make better decisions if they think about criteria for fairness before they begin the actual negotiation about money. You both have indicated that you desire a fair settlement. I need to understand what you mean by fair. Please explain it to me." By discussing criteria first, the disputants have less opportunity to display competitive tactics. If the disputants adopt competitive tactics, the mediator attempts to move from positions to interests by asking questions to determine the facts, moving the discussion to criteria that both will accept in judging the fairness of an outcome, and reminding the former roommates of their common BATNA (Best Alternative to a Negotiated Agreement). The mediator might ask:

- "What prior agreements did you have about the cable?"

- "How was the bill paid in the past?"

- "Is the cable bill in both your names?"

- "You each indicated you may want to have cable service in the future and don't want to lose your credit with the cable company. What criteria can you use in determining how you both can reach that goal?"

- "What will happen if you don't reach an agreement?"

Brainstorming

While some models suggest that every negotiation start with **brainstorming**, we recommend the technique as an option rather than a required first step. When disputants are stalled, the mediator directs them to spend a few minutes brainstorming to discover creative options. Before beginning, the mediator explains the rules of brainstorming.

- Disputants will think of options that could solve the problem and spend five minutes writing them down.

- The mediator will alternate in asking each disputant to contribute one idea.

- None of the ideas will be evaluated as they are listed.

- All ideas will be given the same respect.

- Disputants are encouraged to think about the problem in new ways.

- Building on the ideas of the other party is desirable.

- Wild and creative ideas are good—they may lead to other ideas that are workable.

As each idea is stated, the mediator writes it on a board, separate index card, or large sticky pad. When the disputants have exhausted their supply of creative ideas, the mediator requests the individuals stand and look at all the sticky notes pasted randomly on a wall. Then the mediator asks questions to help the disputants seek mutually agreeable common ground: "Are there ideas on the list that fit your criteria for a fair decision?" or "Are there ideas that can be modified to be part of a solution that works for the two of you?" Through the brainstorming exercise, one divorcing couple with very young children decided that instead of moving the children between mom and dad's houses, the kids would stay in their original home and the parent spend alternate weeks living with the kids. The value of consistency for the children and enabling them to have a stable school district was the most important criteria for the parents. The decision they reached was creative and unlikely to have been considered if a judge had determined the outcome.

ACTIVITY 9.2: Brainstorming

Role-play the mediator leading Jim and John from Case 9.1 through a brainstorming of possible solutions to their issues.

CASE 9.2: Mrs. Graham and the Train

An elderly woman was taking a shortcut to her rural home one dark evening when she drove into a train. The train was parked across the isolated back road. The woman was not injured, but her car was damaged. On hearing of the incident, the family began to wonder whether "Grandma shouldn't drive anymore and maybe we should take her car keys away."

Mrs. Graham decided to sue the train company and called her attorney. Her attorney was a clever man. He researched and found an obscure law saying that it was illegal to park a train across a rural driveway. The attorney approached the train company. Negotiation ensued, and the train company attorney offered to repair the woman's car. When presented with the offer by her attorney, Mrs. Graham replied, "It's not enough."

Her attorney returned to negotiation and came back with repair of the car and $2,000 compensation. Again, she replied, "It's not enough." Thinking the woman was a hard bargainer, her attorney approached the train company and said that his client needed "$10,000 compensation and repair of her car." The company finally acceded, knowing that it could receive bad publicity if the case went to court.

(Continued)

Proud of his work for his client, the attorney presented the $10,000 offer. Once again, she replied, "It's not enough." The attorney was stunned. Finally, he asked a question: "What is it that you need?" She replied, "I want them to write a letter apologizing for leaving the train there and saying it was their fault."

(Randy Lowry of Pepperdine University tells this story.)

Linking and Unlinking

As the negotiation proceeds, the mediator may connect agenda items together if one issue is essential to settlement of another issue. The mediator also may link issues if having more than one item on the table at the same time is advantageous. Competitive negotiators may need to trade concessions on different agenda items to feel that they are standing up to their "opponent." Cooperative negotiators may need to link issues to spur creative thinking and mutual-gains options. If disputants are bogging down in the exact details about damages to an apartment, the mediator might group all of the damages together to negotiate an aggregate amount. Payments of damages might be linked to the landlord's release of a deposit.

Larger issues may need to be unpacked when the items can stand alone and are not contingent on one another. When the criteria that apply to each issue are different, unlinking may help. If disputants began a negotiation focused on aggregate damages to an apartment, the mediator separates the issues if criteria for damage to carpet are different from criteria for landscaping damage.

Logrolling

European settlers in the American continent avowed independence but often needed help from neighbors in tasks that were too hard for one family to accomplish. In clearing land or moving timber to the streamside to go to the lumber mill, these individualists literally meant: "You help roll my logs and I'll help roll your logs." Today, logrolling means "You help me and I'll help you." To facilitate **logrolling** in modern times, each party is coached on how to make concessions on some issues while the other party makes concessions on other issues. Ideally, both are conceding points in areas that have little personal importance and are gaining concessions in areas that are highly important—helping each other and creating a mutually beneficial trade. In Case 9.1, John might agree to pay half of the basic cable bill if he gets possession of the washing machine. To John, who needs a washing machine in his new apartment, paying half the cable bill is cheaper than buying a washer, so the deal fulfills his interests.

Role Reversal

Mediators sometimes ask disputants to engage in perspective taking called *role reversal*. Each party is asked to state what would be fair if he or she were the other person. Disputants can be asked, "What would you think about this offer if you were the other party?" "If you were the other person, what would be a fair outcome for you?" In Case 9.1, the mediator might ask John, "What would you think about the offer you just made if you were Jim?" Variations on the role reversal strategy might find the mediator asking, "What would your coworkers/friends/mother think of this agreement when they find out about it? Will they think it was fair?"

Focus on Future

An effective strategy to move entrenched disputants is changing the focus of discussion to the future. If past grievances are blocking creative negotiation, the mediator changes the frame of the negotiation to their future relationship. The mediator may inquire of coworkers: "What do you want your working relationship to be like in the future?" or "If you had a better working relationship, what would that look like?" Neighbors may be asked: "What would you like in a good neighbor relationship?" By building an idealized image of a good relationship, the mediator assists the parties to move toward a positive goal, rather than to wallow in past grievances. Mediators help disputants understand that holding onto a past grievance story deters the movement to a less stressful future.

Cost-Cutting

If negotiations are stalling on the total cost of the agreement, the parties might brainstorm how they could limit costs. For example, they might agree to drop litigation if the settlement works out, negating the need for expensive attorney fees. Donald G. Gifford (1996) provides another example: "A management attorney who agrees to the wage demands of a certain type of worker might be concerned that in the future the union will expect similarly generous agreements for other workers. The union negotiator may reassure management that she understands that this wage agreement for certain employees stems from special circumstances, such as historical inequities, and that similar wage concessions should not be expected for other employees" (pp. 175–176).

Coaching

Coaching is inherent in many techniques that assist the parties. In a private meeting, the mediator may help an individual think about how to phrase offers, make symbolic gestures, show empathy for the other person's problems, or build **contingency agreements**. In caucus, the mediator might say to John, "You've told me that you're willing to pay half of the cable bill if you get the washing machine. How could you say that to Jim when we go back into session?"

Techniques for Traditional Negotiation

When one or both disputants exhibit traditional, hard negotiation behaviors, the mediator may encourage cooperative negotiation through reframing, controlling the process, and attempting some of the techniques discussed in the previous section. When cooperative negotiation flounders or disputants reach impasse about how to negotiate **scarce resources**, the mediator needs another set of skills.

Traditional negotiation involves a dance with particular rules. According to Gifford (1996), the commonly understood rules for traditional bargaining are as follows:

1. A high initial demand

2. Limited disclosure of information regarding facts and interests

3. Few and small concessions

4. Threats and arguments

5. Real or strategic commitment to positions during the negotiation process (p. 171)

The mediator's task during competitive bargaining is to control the process so the experience is productive and does not regress into face-threatening or degenerative discourse. Lucille M. Ponte and Thomas D. Cavenagh (1999) suggest an approach to the dance of traditional bargaining where the mediator persists in attempting to expand the resources that are on the table for negotiation, pushes for objective criteria, and forestalls early adoption of particularly negative bargaining techniques such as threats or final offers. Several mediator techniques are used when assisting traditional bargainers. In addition, the tactics for promoting cooperative bargaining also may be helpful in some cases.

Create Common Value

David A. Lax and James K. Sebenius (1986) explain that most traditional bargaining focuses exclusively on *private value*—goods or money obtained through a negotiation that one party can enjoy while excluding the other from enjoying the same benefits. Negotiators, however, also can create *common value*—conditions that all parties will share and enjoy simultaneously, such as a better working environment, a safer community, or not having to deal with the other party in the future. One way to moderate extreme competitive negotiation is to focus on the creation of common value during a portion of the agreement.

During a recent trip to the grocery on a cold day, a conflict was observed between a cashier and the customer service clerk. A new, cinnamon-scented pinecone product was placed near the checkout line. The checker, who found the scent overpowering, would prop open the door to let in fresh air. The customer service desk clerk would close the door because she was cold. Customers alternately complained that the scent was overpowering and that it was too cold in the store. Both workers would profit if a third party reminded them of their common goals—serving customers, having a pleasant work environment, being congenial coworkers, or keeping sales up in a flagging economy. During negotiation a mediator who heard repeated demands that the door be open (or closed) might ask, "What do you accomplish if the door is open (closed)?" Given the incentive to create the common value of increasing sales and good customer relationships, the parties could be encouraged to think creatively about other solutions than opening and closing the door.

Fractionate Apparent Differences

Fractionation is defined as breaking something down into its component parts. Fractionating and probing superficial differences can uncover fundamental common-alities. One classic example describes two individuals fighting over an orange. Both may vigorously compete for possession of the orange as their sole property, claiming they can't meet their needs without the orange. The mediator who delves into the underlying *interests,* however, may discover that one party wanted the orange because he was hungry and the other wanted the orange peel for a chemical experiment. Underlying the apparent differences were interests that were not mutually exclusive—if a little creativity is brought to the table.

In Case 9.1, the cable bill could be fractionated to a separate negotiation of each element of the bill: the basic charges, the high-speed Internet charge, the additional sports channels. By fractionating, the party who balks at paying one portion of the bill may see the fairness of paying for a basic line that he also used for an Internet connection. The mediator might ask, "It seems like there are several different costs on the cable bill. Would the two of you consider talking about each line and its related cost?"

Build Contingency Agreements

When outcomes are based on the actions of individuals who are not at the table or other uncertainties, contingency agreements are needed. *Contingency agreements* contain features that only go into effect once other conditions have been met. In Case 9.1, Jim and John could agree who will pay which amounts if the landlord cannot be persuaded to drop some of the late charges in exchange for a speedy resolution. A contingency agreement would be in place for the proportion of payment (or even how to split a reimbursement) if the landlord moderates the demands.

Agreements also can be contingent on information that will be provided by an objective outside party. Roommates in a dormitory might decide to solve their dispute by one roommate buying sound dampening ear buds to block out another roommate's constant cell conversations. A contingency agreement would be negotiated in case the sound-dampening ear buds were too expensive. Employees who both want to use the same equipment might work out a schedule of when each can use the equipment, with a contingency plan in case emergency projects arise. Disputants who do not trust each other can build performance contingencies into agreements as checkpoints. Mediators can help disputants by asking, "What do the two of you want to do if an emergency arises?" or "It sounds like you have an agreeable solution based on a few 'ifs' like the cost of the replacement window—what do the two of you want to do if the window costs more than you think?"

Bring Time into the Agreement

If the parties agree in principle on who is responsible for debts or services, but one party cannot pay the entire amount, a payment or service plan can be parceled out over time. Once an agreement in principle is reached about an amount owed, the mediator can ask, "What will work for the two of you making and receiving the payment? Jim, are you in a position to pay the entire amount right away?" If necessary, an installment plan can be contingent on actions by the other party. John might agree to pay half of the damages to the apartment, contingent on Jim clearing the cable bill so that their credit records are not affected.

Create a Sliding Scale

When issues of relative or proportionate responsibility arise due to the parties' unequal wealth or talents, agreements can be crafted that proportionately tax the parties—according to their abilities or resources. The parties might negotiate to pay 70 and 30 percent of the costs of mediation to balance their abilities to pay. Disputants may agree that they share half of the responsibility for a debt, but one party has few resources to repay the debt. Instead of assuming equal contributions when one party has insufficient means to pay, the parties may agree that the insolvent disputant will contribute a lesser amount and the party who has greater financial resources will pay more (with or without future repayment). Neighbors might allow a skilled carpenter to balance labor in building a common fence against the wealthier individual's purchase of the supplies. The mediator asks questions such as "Given what you've said thus far, what arrangement would feel fair to each of you?" or "Other than cash, what might make the solution workable?"

Maximize Relative Value

The mediator may coach the parties to think about offers that are valuable to the other party but not overly costly to themselves. Because each person is attempting to satisfy personal needs, the items traded in negotiation rarely are of equal value. Case 9.2 illustrates the relative value of an apology. If the insurance company had been more interested in the underlying needs of Mrs. Graham, they could have reduced their total costs.

Elizabeth L. Allen and Donald D. Mohr (1998) label trades that are of low cost to one side and of higher value to the other side a *high-low exchange*. Words can be part of a high-low exchange. An apology or acknowledgment of some positive attribute of the other party may be sincere and easy to say (of low cost to the giver), but be critically important to the recipient (of high value).

Mediators become adept at recognizing and capturing the positive *gems* buried in disputant comments. One party says, "Looking back, I feel badly about some of the things I said when I was angry." Spotting the potential gem in this semi-apology, the mediator might say, "So you feel some regret." If the moment is right, a semi-apology spoken to the mediator may be redirected toward the other individual: "Would you mind saying that directly to Jerry?"

Capitalize on Apologies

Apologies can be pivotal in mediation. All apologies are not alike, however. Carl D. Schneider (2000) proposes that effective apologies have three components: the ritual of apology acknowledges that a past damage was created, the person apologizing appears to be regretful or shamed by the past behavior, and some vulnerability results from the apology. Disputants may need assistance in framing an apology. Sometimes, the mediator can caucus with the parties to explore their feelings of regret, how an apology might be offered, or suggest that the regret privately expressed to the mediator be shared with the other party when the session resumes. Schneider concludes: "An apology may be just a brief moment in mediation. Yet it is often the margin of difference, however slight, that allows parties to settle. At heart, many mediations are dealing with damaged relationships. When offered with integrity and timing, an apology can indeed be a critically important moment in mediation" (p. 277). Schneider cautions that some apologies are problematic, as an apology has a larger acceptance of responsibility when transferred into a legal context than when tendered within general conversation. For example, physicians may only be allowed by their employer to apologize for errors after a patient's lawsuit is completed—hospital attorneys would be concerned that an early apology exposes the hospital to additional legal liabilities.

Avoid Early Commitment

A firm or unreasonable early position leaves little room for creative negotiation. A take-it-or-leave-it offer is a competitive tactic to force concessions from the other party. The mediator should defuse early unproductive offers and demands by ignoring, reframing, or deferring them until later in the session. A recalcitrant renter who is being sued for $5,000 in back rent, damages, and late fees may make an early take-it-or-leave-it statement as the first words out of his mouth: "I have only got $500 in the bank. That's all I can pay—take it or we might as well go see the judge right now." The mediator might reframe to say, "It sounds like you have some willingness to settle this issue; let's take a look at the details."

Discover the Bargaining Range

When parties are negotiating money or the distribution of fixed resources, traditional bargaining frequently is an individual's first impulse. Disputants may behave in the negotiation as if they were buying a car. The dance of competitive negotiation is predictable. Each party tries to get the other to make an offer first. When the first offer is made, the other party claims it is too high/low. An unreasonable counter offer is made. Meanwhile, negotiators have in mind what they are willing to pay and a bottom line—the point at which no deal is better than a negotiated settlement.

The mediator's task is to unpack the unreasonable offers and to determine whether there is a **positive settlement range**. A *settlement range* is the span of overlapping options where parties might be able to come to an agreement.

In small claims court, Paul's landlord was suing for unpaid rent ($900) and late fees ($300) for a total of $1,200. Paul claimed he should not have to pay any of the rent or the late fees ($0) because the apartment had no air conditioning for most of August. In caucus, the mediator helped the landlord determine her bottom line of what was fair to settle the case. The landlord determined she could drop the late fees and take half of the rent if Paul paid it that day ($450). The mediator then met privately with Paul. Paul decided that he might lose the case in court, so he was willing to pay up to 75 percent of the rent ($600). A positive settlement range existed. The landlord would like to receive $1,200 but would settle for $450. Paul would like to pay nothing but would pay up to $600. Both parties were willing to settle within the range of $450–$600 dollars.

Positive Settlement Range

Landlord $450 _____ $1,200
Paul $0 _____ $600

Knowing that a positive settlement range exists, the mediator can work (without revealing privileged information) toward a settlement. However, if Paul were only willing to pay up to $300 and the landlord would accept nothing below $450, a **negative settlement range** exists.

Negative Settlement Range

Landlord $450 _____ $1,200
Paul $0 _____ $300

There is a gap in what has been offered. When a negative settlement range is discovered, the mediator moves the discussion to nonmonetary issues. If Paul and the landlord deadlock at $300 offered and $450 requested (a negative settlement range), then the mediator may ask, "How else can the two of you close the gap in what you are willing to pay and to accept? Are there nonmonetary values that you can enter into the agreement?" Paul may agree to do one day of carpentry work for the landlord.

Discussion Question 9.3

BUYING A car almost always involves traditional bargaining. Do you think the sticker price is a realistic opening offer from a new car dealer? How can you estimate what the dealer's bargaining range is when negotiating a car purchase?

USING THE CAUCUS TO RESPOND TO COMMON PROBLEMS

We've discussed the value of caucusing (private meetings) throughout the book and we've suggested times when it might be useful to speak to the parties individually. A mediator who deems separating the parties advantageous will pause the session and give a rationale for moving to private meetings. The reasons given to the disputants may include:

- "I think at this point it would be useful for me to talk to each of you separately."

- "At this place in the mediation, I typically take a few moments to speak with each of you separately to see how the session is going for you."

- "Let's change the tempo of the session. I'm going to speak with each of you individually for a few minutes."

The mediator should overview the confidentiality pledge as it applies to the caucus with each party before beginning. When the private meeting is finished, the mediator reviews the caucus confidentiality pledge before returning to joint session or conferring with the other party. Reviewing the confidentiality pledge discloses information about whether comments will be shared with the other party and reminds the mediator of the confidentiality standards that apply to private meetings.

To avoid negative mulling, the mediator leaves an assignment with the disputant who will be alone. For example, the mediator might ask a disputant to think about real costs, what bargaining room exists in the situation, or what would happen if the parties were not able to settle. If the session is co-mediated, both mediators may meet with the disputants or the mediators may each meet with one disputant. To avoid appearances of **siding**, co-mediators typically stay together when meeting with each party. Strategic use of the caucus is believed to enhance trust in the mediator (Poitras, 2013).

Not Bargaining in Good Faith

When a disputant continues to repeat an unreasonable position, uses intimidation or coercive tactics, lies, or is otherwise uncooperative about the process of mediation, it is time to call a caucus. In caucus, the mediator probes for the interest underlying the behavior, reality checks the disputant's expectations of the outcome of the dispute, and attempts to persuade the individual to bargain in good faith. BATNA, WATNA (Worst Alternative to a Negotiated Agreement), reframing, goal focus, and open-ended questions are among the techniques that the mediator uses with an uncooperative bargainer. If it becomes clear that the party is unwilling or unable to bargain in good faith, the mediator may withdraw from the session.

Hidden Agendas

At times, the mediator observes that a disputant is unable to move from a position or to accept an outcome that seems to be advantageous. A caucus provides an opportunity for the mediator to check for hidden agendas and to ask, "What else is going on that I am not aware of?" In one case involving unmarried parents attempting to create a visitation schedule for their baby, the mediator could not move the father to consider specific visitation plans. In caucus, the mediator explained what she saw happening and asked for an explanation. The father said, "Well, to tell you the truth, I'm afraid that if we create a visitation schedule, she won't take me back. I'd like to marry her." For the negotiations to proceed, this hidden agenda needed to be set aside or dealt with. The father decided not to talk about it. He agreed to make a visitation schedule for a period of three months, during which time he thought he could talk to her about reconciliation.

Reality Check

Disputants may become overly positional for a variety of reasons—for example, strong emotions, fear, or overconfidence. In these cases, calling a caucus to conduct a reality check may be prudent (see Eddy, 2005). The mediation may ask, "What do you think will happen if the case is not settled today?" or "If this case goes to court, do you think a judge would take your feelings into account or just the facts?" or "You seem to be very fixed on this one point, tell me more about what you're feeling around it. If you lost the rest of the agreement because of this last item, is that going to work for you?"

Lying or Withholding Information

Denial of responsibility is distressingly common. What begins as hard bargaining may become dishonesty if parties are unwilling to disclose key information. For example, one party in a divorce mediation may try to hide assets during the property settlement. Mediators cannot permit the disputants to go forward with an agreement based on false or concealed information. A mediator who senses that one party is lying or withholding information may confront that person in caucus and provide face-saving strategies for the individual to alter problematic behaviors. In caucus, the mediator can ask whether the disputant wants to say anything more about his or her information. The mediator can ask about what seem to be apparent contradictions in the disputant's story by saying, "I'm confused about some of what you've said" or by asking, "Were you uncomfortable about that discussion?" If the disputant clarifies the situation, the mediator can then help the party with a strategy to reveal the information during the session.

Disputants may confess to lies during caucus and then ask the mediator not to tell the other party. Mediators cannot be complicit to lies, even to protect the confidentiality of the caucus. If a party will not provide accurate information during session and expects the mediator to act as if a known lie is the truth, the mediator should end the mediation.

Shuttle

Shuttle mediation occurs when the parties stay in separate rooms and the mediator travels back and forth. Shuttle mediation is used in situations where the disputants are unproductive when together, it is unsafe for them to be together, or when the mediator needs to have extended private talks with each person. In caucus, the mediator probes for BATNA, hidden agendas, or other impediments to settlement while helping the individuals consider their options. In a landlord–tenant case, the mediator might keep explosively angry disputants in separate rooms for the entire session. The mediator could ask the tenant for his opinion about the fairness of living in an apartment for a month and paying nothing for rent—even if the air conditioning didn't work. Then the mediator would move to the issue of what is a fair payment for an apartment with no air conditioning. With the landlord, the mediator might ask whether it is fair to require full rent when the air conditioning didn't work? The mediator would ask about the probability of collecting the full amount even if the landlord won in court. The mediator carries the offers back and forth until an agreement is reached between the parties or the mediator decides that it is unproductive for negotiations to continue.

BREAKING DEADLOCKS

When disputants become firmly locked on contrary positions or have exhausted their ability to negotiate offers, an *impasse* occurs. Impasse is the reason many disputes come to mediation in the first place—they need help. Mediators analyze the probable cause of an impasse and then use specialized techniques to break through the blockage.

Analyze the Impasse

When disputants talk their way to irreconcilable deadlock, the mediator tests the impasse against common causes, such as these suggestions:

- A relationship conflict is sapping the will to negotiate the substantive issues

- Parties remain too emotional

- One or both parties misperceive or stereotype the other

- Communication efforts are inadequate or misperceived

- Negative behaviors persist

- Parties differ on what data are important or how to interpret it

- The parties' interests are mutually exclusive

- One or both parties feel coerced or feel that the proposed outcome is not fair

- The parties hold deeply rooted, different values

- Some of the standard parts of agreements are missing, such as apologies, plans for future communication between the parties, restitution plans, or contingencies

- One party does not trust that the other party will follow through with the agreement

- One or both parties view any change from their earlier position as a loss of face

Once the probable source of the impasse is located, the mediator can select a technique to break through the impasse.

Techniques to Break through Impasse

Depending on the source of the impasse, the mediator may return to the storytelling phase to work through misperceptions or psychological issues. Specific techniques to break through impasse include:

- Return to interests

- Take a break

- Brainstorm

- Go into a caucus to explore the blockage privately

- Separate the parties and shuttle mediate

- Build outside standards to judge information or solutions

- Coach the parties on their negotiation style

- Seek acknowledgments from one party for the other party's feelings or experiences

- Increase identification of commonalities

- Validate feelings

- Ask each party to paraphrase the other's comments before responding

- Separate procedural, psychological, and substantive portions of the negotiation

- Use BATNA; ask what probable outcomes are if they don't settle

- Build contingency plans or accountability steps into the agreement

- Reframe the impasse

Karl A. Slaikeu (1996) recommends the *logjam* metaphor when discussing an impasse with disputants. The mediator asks, "How can we move some of these logs out of the way so the two of you can get on with your business?" Visual descriptions can help the parties see how the process is stuck. Drawing and labeling the "logs" might assist the parties in discovering how moving one log might unclog the negotiation.

FACE-SAVING

One of the reasons disputants cannot manage their conflicts is entrenchment. One or both disputants are mired in firm positions and cannot move from their stance without believing they will appear weak. Another reason disputants cannot manage their conflict is that they cannot transcend hurt feelings or past grievances.

Erving Goffman introduced the concept of *face* in 1967 to describe a person's positive self-image. "*Face* is the part of your identity that you present during interaction and expect will be accepted by others. Maintaining face is part of the ever-present self-presentation goal" (Cupach & Canary, 1997, p. 110). In conflict, disputants might perceive moving from a hard position as a loss of face, particularly when less savory traditional negotiation tactics such as threats, blaming, and personal criticism have been evident (Cupach, Canary, & Spitzberg, 2010). One Hawaii model of mediation builds face-saving into the process by requiring pre-mediation where each party can disclose his or her feelings to the mediator in private and the mediator can coach the disputants on how to proceed (Ogawa, 1999). The balanced mediation model does not require face-saving work during pre-mediation, but it does encourage the mediator to be sensitive to face issues.

Part of the mediator's task is to orchestrate conditions so disputants can move from their positions without losing face. Mediator tactics for face-saving include:

- Coaching parties on how to make offers without denigrating the other person

- Helping disputants create a logical rationale for change

- Coordinating apologies

- Transforming how parties perceive or talk about the actions of others

- Emphasizing the relative value of each party's gains during negotiation

Disputants may refuse outcomes that are advantageous to them economically if they are not advantageous to their **self-concept**. In Case 9.2, Mrs. Graham is more interested in protecting her self-image as an independent person than she is in monetary compensation.

Discussion Question 9.4

HOW IMPORTANT is face to you? Can you remember a time when you did not manage a problem well because your feelings were hurt or you were afraid that settling the issue would make you look weak? How would you recognize a threat to face felt by a disputant?

ENDING THE NEGOTIATION PHASE

When all items on the agenda have reached a tentative agreement, the negotiation phase may be finished. The last question a mediator should ask in this phase is as follows: "Are there other issues we should discuss before going on to work out the details of the general agreements you have reached?" If there are no new issues, the mediator has helped the parties achieve a *soft agreement*—general ideas without all the fine print worked out. During the next phase, the mediator will help the parties determine the specific details of their agreement.

CASE 9.3: The Questionable Gift

Bohn started a job six months ago at a loan company that specializes in mortgage loans. His job is to process loans brought by the independent contractors who solicit business from realtors selling to first-time homebuyers. Bohn noticed that the independent contractors often brought items to the loan processing agents as "thank you" gifts. These gifts range from candy to coveted tickets to football games. The other loan processing agents

(Continued)

love the attention and the gifts and do not want the current system challenged. Bohn is certain that bribery is not legal. Bohn raised the issue with his boss. Bohn explained how uncomfortable it was to receive the gifts and believed it put pressure on him to approve questionable loan contracts.

The boss understands Bohn's concerns but doesn't want to change the system. They agree that Bohn will have a personal policy of not accepting gifts from the contractors and realtors, but that the policy for the rest of the loan processing agents will be up to them.

MEDIATOR ETHICS AND THE NEGOTIATION PHASE

What does the mediator do when the agreement reached by the disputants seems unfair to one party, is socially repugnant, is illegal, or could be harmful to externalities? National mediator professional associations or states with codes of ethics may or may not provide guidance when the mediator believes the interests of external parties are not being included or when the mediator believes the decision is not fair. The Mediation Council of Illinois (2001) advises: "Impartiality is not the same as neutrality in questions of fairness. Although a mediator is the facilitator and not a party to the negotiations, should parties come to an understanding that the mediator finds unconscionable or grossly unfair, the mediator is not obligated to write up a mediation agreement. In the event this occurs, the mediator should inform the participants of his or her decision and indicate that the participants or their attorneys may draft an agreement." Mediators should consult the standards of practice in their state or territory to determine how their jurisdictions treat the interests of parties not at the table and issues of fairness.

Discussion Question 9.6

WHAT SHOULD mediators do if the disputants agree to outcomes that are legal, but the mediator finds personally repugnant? Does the code of conduct for mediators in your state or territory give any advice about how to handle decisions the mediator finds distasteful?

Summary

Competition and cooperation are two opposing approaches to negotiation. Competitive negotiators usually take firm positions; cooperative negotiators search for mutual gains. Each approach to negotiation is associated with different tactics.

Directiveness refers to how tightly the process is controlled, which is different from intruding into the outcome of the negotiation. Mediators using the balanced mediation model are prohibited from intrusiveness, but they may be highly directive.

Eight mediator techniques to foster cooperative bargaining include (1) establishing criteria, (2) brainstorming, (3) linking or unlinking, (4) logrolling, (5) role-reversal, (6) focusing on the future relationship, (7) cost-cutting, and (8) coaching. Additional techniques useful with competitive disputants include creating common value, fractionating, contingency agreements, adding time into the agreement, sliding scales, relative value maximization, avoiding early commitment, and discovering the bargaining range.

Private meetings are useful during the problem-solving and negotiation phase. Mediators may use the caucus to check with disputants about good faith bargaining, hidden agendas, or lying.

If an impasse occurs, mediators will analyze its cause and select a technique to unblock the logjam. Face is an important concept for mediators, and losing face is a common impediment to settlement.

Mediators may use the caucus to check with disputants about unique ethical issues during the negotiation phase. In some jurisdictions, mediators have special obligations if they deem a decision grossly unfair or morally questionable.

Portfolio Assignments

Portfolio Assignment 9.1: Questions to Start Negotiation

Asking questions during the negotiation phase serves several purposes: (1) to get the disputants started, (2) to draw out ideas, and (3) to check ideas or agreement.

List at least four general early negotiation questions. For example, "Earlier, you both expressed an interest in making changes to the fence that would create more privacy. What ideas do either of you have that might create more privacy for both of you?"

Portfolio Assignment 9.2: Going into Caucus

Create a checklist of items to accomplish related to a caucus session. For example, the checklist might include the following:

1. How to tell the parties you are going into caucus. What might you say to the disputants?

2. A review of the confidentiality pledge. What might you say to the disputants?

3. Giving positive homework. What homework might you give to the disputant who is waiting while you are talking to the other party?

CHAPTER 10

Settlement and Closure

Why Write Agreements?   178

Is the Agreement Legally Binding or Legally Nonbinding?   178

A Format for Writing Mediation Agreements   179

Choosing the Phrasing of the Agreement   179

Agreements Use Direct Language   179

Agreements Are Clear   181

Agreements Generally Are Positive   181

Agreements Are Impartial   182

Agreements Are Concrete   182

Agreements Arise from the Parties' Words   183

Creating Durable Agreements   **183**

Contingency Agreements   183

Future Clauses

The final phase of the mediation process establishes the path the disputants will take after the session. Depending on how the negotiation phase unfolds, the mediator helps the parties craft an agreement or ends the mediation without an agreement. This chapter provides the basics of agreement writing, differences in writing agreements and contracts, choosing the language for the agreement, and closing sessions that do not end in settlement. Regardless of how the mediation ends, it will be successful if the parties achieve a greater *understanding* of each other and their interests.

WHY WRITE AGREEMENTS?

Agreements meet the needs of parties to have a record of their decisions. A written agreement memorializes the behaviors that each party agrees to uphold. Future disagreements may be prevented by a written document that addresses key issues. When signed by each party, agreements can add to the disputants' sense of ownership of the outcome. The agreement also reminds the disputants of their negotiation success, offering physical evidence that the parties can and did agree. In most types of mediation, written agreements are required or preferred. In some cases, an informal handshake will suffice.

IS THE AGREEMENT LEGALLY BINDING OR LEGALLY NONBINDING?

The language of agreements can be confusing for new mediators. Any agreement that is written, signed by each party, dated, and witnessed has legal implications. Nonattorney mediators, however, may not write legally binding contracts, which would entail engaging in the unauthorized practice of law. Instead, mediators assist disputants to memorialize the mediation event by writing what they decide in a Memorandum of Understanding.

Nonattorney mediators should include a statement of the mediator's intent within the Memorandum of Understanding form (Figure 10.1), for example: "The mediator's intent was not to draft a legally binding contract. However, any signed agreement may have legal implications. Parties may wish to seek the advice of legal counsel before signing." We further recommend that nonattorney mediators use the phrase "agreement writing" to distinguish from contract writing.

Novice mediators often ask whether the phrasing about the mediator's intent or seeking legal counsel hinders parties from signing agreements. In our experience, the answer is "no." Most people are aware that signing and dating a document in front of witnesses carries legal consequences. This is not a fact that should be hidden from disputants. If asked by disputants whether the agreement is legally binding, the mediator should be forthright and state, "Signing any agreement has legal ramifications. If this is something that concerns you, I encourage you to seek legal advice."

Mediation through some federal programs carries the full weight of legally binding contracts and may limit appeal options. For example, the Department of Education requires states to have mediation processes to resolve special education disputes between parents and school districts. Agreements written during these mediated sessions are directly enforceable in court. Mediators must explain the consequences and enforcement power of those agreements.

A FORMAT FOR WRITING MEDIATION AGREEMENTS

Informal written agreements are common outcomes of successful mediations. Drafting the agreement during the session is beneficial as it allows the parties to be part of the agreement writing and to check the accuracy of the agreement's provisions.

Ideally, the mediator will have access to equipment that will allow all parties to have a personal copy of the agreement once it has been signed. Some mediators use laptop computers and portable printers to copy the agreement, and then all parties will sign all copies. Others use copy machines or scan the handwritten document into an electronic file. If such resources are not available, mediators can handwrite agreements, have the parties sign the handwritten document, then copy it the next day, and mail it to each party. The goal is for all parties to have access to the same information at the same time.

Agreements should include the following features:

1. The title of the type of agreement ("Mediation Agreement" or "Memorandum of Understanding")

2. The first and last names of each of the parties

3. The date that the agreement was created

4. The name of the mediator and/or center

5. Instructions or behavioral guidelines detailing the expectations of each of the parties involved—the agreement

6. Statement of mediator's intent

7. Signature

FIGURE 10.1 Sample Mediation Agreement

Rodriguez Mediation Center Mediation Agreement

Underlined portions would be blank in the form template and are filled in with the details during each specific mediation.

This Memorandum of Understanding between <u>Cindy Bennett and Brian Morgan,</u> dated <u>January 22, 2014,</u> serves to document the following voluntary agreement(s).

1. <u>We agree that Cindy will pay 1/3 of the July 14, 2013 phone bill ($22.38) to Brian on February 1 of this year.</u>
2. <u>We agree that Brian will return all the game software and the computer to Cindy when she brings over the check for the phone bill on February 1 to Brian's house.</u>
3. <u>We agree to sell the couch and the loveseat though a classified ad that Brian will place and pay for and will split the money from the sales 50/50.</u>
4. <u>We agree that if the couch does not sell in one month, Brian will take the couch to the Salvation Army and give the donation receipt to Cindy.</u>
5. <u>We agree that Cindy will not call Brian's mother for any reason.</u>
6. <u>We agree to discuss our differences with calm voices and in private should we have any future disagreements.</u>
7. <u>We agree to return to mediation if we cannot work out our differences together.</u>

We understand that it has not been the mediator's intent to draft a legal contract. However, we understand that signing this document may have legal implications.

Signature: _____ Date: _____

Signature: _____ Date: _____

Mediator: _____ Date: _____

selects words like "will," "shall," and "will not." For example, "Sergio will contact Elsie by e-mail if the supply shipments are delayed." If there may be a time when Sergio could wait to tell Elsie, it is specified in the agreement: "Sergio will e-mail Elsie if the supply shipments are delayed by more than three business days." Direct language allows little room for interpretation, and both parties should be clear about each person's responsibilities.

Agreements Are Clear

The mediator ensures that all parties know what they are expected to do and when they are expected to do it. An agreement that states that one party will pay the other party $500 may be too vague. Clarify the intended outcome through active questioning and discussion between the disputants. Ask the parties questions such as "When will the money be paid?" "How will the money be paid—check, cash, . . . ?" "On the day the payment is made, will that be in person or by postmarked mail or some other way . . . ?" Most disputants appreciate discussions that pin down the details. In the previous example, the parties discussed the mediator's questions and decided "Jessie will pay Margo a total of $500 in two installments of $250. The first cash payment will be on January 15, and the second cash payment will be on February 15. Jessie will pay by 5:00 P.M. at Margo's office on, or before, each due date."

Agreements Generally Are Positive

Even though the agreement may be spurred by past negative behaviors, the mediator crafts the agreement as positively as possible. A "will" statement is much more appealing than a "will not" provision. For example, "Eli will not leave his bicycle behind Mr. King's car" is a negative agreement. When the soft agreement contains negative language, the mediator can ask, "What will Eli do instead of leaving his bicycle behind Mr. King's car?" The discussion among the parties led to a positive future action that can be placed in the final agreement: "Eli will park his bicycle beside the garage."

Agreements Are Impartial

The mediator must consider how the words in the agreement portray each party. Does the language smear one party as the bad one? For example, "Taylor will not cheat on his time cards by guessing what his time was for the past week," is in essence calling him a "cheat." Even if Taylor committed past misdeeds, mediated agreements are forward looking and are promises of *future* behaviors. The phrasing should address the behavior to be changed. "Mr. Taylor will record his time to the nearest five minutes on his time card each day on arriving at work and again just prior to leaving."

The mediator is as even-handed as possible in the portrayal of each individual. Does each party have responsibilities in the agreement or just one side? We recommend starting the specifics of the agreements with a "We agree" preface to each line in the agreement ("We agree that . . .") or by stating both parties' names ("Mr. Zu and Ms. Lee agree that . . ."). Furthermore, agreements should try to address the behavior of both parties instead of only outlining the ways one person will change a behavior.

Finally, the mediator considers how power is portrayed in the agreements. Does one party have a title, and does the other party not have a title? While this may be appropriate in some cases, it may be unnecessary in other situations.

Agreements Are Concrete

The mediator must ensure that all parties have the same interpretation of what the words in the agreement mean. The phrase "Jeff will respect Dea" ignores the probability that parties do not hold the same interpretation of the word "respect." Individuals with high conflict and low trust require more specificity and behaviorally concrete language. Parties with low conflict and high trust may require less specificity and less behaviorally focused language. We recommend that new mediators emphasize concrete and behaviorally specific agreements. Instead of an abstract reference to respect, the mediator might reframe the agreement to focus on behaviors. The mediator asks each party what "respect" would look like, helps them negotiate a mutual perspective, and works their definitions into the agreement. "Dea and Jeff agree to maintain a professional demeanor in their workplace; specifically each will listen quietly during meetings and wait until the speaker is done before asking questions or making a point."

Mediators also consider the audience of the agreement. A statement such as "Ross agrees to be respectful at work" can be open to many interpretations. Will Ross be in violation of the agreement if he does not laugh at the other disputant's jokes? When in doubt, the mediator should err on the side of asking questions to elicit more specific agreements.

A problem may arise if one party requests higher levels of specificity than the other, such as exact dates, specific payment amounts, or precise times in the agreement. In this situation, the mediator must be aware of the needs of each party. Demanding high levels of detail may imply that the other person is not trustworthy. One strategy in this situation would be for the mediator to assume the task of pressing for details so that the level of concreteness seems to be dictated by the mediator rather than the other party.

Language is an important consideration in creating agreements. Because language is *representative* of some idea or thing, we have many options for wording agreements. The terms, "professional," "respectful," "safe," "timely," "reasonable," "occasional," and "acceptable" are extremely abstract terms and are open to varied interpretations. Through our experiences with others, we create a similar understanding of what words mean. However, abstract terms remain highly subjective. Telling a first grader to "clean up her room," only to have the parent disagree when the daughter says it is "clean," illustrates how personal experiences with the word "clean" affect our understanding of that word. Does clean mean putting clutter under the bed or does clean mean putting toys in the basket and clothes in the closet?

It is incumbent on the mediator to determine the proper level of language abstraction necessary in a mediated agreement. For example, all parties may understand the term "safety" because there is a safety statement posted at the work site and everyone gets the same safety briefing each morning. However, without similar experiences with the word "safety," the expectations about what it means to be "safe" must be made more concrete during the final stages of writing the agreement.

Samuel Ichiyé Hayakawa (1990) compared the process of choosing the proper level of abstraction or concreteness to climbing up and down a ladder. At the top rung of the ladder is the most abstract term, such as "professional." As we climb down the ladder to the lower rungs, the description becomes more concrete. When descending each step of the ladder of abstraction, words become less ambiguous. At the top of the ladder are abstract words, such as *well dressed*. At the bottom rung of the ladder are the most concretely descriptive words, such as *blue or black suit*. In each agreement, the mediator helps the parties ground their abstractions in reality by asking questions such as "What do you mean by business attire?" "What does respect mean to you?" "If a room is clean, what will it look like?" Generally, less abstraction is better.

Agreements Arise from the Parties' Words

In general practice, the mediator can use the disputants' words as the starting point to write the agreement. Even if the mediator is not using their exact words, their thoughts and intents are represented. Mediators ask whether the wording is accurate and whether the phrasing is what the disputants want to record. Agreements are more likely to be upheld when the mediator asks questions about what the disputants want rather than when a agreement in Figure 10.1, Cindy and Brian plan to sell the couch and split the money. However, what if the couch does not sell? The mediator prompted the parties to consider this alternative, and they decided to include a contingency plan for what to do with the couch if it did not sell. The disputants have a plan covering two potential futures—sale and no sale of the couch.

Future Clauses

Parties may have poor communication skills or bad habits that exacerbated the conflict. If they will speak with each other when implementing the current agreement or will have a continuing relationship, a plan of how to communicate in the future may be prudent. On many occasions, one party may not feel comfortable talking to the other. A *future communication clause* addresses how the parties will contact each other or rules to govern future communication behaviors. If a disputant has expressed regret at past behaviors, offering them a fresh start opportunity may help. For example, asking, "If you had it to do all over again, what would you do differently?" or "If you were starting out on this project again, how would you want that first meeting to be different?" The ensuing discussion may lead the parties to a positive future communication plan. One divorcing couple regretted the volatile conversations that occurred in the past in front of their daughter. When asked how they wanted their future communication to be different, they discussed several strategies to prevent future outbursts and decided on several rules for their interactions. Their final agreement included (1) We agree that when we pick up or drop off Zoe, we will not engage in conversation about any controversial topics. (2) We agree that we will have a "topic book" to identify issues that needed to be discussed and propose a time to discuss them.

In addition to a communication plan, the mediator might ask the parties if they want to include a *future disagreement clause.* "If there is an unforeseen problem with the mediated agreement or some new issue arises in the future, how do the two of you want to handle it?" Disputants may discuss how they are more likely to talk about matters with one another now that they have been through the mediation, choose to return to mediation, or establish some other method that fits their circumstances.

ACTIVITY 10.1: Fixing Problematic Agreement Phrasing

What could be problematic with the following agreements? Examine the language choices, the behavioral expectations, and how the agreement portrays each party. What questions might the mediator ask to help the disputants decide on more detailed or better phrasing?

1. Julie and Mr. McGraw, disputing neighbors, agree to the following:

   A. Julie will not throw cigarette butts into Mr. McGraw's yard.

   B. Julie's children will not enter Mr. McGraw's yard for any reason.

(Continued)

    C. Julie will turn off her porch light at 9:00 P.M.

    D. Julie will contact Mr. McGraw if his dog, Tiger, is in her yard.

2. Given the desire for Mr. Herra and Ms. Miller to get along at work, Mr. Herra agrees not to be belligerent to Ms. Miller during the sales meetings.

3. Jim will pay his mom back the money he owes her for the damaged car.

4. Tomas and Franklin agree to purchase a car together and share it.

5. Mr. Watson will not use the office computer when Rochelle needs it.

6. Because of past problems and misunderstandings, Charlie and Susan agree not to use the e-mail system to communicate at work.

Reality Testing

Reality testing the specifics of agreements can be a scary proposition for the new mediator. *Reality testing* implicitly asks the disputants, "Are you sure the plan will work?" During the final minutes of the session, the disputants (and mediators) probably are tired—physically and emotionally. However, rushing past reality testing may have disastrous effects. The mediator has a responsibility to the parties to aid them in crafting agreements that will last and meet their needs. The mediator must be realistic without seeming to criticize or disapprove of the ideas put forth by the disputants. In reality testing, the mediator helps disputants consider surprises, unintended consequences, and the overall workability of the plan.

Interests play a crucial role in reality testing. They are the criteria for evaluating the settlement. Mediators bring the interests back into the spotlight to see whether the needs the consequences their decision will have on other people and have disputants talk about possible situations that would test the efficacy of their agreements.

Some reality testing strategies include:

1. *Placing the agreement into the future.* "This agreement will work for you now, but what about a year from now? Do you anticipate any changes in your situation?"

2. *Probing questions to flush out possible problems.* "Have we missed any important issues that might arise?" "What if the cost of repairing the ventilation is more than you initially thought?"

3. *Considering parties not present.* "How will this change in production affect the marketing division?" "How will the children feel about this change in their morning routine?"

4. *Considering hidden costs to the parties in the agreement.* "How will agreeing to fund his trip to the London conference affect your travel budget for other personnel?" "Will agreeing to this payment schedule cause difficulties for you at home?"

5. *Making room for modifications, if needed.* "How can this agreement better meet your need for safety?"

6. *Exploring doubts.* "You seem concerned over the timeline in getting agreement from your constituencies. What exactly concerns you?"

7. *Highlighting changes of heart.* "Earlier you mentioned that seeing your children on Father's Day was important for you. Now you're agreeing to see them the week before. Explain how this works for you."

The purpose of reality testing is to ensure that parties make informed decisions, consider options, explore implications of their choices, and create workable agreements. Do not underestimate the importance of this process in creating durable agreements.

FINAL READING AND SIGNING

When the entire agreement has been crafted, the mediator will read it aloud to the parties. Ideally, the disputants have a draft of the agreement in front of them while it is read. The mediator will ask questions to lead the disputants through any final changes. When the agreement is finished, the disputants may need to have it reviewed by another party prior to signing (such as their attorneys, families, and constituents). If agreements are not signed at the drafting of the document, the signing ceremony might be scheduled for a later date.

In the *signing ceremony,* the mediator facilitates closure among the parties. When parties are in the room together, there is a greater impetus to complete the agreement by signing it than when they receive the agreement in the mail. While not all agreements require signatures, the act of signing provides an extra measure of ownership over the decision. Finally, the signing ceremony provides a chance to ensure that all parties receive copies of the agreement at the same time.

TABLE 10.1   Steps in Writing Agreements

The basic steps in writing agreements are:

1. Record the general decisions during the negotiation phase to create a *soft agreement* in the parties' words (which often are vague and ambiguous). Number the items.
2. At the end of the negotiation phase, read the numbered items in the *soft agreement* aloud to verify that both parties agree to the decisions, in general.
3. Ask, "Are there other issues not yet addressed that need to be considered before we turn to working out the details of your agreement?"
4. During the writing and testing phase, ask questions about each item from the soft agreement to ensure:

   - concreteness
   - behavioral focus
   - timelines
   - contingencies
   - implementation specifics
   - impact on others

5. If the parties have a continuing relationship, the mediator may ask, "If future difficulties come up, how do the two of you want to communicate them to each other?" or "Since you have a continuing relationship, how do the two of you want your communication to be in the future?"
6. Read the entire, numbered agreement back to the parties and ask them whether this is what they agree to do; modify as necessary.
7. Supervise the signing of the agreement.
8. Make sure that all parties receive a copy of the agreement.

Occasionally, a signing ceremony scheduled at a later date may evolve into an extended mediation over some detail of the agreement. The mediator should have a reasonably clear schedule when parties return for a signing ceremony to allow time for any added negotiations.

settlement rate percentages. Disputants may not be able to agree, but that is not necessarily a reflection on the mediator.

The process of ending a nonsettlement mediation should be blame free. The mediator might explain, "Sometimes mediation isn't for everyone or every dispute." Take ownership as the mediator for ending the mediation. Use "I" language. The mediator could explain that the mediation is not making any progress and that the mediator has run out of process options. Validate the disputants' feelings. Explain that their effort in seeking mediation was worthwhile and review their progress. Facilitate the parties in generating options for where to go next. The mediator may need to outline why the process and goals inherent in mediation no longer match their case. Sometimes cases do not settle. The mediator must be prepared for those occasions with a strategy to provide closure for the disputants.

DEBRIEFING THE SESSION

When the mediation is over, bills have been mailed, and case files put away, the afterimages of the session may linger in the mediator's consciousness. The mediator may mull over questions like "How did the session get so angry so quickly?" "Could I have changed that pattern?" or "Did I let my sympathy for the unemployed mother of a young child bias the session?" Discussing what happened and **debriefing** its technical aspects with another mediator is good practice. Regardless of the context, a mediator's work is challenging and requires support from the mediation community (see Choi & Gilbert, 2010).

Most codes of conduct differentiate debriefing a case with another professional to improve technique or foster self-reflection from gossiping about your clients with family and friends. We cannot emphasize too strongly the value of debriefing for all mediators—but especially for beginners. Experienced mediators sometimes form peer consultation groups to foster their continuing education and growth (Minkle, Bashir, & Sutulov, 2008).

Summary

Agreement writing serves an important function in the mediation process. The agreement document provides evidence of the settlement and allows the disputants to have a concrete resource for reviewing the specifics of what is expected of them. When the parties have a large role in agreement creation, it increases their feelings of ownership over the outcome.

Informal written agreements, the focus of this chapter, serve to memorialize the mediation event. Formal legal agreements generally are the domain of attorneys. Nonattorney mediators who embark in contract writing may be guilty of engaging in the unauthorized practice of law.

The language of an agreement should be direct, clear, and phrased positively. Mediators should take care to see that the parties are represented fairly and equitably in the agreement writing. Choosing a proper level of abstraction is necessary to make agreements as strong and clear as possible. Mediators should use the words of the disputants as much as possible.

In creating durable agreements, the mediator reality tests the specifics to ensure agreements are reasonable and workable. Developing contingency agreements is one way to have parties consider alternative futures.

Not all sessions will end in agreements, and mediators should be aware that this is not the mark of a failed mediation. Success is measured in improved relationships, greater understanding, and clarity on where the disputants go next. Strategies for ending mediations positively include the mediator taking some ownership for the mediation ending and helping parties to problem solve their next steps. Mediators should debrief their experiences with professional colleagues.

Portfolio Assignments

Portfolio Assignment 10.1: Memorandum of Agreement Form

Using the sample in this chapter as a model, create your personal Memorandum of Agreement form with lots of room to fill in the details of an agreement.

Portfolio Assignment 10.2: The Referral Sourcebook

Create a roster of resources available at your college and in your community should you need to refer a disputant for additional help to counseling, legal aid, or similar services.

The World of the Mediator

Variations on Basic Mediation	**192**
Co-Mediation	192
Panels	193
Extended Pre-Mediation	193
Mediation and the Internet	194
Mediation as a Profession	**195**
Employment Opportunities for Mediators	196
Standards of Professional Conduct	197
Professional Mediator Competencies	197
Mediation Skills in Everyday Life	**199**
The Promise of Mediation	**200**
Summary	**201**

Our task is not to fix the blame for the past, but to fix the course for the future.

—*John F. Kennedy*

Mediators share President Kennedy's view that it is better to focus on the future than to dwell on the past. After learning the balanced mediation model presented in this book, some readers will complete additional training and become certified mediators. Many readers will integrate the skills of mediation into their daily lives without formally practicing mediation. Whether professional or volunteer, all mediators share a value of building better futures.

This chapter delves into the world of the mediator by discussing some common variations on the basic mediation model, examining mediation as a profession, delineating a checklist of skills for mediators, and suggesting ways to integrate the skills of mediation into everyday life.

VARIATIONS ON BASIC MEDIATION

The model of mediation presented in this book encompasses the phases and skills inherent in most models practiced in the field. While the phases may be labeled differently and technical skills for a specific arena of mediation may be added, the balanced mediation model should serve the novice mediator well. In practice, there are innumerable variations of how mediators conduct their sessions. We elaborate on four alternative formats: co-mediation, panel models, extended pre-mediation, and Internet mediation.

Co-Mediation

As stated several times throughout the book, sometimes a team of two mediators is useful to balance power, culture, or for other reasons. Some professionals prefer to work in teams to expand their strengths and overcome weaknesses or to share the workload. Mediator trainees co-mediate with experienced practitioners as a part of an internship or apprenticeship. Even seasoned mediators find that having a co-mediator is beneficial for professional growth and debriefing difficult cases.

When co-mediating, the mediators should discuss in advance how they will coordinate their work. Mediators need to address procedural and tactical questions similar to those in the following list:

- Will one mediator take the lead role and the other mediator a supportive role?

- Will each mediator take the lead in a particular phase of the session?

- Will both take notes or just one?

- How will the co-mediators signal a desire to speak privately away from the disputants?

- Will the mediators discuss what to do next in the session in front of the parties (to model positive communication) or in private?

- Who will take the lead in formulating the agenda?

- Who will draft the tentative agreements?

- What will happen if one mediator thinks the co-mediator is doing something inappropriate?

When the co-mediators are genuine partners, each should be included in the opening statement so the disputants become accustomed to either mediator directing the process. Co-mediators could each deliver a portion of the mediator's opening statement.

Many co-mediators model positive communication in front of the disputants by discussing what they should do next during the session. For example, if the lead mediator is uncertain about what question to ask next during storytelling and issue identification, he might turn to his co-mediator and say, "Natalie, I feel that we're starting to get a general picture of the circumstance that brought Jamal and Henry here today, but I'm not sure we have all the issues on the table yet. What do you think we should do next?" Natalie might respond by saying, "I'd like to follow-up on the issue of the animals, as we haven't talked about them in detail. What animals do the two of you have?" or "Well, let's find out if there are other issues that they would like to discuss before we move on to the next phase."

Panels

Any format that uses more than two mediators is called a *mediation panel*. Sometimes all of the panelists are highly trained professionals. More often, however, **panel mediation** manifests in programs where only some of the mediators are experts. For example, the original community-board model from San Francisco used three volunteer mediators: two co-mediator lead specialists and one notetaking specialist. Each co-mediator was attentive to one of the disputants at all times. The notetaking specialist recorded issues and commonalties.

accept responsibilities for their actions, and coach the disputants on how to talk to each other. Some transformative mediators believe their success depends more on work during extended pre-mediation than the process implemented when disputants meet face-to-face.

Victim–offender mediation models include extended pre-mediation. After the victim and the offender are interviewed to ensure that they are suitable candidates, a mediator meets several times privately with each person. The mediator works through the phases, including potential outcomes, with the disputants individually and helps each work on productive communication behaviors. Mediators may prepare the offender to accept personal responsibility. Mediators and victims focus on fear or anger management and how to express feelings appropriately in front of the offender. Individual work with the parties can span several sessions or many months. The mediator only will schedule a face-to-face meeting when assured that disputants can be brought together without revictimizing the victim (see Choi & Gilbert, 2010; Umbreit & Armour, 2010). Extensive training is provided by victim–offender programs in the skills of extended pre-mediation.

Mediation and the Internet

Online dispute resolution (**ODR**) began with a focus on long-distance relationship disputes in the 1990s and then transitioned into business conflicts. Through online mediation, individuals in different states or countries negotiate disputes that span geographic boundaries. Judge Arthur M. Ahalt (2012) identified ODR as the largest area of mediation advancement in 2012. He predicted that, "Advances in technology will make ODR a more viable option for the parties and neutrals alike" (para. 2). He surmised that the acceptance of using technology will "make dispute resolution faster, cheaper, and more widely available" (para. 2) Ahalt pointed to web conferencing as a reason for the rising popularity of ODR. The largest source of online mediation probably is the Internet auction company e-Bay, which generates thousands of cases each year when buyers and sellers need assistance to work out the details of their agreement. Organizations such as National Center for Technology and Dispute Resolution act as a clearinghouse for ODR practitioners worldwide. Online mediation advocate James Melamed (2013) comments:

> The growth of online mediation is not generally being driven by mediation professionals, but, rather, by the dispute resolution marketplace. There is, of course, a generational component here. Disputants that are under the age of 35 are literally insulted that they cannot make progress in resolving their disputes online. And in an expanding number of areas, for example elder mediation and online commercial mediation, getting physically together just does not make sense or may be practically impossible. It is rather presumptive to tell people who have done an online commercial transaction that they somehow now need to resolve their online dispute in a face-to-face process. Something does not compute there. ("Enter Online Mediation," para. 4)

ODR is most appropriate when both parties have regular and affordable access to the Internet, all parties (and the mediator) can read and write moderately well or have video capture technology, disputants are prepared in advance, a private (password protected) means of discussion is available, and face-to-face mediation is not an option (Hammond, 2003). Melamed (2013) notes two primary differences from face-to-face and online mediation: (1) There is less access to the multiple channels of communication such as nonverbal signals, and (2) the ability to disengage is greater and may affect a disputant's commitment to the process. Regardless of the difficulties, the trend toward technologically mediated mediation shows no signs of slowing down.

ACTIVITY 11.1: Assessing the Local Professional Mediator Community

Research the mediation community in your area. What volunteer or professional groups exist? Interview a mediator regarding her or his professional memberships and continuing education strategies.

MEDIATION AS A PROFESSION

Fifty years ago, hardly anyone knew that mediation existed and few practitioners considered themselves professional mediators. As Bernard Mayer (2013) notes, "If we knew anything at all about mediation, it was likely to be the context of labor relations or perhaps diplomacy" (p. 34). However, subsequent years brought an increase in the divorce rate, civil unrest, and greater attention on worker's rights—all types of conflict that began to use mediation.

Today, mediation abounds in the public and private sectors. Where once it was seen as "flaky, faddish, unrealistic, unprofessional, and perhaps unethical" (Mayer, 2013, p. 35), mediation has gained institutional legitimacy and prominence in most corners of society. Mediation is part of our institutions, our television programing, and even was featured

TABLE 11.1 Sample Mediation Jobs
Directors of Community Mediation Centers
U.S. Postal Service REDRESS© Mediator
Consumer Protection Advocate
Agency ADR Professional
Hospital or Health Care Dispute Resolution Specialist
Community Law Enforcement Specialist
Real Estate Mediation Coordinator
Foreclosure Negotiation Agent
Directors of Court-Related ADR Programs
University or Corporate Ombudsperson
Mediation Specialist in a Corporate Human Resources Department
Labor Relations Mediator
Mediator for a Private Consulting or Legal Firm
Directors of State-based, Federally Mandated ADR Programs such as Agricultural Mediation or Special Education Mediation

the contexts in which mediation is practiced and on job prospects. Most state mediation associations provide an array of services and information for practitioners.

Employment Opportunities for Mediators

Many mediators also work in another profession such as attorneys, counselors, or providers of consulting and training services. New mediators often volunteer their services until they are experienced enough to seek full-time mediation employment. Table 11.1 lists sample job opportunities for mediators. Examine the jobs section of the Association for Conflict Management website for current listings.

Jobs for mediators also can be found on several professional mediator websites:

- *www.mediate.com*
- *careers.acrnet.org/home/index.cfm?site_id = 9002*
- *www.nafcm.org/Resources/jobs*
- *www.nysdra.org/careers/careers.aspx*
- *peace.fresno.edu/rjjobs.php*

Even when full-time mediation employment is not available or is not the right choice for a specific individual, many people seek mediation training to enhance their employability or as a second income source. Prospective employers usually see the value added when applicants have conflict management skills or mediator credentials.

ACTIVITY 11.2: Find Mediator Jobs

Research local, national, and international jobs posted for mediators. What trends do you see for qualifications required and areas of practice?

Standards of Professional Conduct

We included ethical issues for mediators throughout this book because they are a hallmark of quality. Standards of good practice apply equally to the volunteer and the certified professional. All mediators have responsibilities to those they serve and to the larger community. Mediators should be aware of the standards of practice in their jurisdictional area and keep informed on new developments in the field. Membership in a professional mediation association, at the state, province, or national level is one method of staying current with the community of mediators and a changing legal environment for the profession. Professional mediators are expected to continue their conflict management education and to expand their skills and knowledge through classes, training workshops, or conference discussions.

Many state courts or professional associations have certification requirements for practitioners; i.e., someone who wants to be hired as a mediator in a specific district court must meet that region's certification requirements. National professional associations for mediators include:

- The Association for Conflict Resolution

- The American Bar Association ADR Section

- The Association of Family and Conciliation Courts

- Victim Offender Mediation Association

Community-minded individuals might find fulfillment in serving as volunteers to help neighbors work through their disagreements. Some are more comfortable working with highly technical business cases. Others are accountants who mediate for the Internal Revenue Service or states to resolve tax disputes (Meyercord, 2010). Many mediators will specialize in only one context; others will mediate in multiple contexts. Individual mediators, through guided practice and experimentation, will discover personal strengths and preferred practice areas.

Inset 11.1 presents a checklist of skills for mediators. It is difficult—if not impossible—to master all of these skills during a single class or workshop. The acquisition, development, and mastery of mediator knowledge and skills are a lifelong process. States or courts with certification requirements may have more detailed competency requirements.

For those readers who choose to become mediators, we offer this advice: Mastering new skills is a difficult task. Be diligent. Be persistent. Be creative in finding opportunities to practice. Recognize that mediation is a process. Learn the techniques, but be open to intuitive insights that will help you work with the disputants. As you become more skilled, experiment with different contexts and models of mediation. Work with a mentor or professional mediator. Watch and learn from others. Join a community of mediators and stay connected to that community. Locate like-minded mediators to debrief cases with, refine techniques, and ponder ethical dilemmas. Find areas of practice that meld your personality and skills in a comfort zone that works for you. **Forgive** yourself when you make mistakes. Most of all, be patient as you develop your skills. One day, you may experience the flow and artistry described by Michael D. Lang and Alison Taylor (2012) where all those hours of practice and learning the mediation craft meld into automatic mediator moves, where "intuition" and "talent" allow mediator creativity and effectiveness to flourish. They assert, "The journey from novice to artist is a continuous process of exploration and learning, nurtured by curiosity and the desire for self-improvement. The combination of reflective practice and interactive process will yield artistry" (p. 232).

INSET 11.1 Mediator Skills Checklist

Circle your current competency level in each area.

	Novice	Adequate	Expert
Ability to Analyze			
Distinguish between interests and positions	1	2	3
Differentiate among types of issues	1	2	3
Analyze the problem from the various perspectives	1	2	3
Differentiate emotional from substantive issues	1	2	3
Identify commonalities	1	2	3
Communicate			
Elicit interests from others	1	2	3
Convey the expectation that disputants will be cooperative	1	2	3
Model cooperative behavior	1	2	3
Exhibit impartial regard	1	2	3

INSET 11.1   (Continued)

Check perceptions	1	2	3
Listen to defuse emotions	1	2	3
Listen for facts	1	2	3
Paraphrase and validate emotions	1	2	3
Paraphrase substantive content	1	2	3
Reframe positions and negative comments	1	2	3
Ask "How" and "What" questions	1	2	3
Make "I" statements	1	2	3
Teach disputants how to make "I" statements	1	2	3
Articulate BATNA (Best Alternative to a Negotiated Agreement)	1	2	3
Summarize a disputant's needs clearly	1	2	3
Write agreements in concrete, measurable language	1	2	3
Coordinate			
Facilitate the creation of a pool of possible solutions	1	2	3
Integrate options for solutions	1	2	3
Facilitate the creation of objective criteria for solutions	1	2	3
Set the agenda for negotiation	1	2	3
Exhibit Flexibility			
Be open to creative solutions	1	2	3
Forgive and permit others to save face	1	2	3
Adapt to the style of others	1	2	3
Be sensitive to cultural variations among disputants	1	2	3
Create closure when a mediation terminates	1	2	3
Control			
Redirect unnecessary competition	1	2	3
Deal with emotions	1	2	3
	1	2	3

mediation are invaluable group members in the team approach that abounds in the modern workplace. The skills of reframing and summarizing, among many others, can enhance a group's effectiveness. Collaborative leaders apply many of the same skills as conflict managers (Kuttner, 2011). Teachers can lead peer mediation programs that enhance school climates and child skill development (Cassinerio & Lane-Garon, 2006; Noaks & Noaks, 2009). Some in the medical community consider de-escalation of conflict an ethical obligation of medical professionals and will address a "difficult" patient's concerns with the help of a mediator (Fiester, 2013; Knickle, McNaughton, & Downar, 2013).

Discussion Question 11.1

CONSIDER THE benefits of having someone with dispute resolution skills in these professions: education, health care, real estate, environmental regulation, or human resources.

Some individuals go beyond formal mediation contexts to become conflict coaches or facilitators. Conflict coaches are specialists who help people improve personal communication and conflict management skills (see Donias, 2007; Silsbee, 2010). Facilitators guide work groups and communities through tough conversations (see Noonan, 2007). While coaches and facilitators are different occupations than mediation, they use many of the same conflict management skills.

Individuals trained in mediation also can reap personal benefits. An awareness of the causes of interpersonal conflict, behaviors that provoke defensiveness, or listening provide insight into real-world problems. Stephen B. Goldberg and Margaret L. Shaw (2010) interviewed thirty founders in the mediation movement and reported: "Whatever drew them initially to mediation, once our respondents experienced it, they were captivated. Some were delighted at the constantly changing topics of the disputes in which they became involved; others enjoyed the opportunity to become involved in the lives of others. Nearly all commented on the pleasure involved in assisting participants in mediation to resolve their dispute, often a dispute that had become life consuming" (p. 241).

THE PROMISE OF MEDIATION

While mediation is no panacea for all of the world's ills, mediation does offer hope to individual citizens and communities—hope that difficulties can be resolved without becoming violent or winding up in court. In 2002, the EPA and timber company Boise Cascade settled a Clean Air Act violation case worth $20 million—believed to be the first mediated settlement of the Clean Air Act—saving millions of tax dollars that might otherwise have been spent on litigation (Boise Cascade, 2002). Innumerable individuals and businesses have settled their disagreements with the assistance of a mediator. Small claims and other court-annexed mediation programs speed the process of justice and find outcomes that satisfy the participants while saving taxpayers money (Wissler, 2004). Mediators are drawing some communities closer together by healing neighbor relationships. Through mediation programs tied to the juvenile justice system, recidivism is reduced and children are being given a second chance rather than becoming ostracized from their community (Bradshaw, Roseborough, & Umbreit, 2006; Choi, Green, & Gilbert, 2011).

As new issues emerged, mediation professionals stepped to the forefront to see how they could help. For example, after the perfect storm of inflated home prices and easy credit led to an epidemic of home foreclosures when the economy soured, mediation advocates pushed for procedures where homeowners could renegotiate their debts.

Mayer (2013) highlights many of the passionate debates within the field of mediation that will take the profession into the future (e.g., Can a mediator be truly neutral? Does a mediator have a responsibility to empower the disempowered? Should transforming individuals in conflict take precedence over agreements?). Mediators have many questions to ask about their profession. One aspect of mediation, however, is sure to remain constant—mediators will continue to make a difference in people's lives.

Summary

This book presented information for beginning mediators. The world of the mediator includes many models of professional practice. Variations include co-mediation, panels, extended pre-mediation, and Internet mediation.

Professional mediators are expected to uphold appropriate standards of conduct and to maintain their professional competence. Individuals who learn the skills of mediation have opportunities to exhibit their competence at work and in personal relationships. The job market for new mediators is modest. Many incorporate mediation skills into other professional roles.

Mediation is making a difference and improving people's lives. While we do not wish

Practice Cases

ROLE-PLAYING A MEDIATION CASE

Role-playing is an integral part of learning and often is required in mediator training leading to certification. During role-plays, novice mediators have an opportunity to explore the phases of the balanced mediation model and to develop specific skills. Role-players develop an appreciation for the feelings, styles, and tactics that disputants may bring to the mediation table.

When role-playing as the mediator, you should start with the opening statement and proceed through the phases. Your instructor may focus the role-play on a particular phase of the mediation process, for example, opening statement through the end of the storytelling and issue identification phase. When learning, it is important to work the phases in sequence, rather than skipping to negotiation or solutions too quickly.

When role-playing as one of the parties, your job is to begin with the confidential information provided in the case and then to add details that are in the spirit of the character that you are portraying. If the mediator asks you a question where the information is not provided in the case, answer the question by inventing the detailed answer. For example, The Broken Saw Case does not specify exactly how many years the two have known each _____ _____ specific purchases that have been made in the past. If the

THE CUBICLE CASE

Information Provided to the Mediator

Party 1: Martin/Martha (clerk)
Party 2: Lyle/Lilly (clerk)
Type of Dispute: Workplace

The two parties (Martin/Martha and Lyle/Lilly) have asked you to mediate their case based on a referral from the company where they work. The mediation is not part of a formal grievance, and there will be no report made to the Human Resources Office or information given to their supervisor—what happens is just between the two disputants.

You received these pre-mediation notes from your case developer:

- Both parties are accounts receivable clerks.

- There are 15 clerks total in the department.

- All clerks are in cubicles in the same room.

- The clerks' job is to call to get customers to make payments on their debt.

- Lilly/Lyle has worked at the company for six months and has quickly become the top collector in the department.

- Martin/Martha has been with the department for three years and is considered a solid professional.

- Martin/Martha reported that Lilly/Lyle talks in ways that are keeping everyone else from doing their jobs. Lilly/Lyle seemed to have no idea why he/she had been called in for mediation.

- Both parties want to work this out without getting anyone in trouble with the supervisor.

THE CUBICLE CASE

Confidential Information for Martin (or Martha)

You have a problem with one of the new employees, Lyle (Lilly), and heard about the employee mediation program. You called to ask whether you could use the program without having to file a grievance. They said OK and referred you to a mediator who set up an appointment with the two of you.

You are an accounts receivable clerk who does collection calls to people who owe the state money. You've been with the department for three years and think of yourself as one of the experienced professionals at this type of work. You don't bully the people you call, but you try to help those who are behind understand the possible ramifications if they default and to help them make a plan to become current in their payments.

You work in a "bullpen" with 15 other clerks, each in their own cubicle. You get along well with all of your co-workers on a personal level. The problem is with the employee who joined the group six months ago. Lyle (Lilly) is a real high-energy dynamo. You know because everyone in the office can hear when she/he is on the phone. You think the new employee bullies the people he/she calls, but that isn't your business. The problem is that she/he gets so loud when "motivating" the clients.

Every time his/her voice gets loud, you completely lose your concentration and you know you aren't as effective as you have been in the past. You know that your calls are taking longer now, and over time your case completion rate will go down. You've never been the top performer in the group, but you're probably third or fourth and think of yourself as a solid professional. You don't want your rate to go down. Other clerks have commented to you that Lyle (Lilly) is too loud. You want to do a good job. Lyle's (Lilly's) volume is just "too much" for an open area. You really would like to settle this without going to the supervisor, but these things never work out well for you when you try to talk to the person directly. So, you've asked for some help.

Your Positions: Lyle/Lilly is too loud and not a team player.

Your Interests: You need quiet to get your work done. You want to be a team player. You _____ the group even though you know you'll probably

THE CUBICLE CASE

Confidential Information for Lyle (Lilly)

You are an accounts receivable clerk who does collection calls to people who owe the state money. You've been with the department for six months and have become the top collector almost immediately after your training finished. You love your job. Sometimes the people on the other end of the line need a little motivation, and you tell them in no uncertain terms what will happen if they don't pay. You are from a second-generation Italian family where being exuberant and a little loud is the norm and you learned how to "say it like it is" at the family dining table. You can hold your own with anyone.

You like all of your co-workers. You work in a "bullpen" with 15 other clerks, each in their own cubicle. You were surprised when you got a call from a mediator saying there was an issue that your co-worker, Martin (Martha), wanted to talk about. You really have no idea what this is about, but you've always been a team player and said you would go along to be helpful. You are hurt that Martin (Martha) is bringing a stranger into what must be some kind of personal problem; you wish he/she had talked to you personally.

Whatever it is, you don't want the supervisor to be involved or for anything to get into your record. As the top performer, it probably is right that you should help out the other employees.

Your Positions: Martin (Martha) should have talked to you first. You don't have a problem.

Your Interests: You want to do your job your way. You want to stay the top performer. You want to be a team player and be helpful if it doesn't get in the way of your personal achievement goals. You don't want the supervisor to be involved.

What You Might Be Willing to Accept During the Negotiation Phase: As long as it isn't phrased as if you've done anything wrong, you are happy to help a co-worker out.

THE SAVING KIDS PROJECT CASE

Information Provided to the Mediator

Party 1: Director of the City Juvenile Justice programs
Party 2: President of the Neighborhood Association
Type of Dispute: Court Referred

You were hired by the court to mediate a dispute between the City's Juvenile Justice department and a local neighborhood association concerning the use of a building for a Juvenile Justice department program. The neighborhood association filed a suit against the city. The judge in the case mandated mediation prior to litigation. The mediation will occur between the Director of Juvenile Programs for the city and the President of the Neighborhood Association. No attorneys will be present.

THE SAVING KIDS PROJECT CASE

Confidential Information for the City Director of Juvenile Projects

You are the Director of Juvenile Projects for the city. Last year, you learned of a building owned by the city formerly used as a small machine repair shop and training facility. That department was closed, and the building has been empty for six months. The facility is still usable with only small updates.

For some time now, you've been looking for a training program to put juvenile offenders through. After careful consideration, you decided to partner with Saving Kids Incorporated, a group that provides a second chance to juveniles who have been involved with the legal system or juvenile court, or who are identified as at risk. These are kids that have been in some trouble, but they don't need to be in a lock-down situation 24 hours a day. Saving Kids proposes to run a grant-funded program to train these kids in small engine repair (lawn mowers). The kids will be local or from other parts of the state. You see this as a great partnership opportunity. The Saving Kids company sees your city as a good place to locate; you can achieve some of your goals for getting local kids into a useful training program; and the city gets to collect rent on an unused building instead of having it fall into disrepair.

Saving Kids has opened similar programs in other communities involving different types of equipment repair programs and has received good recommendations from those communities. One of their programs is just across the state line in another city.

Saving Kids proposes to operate its program from 9:00 A.M. to 8:00 P.M., six days a week, although it may take a year or two to reach that level of operation. They will provide one-on-one counseling from 9:00 A.M. to 3:00 P.M. for up to 25 students on a rotating basis, hold training classes for groups of eight, and have students involved in supervised repair work the rest of the time. They also intend to build a basketball court in the back of the facility for break times and recreation for the students. The students will be supervised at all times. The current plan is to bus the students in from central locations downtown each day.

The local neighborhood association's lawsuit blindsided you at the last stages of the contract negotiation with Saving Kids. Fortunately, the judge referred the case to mediation. You really don't understand what the neighborhood association's problem is. You are authorized to negotiate with the neighborhood association and do not need to consult with your superiors before making any agreements. You still can make minor modifications to the planned contract with Saving Kids, if the changes aren't too severe.

Your Position: This is a great program, and you want it in your city.

Your Interests: Helping kids become better people, saving the city money by not going to court, and being able to rent the building.

What You Might Be Willing to Accept During the Negotiation Phase: Minor changes to the contract hours or ways to help the neighborhood feel more comfortable if they seem reasonable.

THE SAVING KIDS PROJECT CASE

Confidential Information for the Neighborhood Association President

You have been asked to represent the neighborhood association at a meeting with the city group that wants to put juvenile delinquents in your backyard. You sued the city to prevent the project, and the judge referred the case to mediation.

The association is aware that the city wants to rent one of their old buildings in your neighborhood to some out-of-state group. You've heard it will be leased to an organization that provides services to bad kids—probably kids with mental illnesses or from gangs and who should be in jail. You are angry and frightened. As far as you are concerned, this kind of activity has no place in your quiet residential neighborhood. If this mediation doesn't work out, you'll continue your lawsuit and start a publicity campaign against the city.

At a recent meeting of your association, the following demands were drawn up:

1. The city should not be allowed to rent its space for any use that would disturb your neighborhood. Many of you have lived here for years and have faithfully kept the neighborhood up. You deserve a safe place to live.

2. If these bad kids are allowed in the neighborhood, there is bound to be trouble. Some of the neighbors are elderly and have no ability to defend themselves. There is a school just down the street with small children. You're concerned about whether it will be safe to walk to the store or for local children to walk to school.

3. There have been a few burglaries in the area. You suspect the facility will increase crime.

4. You are opposed to any new activity in the neighborhood that increases parking and traffic hazards. There is enough traffic on your streets already. The increase in noise and traffic will diminish the value of your homes. You don't want kids driving fast cars through the neighborhood.

5. You are really mad that the city didn't talk to you before making the decision to rent the building.

6. You've heard there won't be full-time supervision of the disturbed students. You're concerned that these students will be wandering the streets.

7. If the city's plan goes forward, you think these conditions should be imposed:

    - No early morning noise or traffic when kids are around. Hours of operation must be limited to 10:00 A.M. to 2:00 P.M., four days a week with no weekend or Friday activities.

    - No more than ten people in the building at any time.

- No parking cars on the street.
- The city must accept responsibility for all damages in the neighborhood caused by strangers.
- The city has to pay to pick up any trash that the kids have thrown around.

You are authorized to negotiate without taking offers back to your group.

THE LUNCHROOM DISCONTENT CASE

Information Provided to the Mediator

Party 1: J. Fascilla, new employee
Party 2: Supervisor B. Patel
Type of Dispute: Workplace

You were hired by the Human Resources department to mediate a dispute between a supervisor and an employee. The employee is relatively new and reported the supervisor yelled inappropriately and is too hard on him/her. The supervisor commented that the employee does not listen and has not reached the standards for food safety behavior. At this point, the results of the mediation will not be placed in anyone's employee file.

THE LUNCHROOM DISCONTENT CASE

Confidential Information for J. Fascilla

You are a relatively new employee at the state cafeteria. You are grateful that the state hired you because you have some significant long-distance vision difficulties, and they were willing to accommodate you. You've been working here for two months. You fudged a bit on your application in saying that you had lots of restaurant experience when you really just cooked at home, helped out at church bazaars, and worked at a hotdog stand at the state fair. You are pretty quick, though, and pick things up fairly easily.

Your training was pretty skimpy. You just followed another employee around, and she said to ask her anything if you had a problem, but then she left for vacation and never came back. The supervisor, Mr./Ms. Patel, was on vacation when you were hired. You get along well with the customers. You already know many of the regulars by name and what they like to order for lunch.

Your job is to put the burgers or hotdogs together, add whatever the customer wants on the item, put on some chips, and put the plate on the counter. It's not rocket science. When things are slow, your job is to keep the entire service area (except the grill area) clean; you wipe things down regularly. You are doing the job you were given.

The only drawback to the job is Mr./Ms. Patel, the supervisor. Patel watches you all the time and loves to catch you making a mistake. Sure, you might not do things exactly like the specification sheet says, but you know many customers only have half an hour for lunch, so speed is of the essence. Some of the rules are really dumb—like the burger goes on the front of the plate when you set it down so it is toward the customer and the chips are on the back; not putting your thumb on the plate; or using some fancy rag to wipe up the counters.

The supervisor constantly nags and bullies you. One day he/she got really mad at you and yelled so everyone in the whole place heard—OK so you licked your finger when some ketchup got on it, but you didn't put that finger on the plate! Maybe you don't always have time to wash your hands after wiping up, or forget which rag to use clean the counters, or don't put your gloves on—but the customers should come before these silly rules.

After the supervisor yelled at you, you called Human Resources and complained that he/she was a bully. HR suggested mediation, so here you are.

Your Positions: The supervisor should lighten up and leave you alone. You want the rules to go away because they are stupid. You don't want to be yelled at.

Your Interests: You need this job to support your two kids; you want to do a good job; you want to be valued at work; and you want to work in a stress-free environment.

What You Might Be Willing to Accept During Negotiation: You are willing to do things differently if you understand the reasons for them and the supervisor is nicer.

THE LUNCHROOM DISCONTENT CASE

Confidential Information for Supervisor B. Patel

You've been supervising employees for some time at the state cafeteria. The newest employee, J. Fascilla, was hired while you were on vacation, and you're starting to think somebody made a mistake. You think the big boss is going to retire soon and you might be in line for his/her job. You don't want a bad employee to make you look like a poor supervisor. If Fascilla won't follow the rules, you'll have to start disciplinary action. You know Fascilla has a vision impairment, but you don't think that has anything to do with the problem—it's his/her attitude.

To give him/her credit, Fascilla is a fast worker and very personable. He/she gets along with the customers and other employees. Fascilla's problem is he/she won't follow the food safety and hygiene rules. You've been watching and observed the following rule violations in just the last week!

- Placing a plate down in front of the customer with the chips toward the customer. The rule is the burger or hot dog goes toward the customer so the chips don't fly off onto the counter when the customer picks up the plate.

- Putting his/her thumb on the plate when lifting it up instead of lifting it from below. Since he/she forgets to put the plastic gloves on about half the time, this is a real food safety problem that will get the cafeteria cited if the health inspectors see it.

- Using any dirty rag lying around to wipe up the counters instead of the cloth with the special anti-bacterial cleaning solution. This is another violation of the health code because it spreads the germs around, and it could make people sick!

- Fascilla forgets to wash his/her hands after wiping up the counters, which transfers bacteria to everything else he/she touches.

You've been telling Fascilla not to do these things when you see them. "Don't put your thumb on the plate." "Put your gloves on." "Wash your hands." But it is like talking to a brick wall. He/she just rolls his/her eyes and says he/she is too busy. You did yell at him/her one day in front of others when you saw him/her lick a finger that had some ketchup on it. You feel a little badly about that, but you were so frustrated!

HR called and said that your supervisor wanted the two of you to go to mediation and work things out. So here you are.

Your Positions: You want Fascilla to follow the health rules or leave.

Your Interests: You don't want a bad mark on your record—either because you get a health inspection downgrade or you had to fire an employee. You need people who eat in your establishment to be safe and not get sick.

What You Might Be Willing to Accept During Negotiation: You might work on Fascilla's training and not yell at him/her, but only if you see an indication that he/she is willing to follow the health rules.

CONFUSION IN THE STUDENT PROJECT CASE

Information Provided to the Mediator

Party 1: Sam/Samantha, student
Party 2: Jerry/Jeri, student
Type of Dispute: Student group project

Sam/Samantha approached you as a student mediator to help with a problem she/he is having with a group project. The other person in the group is Jerry/Jeri. You called Jerry/Jeri who agreed to come to a mediation session.

You only had a very brief conversation with Sam/Samantha and Jerry/Jeri on the phone for your pre-mediation casework. You learned that:

- They are in this project as part of an Organizational Communication class.

- The professor of the class considers students working out their problems as part of the assignment, and the professor will not intervene to solve the problem.

- Both claimed that the other person was missing meetings.

- Both expressed a desire to complete a really good project.

CONFUSION IN THE STUDENT PROJECT CASE

Confidential Information for Sam/Samantha

You, Sam/Samantha, were assigned by the instructor to work with Jerry/Jeri on a group project. The project requires you to interview two business owners about their leadership philosophy and how the current economy is affecting their business.

The problem is Jerry/Jeri isn't pulling his/her weight. This project is really important to you, and you had your interview all lined up for last Thursday. You and Jerry/Jeri were supposed to meet at the coffee shop in the campus library at 7 P.M. last Thursday to finish up the interview questions so you both could use the same questions. Jerry/Jeri never showed up. He/she probably hasn't even called anybody, and you heard from other students that he/she has blown off projects in the past and left a group holding the bag. After waiting for half an hour, you called his/her cell—no answer, so you left a not-so-nice message about him/her slacking off.

You need to get a good grade—your scholarship depends on it. Your life would be perfect if Jerry/Jeri would just drop the class so you could do the project by yourself. The instructor refuses to get in the middle of group project problems, so you've gone to the student mediation club for help.

Your Position: Jerry/Jeri needs to quit slacking off.

Your Interests: You need a good grade in the class.

What You Might be Willing to Accept During Negotiation: Working with Jerry/Jeri, if you have assurances that he/she will get the job done.

CONFUSION IN THE STUDENT PROJECT CASE

Confidential Information for Jerry/Jeri

You and Sam/Samantha were assigned by the instructor to work together on a group project. The project requires you to interview two business owners about their leadership philosophy and how the current economy is affecting their business.

In the past, you've not been a very diligent student. But, this semester, you really started to think about getting a job after graduation and have been hitting the books hard since day one. You were excited about this project because it would give you a chance to interview a business owner that might lead to a job opportunity. In fact, you'd planned to do three interviews even though only one was required and then pick the best one to use in the project.

The problem is Sam/Samantha. You were all ready to start, but he/she didn't show up for your last meeting at the off-campus coffee shop at 7 P.M. last Thursday. You were stunned. You thought Sam/Samantha was a good student—that's why you wanted to work with him/her. Now you know how people must have felt in the past when you were lax about your work. Sam/Samantha left a really angry message on your phone about you slacking off, which must be some kind of weird displacement because you were at the meeting and he/she wasn't!

A member from the student club called and said that Sam/Samantha wanted to mediate to see whether you can save the group project. You're glad that the two of you are going to talk.

Your Position: Sam/Samantha should stop blaming you for bring the project down.

Your Interests: You want to get a good grade on the project.

What You Might Be Willing to Accept in the Negotiation Stage: Working with Sam/Samantha if you have some assurances he/she will get the job done.

THE BROKEN SAW CASE

Information Provided to the Mediator

Party 1: J. McGuire, framing/construction contractor
Party 2: H. Hughes, owner of H&H Hardware
Type of Dispute: Customer complaint

J. McGuire called to work out an agreement over a broken saw the contractor claims was under warranty. The disputants have had one interaction, which did not resolve the problem. Both parties have strong feelings about how each has treated the other during their last interaction.

THE BROKEN SAW CASE

Confidential Information for J. McGuire, the Customer

You own a small construction/framing company and purchase your tools from H&H Hardware in your small community. You believe in supporting the "Mom and Pop" businesses, rather than in the warehouse retailers, even though you know that they can't buy their stock in bulk. Subsequently, you pay a little more for your tools, but supporting your local economy and other small business owners is important to you.

One and half years ago you bought a 9 inch, ¼ horsepower circular saw ($149.99) from H&H Hardware. The kid salesman you bought it from stated that it had a full three-year warranty. You have other saws that you primarily use in your framing work, and you wanted a "back-up" saw for those occasional jobs where you had an extra worker. The saw gets used about four times a month and only for minor cuts.

You were cutting a board last week, and the saw seized up and quit. When you went back to the store, you found that the original "sales kid" went away to college. After telling your story first to one young man, and then the "head" of sales, you were referred to H. Hughes, the owner. By this point you were a bit grumpy and short tempered. You insisted that the store needed to fix this saw and loan you one until you got the saw fixed.

The owner told you that the warranty didn't apply because you were a professional and that the conversation with the original sales kid didn't have a bearing on the "here and now."

As a framing/construction business owner, you *know* the expected quality of your equipment. You also know that the saw was used less than what many "nonprofessionals" would use it. You feel that the hardware store not only misrepresented the saw but also has handled your complaint poorly. You feel like telling everyone you know about your experiences with the hardware store.

A friend told you about mediation, and you thought you would give it a try. You called the mediation center.

Your Positions: Have H&H Hardware fix the saw and loan you another until it is fixed (even though you don't really need it).

Your Interests: You want to have the owner recognize that you bought the saw because of your belief in supporting a small-town business. Frankly, you didn't read the warranty until the saw broke. It does specify that this warranty is for nonprofessional use only. You don't want to make an enemy of the store owner. This could hurt both of your businesses.

What You Might Be Willing to Accept in the Option-Generating Stage: You would pay the cost to have the saw fixed, after H. listens to you. If you feel like the store owner is really listening to you, you would be open to other reasonable solutions.

THE BROKEN SAW CASE

Confidential Information for H. Hughes, Store Owner of H&H Hardware

You have owned a small hardware store for 23 years. You have survived the influx of large companies who have a questionable customer-service reputation but generally have lower prices. Your reputation is important to you, and you are well respected in this small community.

J. McGuire owns a framing/construction company and purchases many tools and supplies from your store. About a year and a half ago, J. McGuire bought a 9 inch, ¼ horse-power circular saw ($149.99). The sales kid who sold it was a real swindler. You have an incentive program for your sales staff, and this kid, Roger, would lie to his own mother to get a sale. You were pleased when he finally left the store to go back to college a month ago. You still have some anger left over about Roger's sales tactics. There have been several repercussions to his work since he left. And now J. McGuire is another one.

In most cases you "go to bat" for customers who experience problems with their tools, just to keep the customer happy. But J. McGuire is a different story.

McGuire is a professional and should have known the limitations on the warranty. The owner's manual clearly states that the saw is not intended for commercial use. You feel that regardless of the former sales kid's claims, McGuire voided his warranty through the professional use of this saw. In addition, you are still a little miffed at him/her for being rude with you when you last spoke. McGuire insisted that the store needed to fix this saw and loan another saw until the current one got fixed.

You are concerned about the negative image that this customer has of your store, and you know McGuire Construction is well liked in the community. You are afraid that she/he may bad-mouth the business and hurt the store's reputation. You have been in business for a long time and you *know* the quality of the tools you sell.

Honestly, you think that with the pull you have with your vendors and sales reps that you could probably get the saw repaired or replaced under warranty. McGuire's current attitude precludes you from giving any special treatment. The mediation center called you to set up a meeting, and you hope to work some way out of this situation.

Your Positions: J. McGuire should have known that his saw was not under warranty and shouldn't expect you to do anything.

Your Interests: You are afraid of having your reputation tarnished. You don't want to make an enemy, and you would like to continue having McGuire Construction's business.

What You Might Be Willing to Accept in the Option-Generating Stage: Getting the saw fixed—and absorbing that cost if necessary—if he/she won't talk down the company. If you feel that McGuire is really listening to you, you would be open to other reasonable solutions.

THE AD AGENCY AND THE INTERN CASE

Information Provided to the Mediator

Party 1: M. Olivero, intern
Party 2: Pat Harrington, agency owner
Type of Dispute: Intern and field supervisor conflict

M. Olivero is a student who is enrolled in an internship for Harrington, Inc., an advertising agency. Olivero has just been informed that she/he will not be receiving a high grade for an internship. Harrington claims that the work initially was high quality, but it is no longer deserving of high marks. The chair of the academic department has referred the case to the campus mediation program.

THE AD AGENCY AND THE INTERN CASE

Confidential Information for M. Olivero, the Intern

You are a senior who took a one-year internship at an advertising agency at Harrington, Inc. You briefly thought about going into advertising, but after this internship, you are certain that this is not the career for you. You find the people you've worked with to be flighty and phony. Pat Harrington, a nice enough person, who owns Harrington, Inc., hired you. Harrington wanted an energetic student (probably as a frugality since an intern isn't paid as much as a regular employee). The first few months at the agency were great. You were treated well by Pat and Pat's spouse, Chris (who did all of the accounting/bookkeeping). They even ordered you cards that gave you new responsibilities as the "Media Director."

You never worked in advertising before and had to learn most of the job by yourself. The woman you replaced spent one afternoon showing you the "ropes" of how to buy time from radio, television, and print media sources, and she gave you a book that had the station ratings. However, the media world is a lot like buying a used car. When you call an account representative from a radio station, you "barter" for the best buy. It took you a long time to feel competent in your demanding role. You knew you were being used as an employee rather than as an intern, but you also knew that the experience was rich, so you didn't complain. After five months, you are almost to the point where you don't have to look everything up for each media placement—you've just about got it down.

Early on, you even made some changes in how the clients' accounts were billed, streamlining the process so that the agency would get money faster from clients for the media time. Because of your ingenuity, you were given more responsibility for some of the monthly billings. You felt important and respected. Then it happened: Harrington decided to merge with a local graphic artist, Teresa, and the growth of the business had a bad effect on the atmosphere at work. You are ready to leave at the end of the semester, instead of finishing the year like you had told Pat you would. You feel badly, but you just can't take it anymore.

The business went from being a three-person operation to an office of ten in just one month. While you were able to handle the responsibilities given to you before the merger, you are overwhelmed now. Before you had time to look up everything (or ask, because Pat was around more often), but now you find yourself either working too slowly or making mistakes because you are expected to do too much. You are really upset that your work is not the best you can do, but you are in survival mode now. It seems that the artist, Teresa, is always calling you on the carpet for some minor thing. To top it off, you know that Teresa doesn't like you and has even told you that you are incompetent. Well of course you are! You're an intern who hasn't been appropriately trained!

The semester is ending, and you are hoping to get a decent grade out of this internship. You have decided to go to graduate school next year, but know if you get a "C" on this internship, you may lose your shot at a very competitive graduate school. Your last evaluation, a "D," included feedback from Teresa, and you are worried that she will have a big impact on your final grade. You already told the agency that you will be ending the internship this semester and will not stay the next semester as you had originally planned. They were given two weeks' notice of your intentions to vacate the position. You don't have another internship lined up, but anything has to be better than this. It's just not fair that your grade can't be based on the job you took, instead of the nightmare it turned out to be.

Your Positions: Teresa shouldn't evaluate you. You should be evaluated on the original internship job description. You want an "A" for the internship because you did a great job without sufficient supervision.

Your Interests: (Only reveal interests after being properly validated or questioned by the mediator.) You want a good letter of reference. You want to be recognized for your hard work. You don't want the internship to hurt your chances at graduate school by getting a five-credit C.

What You Might Be Willing to Accept in the Option-Generating Stage: Have Pat be the only one to evaluate you—once you feel Pat understands your "side." If you feel that Pat is really listening to you, you would be open to other reasonable solutions, including maybe staying longer.

THE AD AGENCY AND THE INTERN CASE

Confidential Information for Pat Harrington, the Agency Owner

You and your spouse, Chris, always dreamed of having a successful advertising agency. The year has been tough financially, but you survived—barely. You have been hiring students because they aren't as expensive to pay, and they are willing to work part time so you don't have to pay benefits. The intern position started out just helping, but what you really needed was a "Media Buyer." Really, the job of Media Buyer isn't that difficult, so up until now, there haven't been any problems when you moved your interns into that role as soon as you thought they were competent. You had the student intern that previously worked for you train M. Olivero before leaving. The training was completed in an afternoon.

M. Olivero answered your ad at the university for an intern. You liked how he/she could take a joke and keep up with the artsy characters that hang out in an ad agency. Olivero asks lots of questions about things you think are simple but that's how you learn new things, and she/he showed great initiative by helping streamline the billing process.

This fall, business really started to pick up. You landed a big car dealership as an account and ended up working with a talented graphic artist, Teresa. You recognized that Teresa has a lot of potential, and the two of you decided to merge your clients and business. This has been a very successful venture and has taken a three-person operation (you, your spouse, and an intern) to an office of ten people—bringing in that much more business!

However, you are not able to be around the office as much as you used to be. Olivero, you felt, had learned enough of the media-buying business to go it alone. Instead, you are being told by Teresa that he/she is making lots of mistakes. At first you were skeptical about the bad reports because this intern had been so "on top of it." But, sure enough, when you double-checked Olivero's efforts, the work was not of the high quality you had come to expect. And to top it off, M. just announced that she/he will be leaving in two weeks instead of staying for the year, like you had originally thought. The holidays are coming up, and this is a terrible time to leave. You think that the announcement is meant to get back at the company for some reason. You are really hurt that you are being "dumped"—particularly during the busy season!

It's too bad because you really like Olivero, but you are finding that because the work is not of the high quality it once was and that you are getting bad reports from Teresa, you will have to grade the internship a D or maybe a C–. You know that Teresa does tend to believe the worst about people, but you don't want to offend her this early in your partnership together. Additionally, you don't want to fudge on grades because you have had a good working relationship with the department at the university, and you want to keep the good interns coming.

Your Positions: Olivero should not be rewarded for substandard work and should have talked to you if there were a problem.

Your Interests: (Only reveal after being properly validated and questioned by the mediator.) You don't want to be left short-staffed during the busy season. You don't want this situation to taint the relationship with the university. You want to evaluate fairly.

What You Might Be Willing to Accept in the Option-Generating Stage: Keep Teresa out of the evaluation process and re-evaluate Olivero in light of what was discussed here today. If you feel that Olivero is really listening to you and makes some concessions, you would be open to other reasonable solutions.

THE DAYCARE DILEMMA CASE

Information Provided to the Mediator

> **Party 1:** Wiggins, parent of two children, ages two and four
> **Party 2:** Nearhoof, daycare provider
> **Type of Dispute:** Business provider and customer

Wiggins called your office to mediate a dispute with his/her daycare provider, Nearhoof. Currently the kids are at home and Wiggins took off one week to be with them until this dispute is settled. The caseworker contacted Nearhoof to set up the mediation time but was unable to gather any details about the issues in the case.

THE DAYCARE DILEMMA CASE

Confidential Information for F. Wiggins, Working Parent of Two Children

You are a working parent with two children, Mike and Jessica, ages two and four. You originally wanted to stay home while your spouse worked full time, at least until the children got into school, but you ended up getting a great job that you just can't afford to quit. However, you do feel some guilt about not being home with your kids. You have a neighbor, Mr./Mrs. Nearhoof, who runs an "in-home" daycare where you take your kids.

Initially, you took them to a large daycare, but you felt that your children were getting lost in the crowd. You were thrilled when you saw your neighbor taking in kids. You like Nearhoof's child, Benny. Benny is well behaved and clean, and you think that Nearhoof is a good parent. Your kids really love being at the Nearhoof house and seem content.

Your children are, of course, beautiful. The problem lies in that one of the other children at the daycare is intellectually gifted. Alex is almost four and is far ahead of children in his age group. He was talking in full sentences by 18 months and reading at 2 ½. He is really amazing. You think that it is pretty cool that your kids are around such a smart kid all of the time, and you think that the Nearhoof house is very enriching. However, you feel that Alex is getting a lot more attention than your kids and that Nearhoof is "playing favorites." When you come in to pick up your kids, it seems that Nearhoof spends more time talking about Alex's achievements that day rather than your own kids' achievements. Granted, you were really interested at first and probably encouraged such talk, but now you are tired of it.

Nearhoof takes the kids down to the park (about one block away) at least three times a week. About a month ago, your oldest, Jessica, fell off of the monkey bars and cut her leg badly enough to warrant stitches. You were upset that she was climbing so high, and you told Nearhoof that you would appreciate if your kids were watched more closely. You think that you hurt his/her feelings, but you needed to say something.

Finally, you are tired of the way that Nearhoof does business. As Nearhoof is the only adult at his/her home daycare, if she/he is sick, there is no one else to watch the kids—he/she has been sick two times in the last six months. If Nearhoof's son, Benny, is sick, you get a call telling you not to bring your kids over (you leave for work at 7:30 A.M.). One time Nearhoof called you at 6:30 in the morning to tell you not to bring the kids over! She/he also has made it very clear that you can't bring your kids over if they are sick (running a fever or a nose that isn't running clear). But, you have noticed that Alex was there last week, and he was obviously really sick. When your kids can't be in daycare, you have to rely on the kindness of your mother-in-law, who has agreed to be a "backup" for your daycare. However, she lives 35 miles away from your workplace, and you hate not being able to give her any warning.

The final straw came on Friday of last week. You had a very important meeting and were called in the middle of it to "come get your kids." Michael (your two-year-old) was running a fever and had been throwing up at daycare. There were only two hours left in the workday and you were swamped. Your spouse, a high school coach, was away at a game that day. You told him/her that you couldn't come over right then, that you were in the middle of an important meeting, and that your kids would have to stay there. The reply was a little testy, so you reminded Nearhoof that she/he made exceptions for Alex, and could make an exception for your kids just this once. You abruptly said, "Goodbye," and got back to your meeting.

When you picked up your kids two hours later, Nearhoof told you that she/he can't be taken advantage of and that you need to be more considerate or find another daycare provider. You left and haven't brought your kids back since.

However, you can't find another place to watch your kids, and your kids are missing the Nearhoof house and the other kids. You really want them to go back, but you need some ground rules set. That is why you have come to mediation.

Your Positions: You want the same rules for everyone. You want to know the night before if Nearhoof can't watch your kids. You want Nearhoof to keep your kids if they aren't *that* sick.

Your Interests: (Only reveal after being properly validated and questioned by the mediator.) You really don't want to change daycare providers; your children love the Nearhoof house. You want to be treated fairly, and you want assurances that your kids matter as much as Alex. You want to hear about what your kids do each day because you feel badly when you miss hearing something.

What You Might Be Willing to Accept in the Option-Generating Stage: Getting a call as early as possible when your children can't go to daycare the next day, even if that means in the middle of the night. You might be okay with arranging for a third party to pick up your kids if they are sick. You'd like daily reports about how and what your kids do each day, even if it is in the form of a three-minute chat at the end of the day. If you feel that your neighbor is really listening to you, you would be open to other reasonable solutions.

THE DAYCARE DILEMMA CASE

Confidential Information for E. Nearhoof, Daycare Provider

You are a single parent who has one son, Benny (age four). You had Benny while you were still in high school and worked hard to finish your high school degree. When you finished, you found that you could only get minimum wage jobs, which would barely pay for daycare. You decided to open a daycare of your own so that you could be with your son. You love what you do, and with the few kids that you take in, you are able to make ends meet financially.

You were excited when Mr./Mrs. Wiggins started bringing in his/her two kids, Mike and Jessica (ages two and four). That family obviously makes a good living, and with the addition of Mike and Jessica, you now are feeling more financially secure. Besides, you have grown to love Mike and Jessica, as you do all of the kids. Jessica is quite the storyteller and keeps everyone entertained. Mikey (the two-year-old) is enthralled with toy cars and is so easy to keep happy. You really don't want the kids to go.

There is another boy, Alex (aged four), who is intellectually gifted. He was talking in full sentences by 18 months and reading by 2 ½ years of age. He is a handful, and his parents are a pain. But he is a good kid, and you like the community of children you have at your home every day. You really are amazed at Alex's achievements—you've never seen such a bright kid.

You take all of the kids down to the park (about a block away) at least three times a week. About a month ago, Jessica (Wiggins's oldest child) fell off the monkey bars and cut her leg badly enough to require stitches. You felt horrible, but the accident could have happened to anyone. You were watching the kids and were really offended when Wiggins told you that you "needed to watch the kids more closely." This hurt your feelings, but you never said anything else about it.

You also know that Wiggins is angry about the way you run your daycare. You do this all by yourself, with no back-up help. Twice in the last six months you had migraine headaches—so painful that you couldn't really see. You didn't want to have kids around because you were afraid that you couldn't watch them carefully. So you called each parent as soon as you thought everyone would be up, around 6:00 A.M. Also, you called everyone once a couple of months ago when your son was sick. You had been up all night with him at the hospital. He had a respiratory infection, and you were scared when his breathing became shallow. You called everyone from the hospital around 6:30 A.M. The only parent who was really grumpy with you was Wiggins—in fact, you didn't even get to tell the entire story before he/she had to hang up.

You have a pretty strict policy regarding parents bringing sick kids to daycare. If they are running a fever or have other infection symptoms, you insist that they pick up their kids. Alex was sick last week, and you tried to call his folks to pick him up. But they were not at their work numbers. Alex's dad was away at a conference, and Alex's mom wasn't answering her cell phone (she's a real estate agent). You were really upset with her because you didn't want Alex there, and you let her know when she did show up that she needed to be available at all times. You don't think that this problem will happen again with Alex.

Last Friday, Michael started to run a fever and was vomiting. You called Wiggins around 3:00 P.M. to come and get him because he was sick. He/she was in the middle of a meeting and couldn't come and get him until 5:00. Wiggins then told you that you seem to make a lot of exceptions for Alex, and the least you could do was keep Mikey for two more hours; then she/he abruptly said "Goodbye," and hung up. You couldn't get past the secretary when you called back.

When Wiggins picked up the kids at 5:00 P.M., you told her that you couldn't be taken advantage of and that you didn't want Mikey to infect the other kids. If she/he didn't like those rules, Wiggins needed to find another provider. You haven't seen Michael or Jessica since.

Your Positions: Kids should not be at daycare when they are sick. Parents need to be able to pick them up when called. Parents should have a back-up plan when they can't pick up their kids or you can't provide care.

Your Interests: (Only reveal after being properly validated and questioned by the mediator.) Looking back on the whole situation, you wish that you and Wiggins could work something out. You miss his/her kids and frankly are scared about making ends meet without them. You agreed to come to mediation so that you could set this matter straight. You want to be fair to everyone but not be taken advantage of.

What You Might Be Willing to Accept in the Option-Generating Stage: Calling parents as soon as you know you won't be able to watch their kids. Having a "sick room" for emergencies. If you feel you've been heard and understood, you might be open to other reasonable solutions.

Glossary

The glossary gives general definitions for common terms used in the alternative dispute resolution community.

A

Abstract: Ideas that are not specific or are vague.

Accommodation cultural conflict style: A preference for indirect speech and restrained emotions during conflict.

Active listening: The process of purposefully attending to the speaker's expressed and unexpressed messages.

Adjudication: Litigation or legal processes.

Agenda: The list of issues to be negotiated.

Agreement to mediate: A document informing disputants of the nature and terms of a mediator's work that is signed prior to the mediation session.

Alternative dispute resolution (ADR): Conflict resolution processes such as mediation or arbitration that provide alternatives to legal actions.

Anger: A secondary emotion where one is irritated, annoyed, upset, or enraged by a stimulus that, upon deeper analysis, was rooted in fear, hurt, or some other primary emotion.

Appreciative listening: Attending to the artfulness of a message.

Arbitrator: A third party who investigates and makes a decision for the parties in a conflict (binding or nonbinding arbitration).

Assertiveness: The ability to advance one's thoughts or goals directly without aggression.

Attitude: A relatively stable predisposition to act or believe in specific ways.

Attribution theory: The concept that people consistently make sense of the world by assigning meaning and motives to others' behavior.

Avoidance: A style not to engage directly in conflict.

B

Balanced mediation model: A mediation model that considers conciliation and problem-solving approaches equally valuable depending on the circumstances.

Bargaining: Interactions between parties for the purpose of individual and/or joint goal attainment (also called negotiation).

Bargaining chip: Something of value that is traded during a negotiation session.

Bargaining range: The areas of overlap in the parties' goals where a beneficial outcome might be reached.

BATNA: Best alternative to a negotiated agreement.

Brainstorming: A structured technique to spur creativity while generating possible solutions during problem solving.

C

Caseworker: A person other than the mediator who performs intake or pre-mediation activities.

Caucus: A time during a mediation session when the mediator meets separately with each party.

Civility: Showing respect for others.

Close-ended questions: Questions with limited answer options, such as "yes" or "no."

Closure: The final phase of a mediation session that provides a sense of being finished.

Coerced: Forcing others to comply (coercion; also called power-over).

Collectivist culture: A society that values the group above the individual.

Co-mediation: A session with two mediators.

Commonality: An issue, circumstance, or goal shared among the disputants.

Communication accommodation theory: A theory that explains how individuals adapt to another person's style by copying it, diverging from it, or overaccommodating to it.

Communication privacy management theory: A theory explaining how individuals create boundaries that ensure psychological privacy.

Community mediation: Neighbor or local issue mediation, often conducted by trained volunteers.

Competitive worldview: A social construct in which the way humans interact is based on the assumption that the only choices are win, lose, or tie (also called distributive).

Comprehensive listening: Attending to acquire the overall meaning of a message (see also content paraphrasing).

Compromise: A style or tactic in response to conflict where each party gives up some part of goal achievement to reach agreement.

Concessions: Things given to the other party in a negotiation.

Concrete: Very specific, unambiguous terms describing ideas or behaviors.

Confidentiality: A pledge made by the mediator not to share information from the mediation session unless legally compelled to do so.

Conflict management style: An individual's preferred or habitual responses to conflict situations.

Constituencies: Groups one belongs to or reports to.

Content paraphrasing: A communication technique to summarize specific facts or offers.

Contingency agreements: Settlement clauses that only go into effect when other conditions are met.

Conversational style: Speech habits, vocal patterns, and preferred means of expression.

Cooperative worldview: The view that with work and creativity, the needs of all people can be met (also called mutual gains, interest-based, and win-win).

Court-annexed mediation: Any mediation managed by a court or referred by a court, frequently associated with small claims, child custody, and illegal detainer courts.

Critical listening: Evaluating the message while listening.

Cultures: Populations that share common assumptions, values, experiences, and communicative styles.

D

Debriefing: Discussing or analyzing what happened during a case with other professionals (not to be confused with general gossip about a case).

Defense-provoking/Defensive climates: Types of communicative behaviors posited by Jack R. Gibb to provoke protective or negative reactions and a climate of distrust.

Demographic information: Data about the disputants such as age, sex, or occupation.

Denotative meaning: The literal definition of a word.

Directiveness: In mediation, how tightly the mediator controls the process and communication during a mediation session.

Directness: How open and clear an individual is about thoughts, goals, or interests.

Discussant cultural conflict style: A preference for direct speech and restrained emotions during conflict.

Disputants: The individuals invested in the outcome of a conflict or a mediation.

Dual-role relationships: The practice of acting in two professional roles simultaneously, such as mediator and counselor for one party.

Dynamic cultural conflict style: A preference for indirect speech and expansive emotions during conflict.

E

Emotional contagion theory: A theory that explains when one person mimics or adopts the tone of the other person's behavior.

Emotional intelligence (EQ or EI): A counterpart to intellectual intelligence (IQ) which holds that individuals possess measurable levels of social skills and self-awareness.

Emotional paraphrasing: A listening technique to show empathy and validate the feelings of others, often to the effect of decreasing the emotional display.

Empathy/Empathic listening: The ability to understand, but not necessarily share, another person's view or emotional state.

Engagement cultural conflict style: A preference for direct speech and expressive emotions during conflict.

Escalation: A communication behavior where a response is designed to expand the size, scope, or intensity of the conflict.

F

Face: The public or private image one holds about oneself.

Feeling paraphrase: A listening technique to show empathy and validate the emotions of others, often to the effect of decreasing the level of emotional affect in others.

Forgive: Letting go of negative feelings caused by another person.

Fractionate: Breaking negotiable issues down into smaller parts for problem solving (also fractionation).

Future-focused questions: A conflict management technique that requires disputants to attend to the changes to be made in the existing circumstances instead of focusing on past events, previous problems, or root causes.

G

General inquiry questions: Questions with broad possibilities for response that build a general background of the situation.

Genuinely curious questions: A question with phrasing and intonation indicating sincere curiosity about a disputant's history, feelings, or thoughts.

Ground rules: Behavioral guidelines that govern disputant communication.

H

Hearing: An automatic, physiological process of receiving sounds.

I

"I" statements: Statements that take responsibility for one's personal feelings or thoughts phrased using the word "I."

Impartial: A third party who has no stake in the outcome of a dispute.

Impasse: When the parties are stuck and can make no progress toward resolution.

Incompatible: Goals or other actions that do not fit well together.

Individualistic culture: A society that values the individual over the group.

Informed consent: A condition where disputants have enough relevant information to make decisions (also called informed choice).

Interest-based: Negotiating or mediation processes focused on each person's underlying needs rather than purely on procedural or rights-based levels.

Interests: The needs that underlie issues.

Internal attributions: Assuming a behavior was caused by factors inherent to the person, such as personality, values, or characteristics, and not some external situation.

Interpersonal conflict: A struggle among a small number of interdependent people (usually two) arising from perceived interference with goal achievement.

Intrusive: A mediator who makes suggestions to the parties on what the solution could or should be.

Issue: In conflict, that which must be resolved.

L

Listening: The physical and psychological processing of sense stimuli.

Logrolling: A negotiation tactic where one party helps the other if there is reciprocity.

M

Med-Arb: A process where mediation occurs up to a predetermined deadline, and then the process switches to arbitration.

Mediation: The assistance of a neutral and impartial third party who facilitates the parties in creating their own mutually agreeable outcome.

Mediation model: A set of rules on how to conduct a mediation session arising from a specific philosophical approach to mediation.

Mediator monologue: A presentation of the opening statement by the mediator without interruption from the parties.

Mediator privilege: A legal right granted to mediators in some states that preclude disputants from subpoenaing the mediator to testify about the details of a mediation session.

Metacommunication: Focusing discussion on the interaction process; communication about communication.

Mixed motive: Situations where an individual's goals are somewhat cooperative and somewhat competitive.

Mulling: Reliving or obsessively replaying a past interaction.

Multitasking: The ability to rapidly switch one's attention from one task to another.

Mutual gains: The view that through interest-based negotiations the needs of all parties can be met to some extent (also called cooperative, integrative, win-win, and interest-based bargaining).

N

Negative settlement range: In negotiation, a gap between the bargaining ranges of the individuals where there is no overlap in their preferred outcomes.

Negotiated rule-making: A process that brings all interested parties together to negotiate workable terms for a regulation or policy.

Negotiation: Interactions between parties for the purpose of individual and/or joint goal attainment (also called bargaining).

Neutral: A third party who has no relationship to the disputants and no preference for either party.

O

ODR: Online dispute resolution.

Open-ended questions: Questions with no particular expected answer that are designed to elicit the disputant's perceptions and personal experiences; opposite of close-ended questions.

Opening statement: The first phase of a session where the mediator outlines the process, guidelines, and expectations to be followed (also called mediator monologue).

P

Panel mediation: A session with three or more mediators.

Paraphrasing feelings: A listening technique to show empathy and validate the emotions of others, often to the effect of decreasing the level of emotion.

Parties: The individuals in a conflict (also called disputants).

Personality attribution: Assuming someone's behavior is driven by their inner personality.

Personality style: A relatively stable pattern of thinking and processing information that impacts behavior.

Perspective taking: Looking at the world from another person's viewpoint.

Position: A demand, proposed solution, or fixed outcome statement.

Positive settlement range: The overlap in bargaining positions in which a settlement may be created.

Post-mediation: Any activities conducted by the mediator or mediation agency after the session is completed.

Postponement: A tactic of deferring discussion.

Power: The ability to influence another person.

Power distance: A culture measurement of how comfortable individuals are with social stratification and authority.

Pre-mediation: Any interviews, casework, or other official contact with the parties prior to the beginning of the mediation session.

Private meeting: During a mediation session, a time when the mediator meets separately with each party.

Probing questions: Questions aimed to uncover additional details.

Problem-solving mediation: Mediation models that focus more on the disputant's tangible issues than on relationships or emotions.

Procedural interests: A need to have things done in particular ways or involving procedures, criteria, or other process-related choices.

Procedural issues: Conflicts about how to accomplish tasks, structural elements, rules, or criteria.

Promise: A tactic of stating a positive reward will occur if the other party complies with certain conditions.

Psychological interests: A need to have emotions recognized, to save-face, or other needs related to emotions.

Psychological issues: Conflicts involving embarrassment, feelings of entitlement, or other emotional states.

Pure content paraphrasing: A communication technique to summarize specific facts or offers.

R

Rapport: A feeling of mutual understanding built through positive communication.

Reality testing: Comparing decisions to feasibility and workability criteria.

Recency: The timeliness of the conflict; if events in the conflict are new or old.

Reconciliation: The rebuilding of a relationship broken or tarnished in conflict.

REDRESS©: A U.S. Postal Service employee mediation program.

Reformulation: The response to another person's comment that changes the original tone, comment, or conversational direction.

Reframing: A technique to move an issue or topic from a narrow interest or negative frame into a larger or neutral frame where defensiveness is decreased and productive negotiation is encouraged.

Restorative justice: A view that justice is served by bringing balance to a community or a victim by requiring reparations and or acknowledgments by the offender in addition to or in lieu of punishment by the judicial system.

Rights-based: Resolution criteria based on legal or other institutionalized rights.

Ripeness: A condition where the disputants are sufficiently motivated to work on a conflict in good faith.

Root culture: The cultural group a person was born into or received the most influence from as a child.

S

Save face: Communication to manage personal embarrassment (also called face-saving).

Scarce resources: Anything that is perceived to be in short supply.

Second party paraphrase: Paraphrases that repeat one person's characterization of another person ("You feel that he . . .").

Self-concept: A relatively stable set of perceptions, values, attitudes, and beliefs an individual holds about oneself (also called face).

Self-determination: The ability of the parties to make decisions and to do so without pressure from the mediator.

Self-serving bias: In attribution theory, where one ascribes positive motivations or explanations to personal behavior even when the same behavior is criticized in others.

Shuttle mediation: The practice of keeping parties apart in separate rooms with the mediator going back and forth between the rooms to convey communication and offers.

Siding: When a mediator advances the position of one party over the other—taking one party's side.

Situational attribution: Assuming someone's behavior is influenced by circumstances in the situation.

Specific inquiry questions: Questions that probe for precise details.

Stakeholder: Any person with a substantial and direct interest in a conflict.

Stereotypes: Generalizations that ascribe the same characteristics to all members of a group.

Storytelling: The relating of events and issues by disputants in their own words, typically during the first phase of a mediation session.

Structure: The external framework, rules, setting, and processes in which a conflict occurs; or, the framework for the organization of a mediation session.

Style: A person's habitual and/or preferred way of operating in the world.

Subpoena waiver: A document where disputants agree not to subpoena the mediator to testify about the details of a mediation session.

Substantive issue: Conflict involving tangible or measurable things such as money, goods, or other genuinely scarce resources.

Supervisor mediation: A variation of mediation where trained supervisors mediate cases with subordinates who are in conflict. In these sessions, the mediator is not impartial.

Supportive climates: Environments where communication behaviors encourage trust and openness.

T

Theories: Tentative explanations for observed behaviors.

Third party: A person who is not involved in the conflict who assists the disputing parties in reaching a settlement.

Threat: A tactic promising negative sanctions will occur if the other party does not comply (see coerced).

Transformation: Moving from one state to another; changing a key element that sustains a conflict.

Transformative mediation: A philosophical approach to mediation that focuses on the parties' self-discovery process to transform the situation or people in conflict.

Two-way commonality statement: A statement by the mediator that links the goals or needs of the parties together in one statement.

U

Unauthorized practice of law: A violation occurring when a lay mediator gives legal advice or engages in other activities reserved for attorneys.

Uncertainty avoidance: A cultural measure of how comfortable a group is with change or ambiguity.

Uniform Mediation Act: Legislation recommended to state legislatures to make the rules for mediation uniform across state boundaries.

V

Validation: A technique to recognize another person's thoughts or feelings without agreement or criticism (see empathic listening, emotional paraphrase, and feeling paraphrase).

Values: Deeply seated beliefs and core ideas about right and wrong.

Verbally aggressive: Ultra-argumentativeness using personal attacks, name-calling, and other aggressive tactics.

Victim–Offender mediation (VOM): The referral of selected cases, usually at some point during a formal prosecution process, to mediation with the victim to create a restitution plan that is approved by a judge (also called victim–offender dialogue and restorative justice).

W

WATNA: Worst alternative to a negotiated agreement.

Whole picture questions: Questions that put events into their past, present, or future contexts.

References

Ahalt, A. (2012). 2012: The move to online dispute resolution. Retrieved February 2012 from http://www
.mediate.com/articles/AhaltA1.cfm.

Allen, E. L., & Mohr, D. D. (1998). *Affordable justice: How to settle any dispute including divorce, out of
court*. Encinitas, CA: West Coast.

Americans with Disabilities Act (ADA) mediation. (2011). Questions and answers for mediation providers: Mediation and the Americans with Disabilities Act. Retrieved April 2012 from http://www.eeoc
.gov/eeoc/mediation/ada-mediators.cfm.

Antes, J. R., Hudson, D. T., Jorgensen, E. O., & Moen, J. K. (1999). Is a stage model of mediation necessary?
Mediation Quarterly, 16 (3), 287–301.

Arkansas Alternative Dispute Resolution Commission. (2011). Requirements for the Conduct of
Mediation and Mediators. Retrieved March 14, 2012, from https: //courts.arkansas.gov/adr/
documents/ conduct_requirements_revision_2011.pdf.

Association for Conflict Resolution. (2002). *Report of the Task Force on the Unauthorized Practice of
Law*. Reston, VA: Author.

Astor, H. (2007). Mediator neutrality: Making sense of theory and practice. *Social & Legal Studies, 16*
(2), 221–239.

Baksi, C. (2010). Family mediation pilot achieves mixed results. *The Law Society Gazette*. Available at
http://www.lawgazellet.co.uk.

Ballis Lal, B. (1995). Symbolic interaction theories. *American Behavioral Scientist, 38* (3), 421–441.

Beall, M. L. (2010). Perspectives on intercultural listening. In A. D. Wolvin (Ed.), *Listening and human
communication in the 21st century* (pp. 225–238). Hoboken, NJ: Wiley.

Beck, C. J. A. (1999). *Family mediation myths and facts*. Unpublished doctoral dissertation, University
of Arizona.

Beer, J. E., & Stief, E. (1997). *The mediator's handbook* (3rd ed.). Gabriola Island, BC, Canada: New
Society.

Binder, D. A., Bergman, P., & Price, S. C. (1996). Lawyers as counselors. In E.W. Trachte-Huber &
S. K. Huber (Eds.), *Alternative dispute resolution: Strategies for law and business* (pp. 51–68).
Cincinnati, OH: Anderson.

Blake, R., & Mouton, J. (1964). *The managerial grid: The key to leadership excellence*. Houston, TX: Gulf.

Bodine, S., & Ornish, D. (2006). *Mediation for dummies*. Hoboken, NJ: Wiley.

Boise Cascade, EPA settle air quality dispute. (2002, March 14). *The Idaho Statesman*, p. B1.

Bollen, K., Euwema, M., & Muller, P. (2010). Why are subordinates less satisfied with mediation? The
role of uncertainty. *Negotiation Journal, 26* (4), 417–433.

Borisoff, D., & Hahn, D. F. (1997). Listening and gender. In D. Borisoff & M. Purdy (Eds.), *Listening in
everyday life: A personal and professional approach* (2nd ed., pp. 59–85). Lanham, NY: University
Press of America.

Borisoff, D., & Victor, D. A. (1998). *Conflict management: A communication skills approach* (2nd ed.).
Englewood Cliffs, NJ: Prentice-Hall.

Bradshaw, W., Roseborough, D., & Umbreit, M. S. (2006). The effects of victim offender mediation on juvenile offender recidivism: A meta-analysis. *Conflict Resolution Quarterly, 24* (1), 87–98.

Brigg, M. (2003). Mediation, power, and cultural difference. *Conflict Resolution Quarterly, 20* (3), 287–307.

Brownell, J. (2010). The skills of listening-centered communication. In A. D. Wolvin (Ed.), *Listening and human communication in the 21st century* (pp. 141–157). Hoboken, NJ: Wiley.

Brownfields and Land Revitalization. Retrieved March 13, 2012, from http://www.epa.gov/brownfields.

Bush, R. A. B., & Folger, J. P. (1994). *The promise of mediation: Responding to conflict through empowerment and recognition.* San Francisco, CA: Jossey-Bass.

Cassinerio, C., & Lane-Garon, P. S. (2006). Changing school climate one mediator at a time: Year-one analysis of a school-based mediation program. *Conflict Resolution Quarterly, 23* (4), 447–460.

Choi, J. J., & Gilbert, M. J. (2010). "Joe everyday, people off the street": A qualitative study on mediators' roles and skills in victim-offender mediation. *Contemporary Justice Review, 13* (2), 207–227.

Choi, J. J., Green, D. L., & Gilbert, M. J. (2011). Putting a human face on crimes: A qualitative study on restorative justice processes for youths. *Child and Adolescent Social Worker Journal, 28* (5), 335–355.

Cloke, K. (2001). *Mediating dangerously: The frontiers of conflict resolution.* San Francisco, CA: Jossey-Bass.

Cohen, C. F. (1999). When managers mediate. *Dispute Resolution Journal, 54* (3), 65–69.

Cohen, O. (2009). Listening to clients: Facilitating factors, difficulties, impediments, and turning points in divorce mediation. *Family Therapy, 36* (2), 63–82.

Cohen, O., Dattner, N., & Luxenburg, A. (1999). The limits of the mediator's neutrality. *Mediation Quarterly, 16* (4), 341–348.

Cohen, R. (2005). *Students resolving conflict: Peer mediation in schools.* Glenview, IL: GoodYear Books.

Cooks, L. M., & Hale, C. L. (1992). A feminist approach to the empowerment of women mediators. *Discourse & Society, 3* (3), 277–300.

Cooley, J. W. (2000). *Defining the ethical limits of acceptable deception in mediation.* Retrieved from http://www.mediate.com/articles/.

Cupach, W. R., Canary, D. J., & Spitzberg, B. H. (2010). *Competence in interpersonal conflict* (2nd ed.). Prospect Heights, IL: Waveland Press.

Cruthirds, K. W. (2006). The impact of humor on mediation. *Dispute Resolution Journal, 61* (3), 33–41.

Da Silveira, M. A. (2007). Impartiality v. substantive neutrality: Is the mediator authorized to provide legal advice? *Dispute Resolution Journal, 62* (1), 26–32.

Davidheiser, M. (2008). Race, worldviews, and conflict mediation: *Black and White Styles of Conflict* revisited. *Peace & Change, 33* (1), 60–89.

Domenici, K., & Littlejohn, S.W. (2001). *Mediation: Empowerment in conflict management* (2nd ed.). Prospect Heights, IL: Waveland Press.

Donais, B. (2007). Training managers in handling conflict. *Canadian HR Reporter, 20* (5), 13.

Donohue, W. A., Diez, M. E., & Weider-Hatfield, D. W. (1984). Skills for successful bargainers: A valence theory of competent mediation. In R. N. Bostrom (Ed.), *Competence in communication.* Beverly Hills, CA: Sage.

Eastman, H. B. (2008). Future trends in civil mediation. *Bar Bulletin Focus.* Maryland State Bar Association.

Eddy, W. A. (2005). High conflict personalities. *ACResolutions, 4*(4), 14–17.

Erickson, S. K., & Johnson, M.E. (2012). ADR techniques and procedures flowing through porous boundaries: Flooding the ADR landscape and confusing the public. *Practical Dispute Resolution, 5*(1), 1–15.

Fiester, A. (2013). De-escalating conflict: Mediation and the "difficult" patient. *The American Journal of Bioethics, 13* (4), 11–26.

Fisher, R., & Brown, S. (1988). *Getting together: Building relationships as we negotiate.* Boston, MA: Penguin.

Fisher, R., & Ury, W. (2011). *Getting to yes: Interest-based conflict management* (3rd ed.) New York, NY: Houghton Mifflin.

Folger, J. P., Poole, M. S., & Stutman, R. K. (2013). *Working through conflict* (7th ed.). New York, NY: Longman.

Fraser, B. (2007). Pragmatic tactics in mediation. *Lodz Papers in Pragmatics, 3* (1), 61–78.

Galton, E. R. (1996). Mediation checklist. In E. W. Trachte-Huber & S. K. Huber (Eds.), *Alternative dispute resolution: Strategies for law and business* (pp. 369–375). Cincinnati, OH: Anderson.

Galtung, J. (1969). Violence, peace and peace research. *Journal of Peace Research, 6* (3), 167–191.

Garcia, A. C. (2000). Negotiating negotiation: The collaborative production of resolution in small claims mediation hearings. *Discourse & Society, 11* (3), 315–343.

Gewurz, I. G. (2001). (Re)designing mediation to address the nuances of power imbalance. *Conflict Resolution Quarterly, 19* (2), 135–162.

Gibb, J. R. (1961). Defensive communication. *Journal of Communication, 11* (3), 141–148.

Gifford, D. G. (1996). A context-based theory of strategy selection in legal negotiation. In E. W. Trachte-Huber & S. K. Huber (Eds.), *Alternative dispute resolution: Strategies for law and business* (pp. 170–177). Cincinnati, OH: Anderson.

Girdner, L. K. (1990). Mediation triage: Screening for spousal abuse in divorce mediation. *Mediation Quarterly, 7* (4), 363–376.

Goldberg, S. B., & Shaw, M. L. (2010). The past present and future of mediation as seen through the eyes of some of its founders. *Negotiation Journal, 26*(2), 237–253.

Hammer, M. R. (2002). *Resolving conflict across the cultural divide: Differences in intercultural conflict styles.* Minneapolis, MN: Hammer Consulting.

Hammer, M. R. (2005). The intercultural conflict style inventory: A conceptual framework and measure of intercultural conflict resolution approaches. *International Journal of Intercultural Relations, 29*, 675–695.

Hammond, A. M. G. (2003). How do you write "Yes"?: A study on the effectiveness of online dispute resolution. *Conflict Resolution Quarterly, 20* (3), 261–286.

Hatfield, E., Cacioppo, J. T., & Rapson, R. L. (1993). *Emotional contagion: Studies in emotion and social interaction.* Boston, MA: Cambridge University Press.

Hayakawa, S. I. (1990). *Language in thought and action* (5th ed.). New York, NY: Harcourt Brace Jovanovich.

Haynes, J. M. (1994). *The fundamentals of family mediation.* Albany: State University of New York Press.

Hebein, R. (1999). The prevention and cure of campus disputes. In S. M. Richardson (Ed.), *Promoting civility: A teaching challenge* (pp. 87–95). New Directions for Teaching and Learning, vol. 77. San Francisco, CA: Jossey-Bass.

Heider, F. (1958). *The psychology of interpersonal relations.* New York, NY: Wiley.

Heisterkamp, B. L. (2006). Conversational displays of mediator neutrality in a court-based program. *Journal of Pragmatics, 38* (12), 2051–2064.

Hughes, M., & Terrell, J. B. (2012). *Emotional intelligence in action* (2nd ed.). San Francisco, CA: Pfeiffer.

Inman, M., Kishi, R., Wilkenfeld, J., Gelfand, M., & Salmon, E. (2013). Cultural influences on mediation in international crises. *Journal of Conflict Resolution, March 7,* 1–28.

Irving, H. H., & Benjamin, M. (1995). *Family mediation: Contemporary issues.* London, UK: Sage Ltd.

Irving, H. H. & Benjamin, M. B. (2002). *Therapeutic family mediation: Helping families resolve conflict.* Thousand Oaks, CA: Sage.

Isenhart, M. W., & Spangle, M. L. (2000). *Collaborative approaches to resolving conflict.* Thousand Oaks, CA: Sage.

Jenkins, M. (2011). Practice note: Is mediation suitable for complaints of workplace bullying? *Conflict Resolution Quarterly, 29*(1), 25–38.

Johnston, M. K., Weaver, J. B., Watson, K. W., & Barker, L. B. (2000). Listening styles: Biological or psychological differences? *International Journal of Listening, 14,* 32–46.

Judicial Council of Virginia. (2011). *Standards of ethics and professional responsibility for certified mediators.* Adopted July 1.

Kansas Supreme Court Dispute Resolution Advisory Council. (2002). Model Local Court Dispute Resolution Procedures. Retrieved from http://www.kscourts.org/pdf/adr/disresmanual.pdf.

Keltner, J. W. (1987). *Mediation: Toward a civilized system of dispute resolution.* Annandale, VA: Speech Communication Association.

Khader, S. H. (2010). Mediating mediations: Protecting the homeowner's right to self-determination in foreclosure mediation programs. *Columbia Journal of Law and Social Problems, 44* (1), 109–144.

Kheel, T. W. (2001). *The keys to conflict resolution: Proven method of resolving disputes voluntarily.* New York, NY: Four Walls Eight Windows.

Knickle, K., McNaughton, N., & Downar, J. (2013). Beyond winning: Mediation, conflict resolution, and non-rational sources of conflict in the ICU. *Critical Care, 16* (3), 308.

Kosmoski, G. J., & Pollock, D. R. (2005). *Managing difficult, frustrating, and hostile conversations* (2nd ed.). Thousand Oaks, CA: Corwin Press.

Kritek, P. B. (2002). *Negotiating at an uneven table: Developing moral courage in resolving conflicts* (2nd ed.). San Francisco, CA: Jossey-Bass.

Kuttner, R. (2011). Conflict specialists as leaders: Revisiting the role of the conflict specialist from a leadership perspective. *Conflict Resolution Quarterly, 29* (2), 103–126.

Lang, M. D., & Taylor, A. (2012). *The making of a mediator: Developing artistry in practice.* Hoboken, NJ: Wiley.

Lax, D. A., & Sebenius, J. K. (1986). *The manager as negotiator: Bargaining for cooperative and competitive gain.* New York, NY: Free Press.

Leitch, M. L. (1987). The politics of compromise: A feminist perspective on mediation. *Mediation Quarterly, 14/15,* 163–176.

Love, L. P. (2000). Training mediators to listen: Deconstructing dialogue and constructing understanding, agendas, and agreements. *Family and Conciliation Courts Review, 38* (1), 27–40.

Lulofs, R. S., & Cahn, D. D. (2000). *Conflict from theory to action* (2nd ed.). Boston, MA: Allyn & Bacon.

Ma, R. (1992). The role of unofficial intermediaries in interpersonal conflicts in the Chinese culture. *Communication Quarterly, 40* (3), 269–278.

Mayer, B. (2000). *The dynamics of conflict resolution: A practitioner's guide.* San Francisco, CA: Jossey-Bass.

Mayer, B. (2013). Mediation: 50 years of creative conflict. *Family Court Review, 51* (1), 34–41.

McCorkle, S. (2005). The murky world of mediation ethics: Neutrality, impartiality, and conflict of interest in state codes of conduct. *Conflict Resolution Quarterly, 23* (2), 165–184.

McCorkle, S., & Reese, M. J. (2010). *Personal conflict management.* Boston, MA: Allyn & Bacon.

Mediation Council of Illinois. (2009). *Standards of practice for mediators.* Retrieved from http://www.mediationcouncilofillinois.org.

Melamed, J. (2013). SYNC, UN-SYNC, RE-SYNC—An emerging paradigm for online mediation. Retrieved from http://www.mediate.com/articles/MelamedSynch.cfm.

Merry, S. E. (1990). The discourses of mediation and the power of naming. *Yale Journal of Law and the Humanities, 2,* 1–36.

Meyercord, L. (2010). Avoiding state bankruptcy: Mediation as an alternative to resolving state tax disputes. *The Review of Litigation, 29* (4), 925–950.

Minkle, B., Bashir, A. S., & Sutulov, C. (2008). Peer consultation for mediators: The use of a holding environment to support mediator reflection, inquiry, and self-knowing. *Negotiation Journal, 24* (3), 303–323.

Moore, C. W. (2003). *The mediation process: Practical strategies for resolving conflict* (3rd ed.). San Francisco, CA: Jossey-Bass.

Mosten, F. S. (2001). *Mediation career guide: A strategic approach to building a successful practice.* San Francisco, CA: Jossey-Bass.

Murray, J. S. (1996). Understanding competing theories of negotiation. In E.W. Trachte-Huber & S. K. Huber (Eds.), *Alternative dispute resolution: Strategies for law and business* (pp. 149–151). Cincinnati, OH: Anderson.

Nabatchi, T., & Stanger, A. (2013). Faster? Cheaper? Better? Using ADR to resolve federal sector EEO complaints. *Public Administration Review, 73* (1), 50–61.

National Conference of Commissioners on Uniform State Laws. (2003). *Uniform Mediation Act.* Approved by the American Bar Association, Philadelphia, PA.

Nichols, M. P. (2009). *The lost art of listening: How learning to listen can improve relationships* (2nd ed.). New York, NY: Gilford.

Noaks, J., & Noaks, L. (2009). School-based peer mediation as a strategy for social inclusion. *Pastoral Care in Education, 27* (1), 53–61.

Noce, D. J. D., Bush, R. A B., & Folger, J. P. (2002). Clarifying the theoretical underpinnings of mediation: Implications for practice and policy. *Pepperdine Dispute Resolution Law Journal, 3* (1), 39–65.

Noonan, W. R. (2007). *Discussing the undiscussable.* San Francisco, CA: Wiley.

Ogawa, N. (1999). The concept of facework: Its function in the Hawaii model of mediation. *Mediation Quarterly, 17* (1), 5–20.

Oregon Mediation Association. (2005). *Core Standards of practice.*

Patterson, K., Grenny, J., McMillan, R., & Switzler, A. (2002). *Crucial conversations: Tools for talking when stakes are high. New* York, NY: McGraw-Hill.

Peacemaking program of the Judicial Branch of the Navajo Nation. (2012). Retrieved from www .navajocourts.org/peacemaking/plan/ppp02013-2-25.pdf.

Pepperdine University Institute for Dispute Resolution. (1995). *Advanced mediation practice: An interactive training program.* Malibu, CA: Pepperdine University School of Law.

Petronio, S. (2002). *Boundaries of privacy: Dialectics of disclosure.* Albany: State University of New York Press.

Phillips, B. (1999). Reformulating dispute narratives through active listening. *Mediation Quarterly, 17* (2), 161–180.

Picard, C. A. (2002). *Mediating interpersonal and small group conflict* (Rev. ed.). Ottawa, ON, Canada: The Golden Dog Press.

Pinto, J. (2000). Peacemaking as ceremony: The mediation model of the Navajo nation. *The International Journal of Conflict Management, 11* (3), 267–286.

Poitras, J. (2013). The strategic use of caucus to facilitate parties' trust in mediators. *International Journal of Conflict Management, 24* (1), 23–39.

Ponte, L. M., & Cavenagh, T. D. (1999). *Alternative dispute resolution in business.* Cincinnati, OH: West Educational.

Pynchon, V., & Kraynak, J. (2012). *Success as a mediator for dummies.* Hoboken, NJ: Wiley.

Ridge, A. (1993). A perspective of listening skills. In A. D. Wolvin & C. G. Coakley (Eds.), *Perspectives on listening* (pp. 1–14). Norwood, NJ: Ablex.

Roberts, M. (1997). *Mediation in family disputes: Principles of practice* (2nd ed.). Aldershot, UK: Arena.

Ruell, E., Burkardt, N., & Clark, D. R. (2010). Resolving disputes over science in natural resource agency decisionmaking. Technical Memorandum 86–68211–10–01. Denver, CO.

Saposnek, D. T. (1998). *Mediation child custody disputes: A strategic approach* (Rev ed.). San Francisco, CA: Jossey-Bass.

Schneider, C. D. (2000). What it means to be sorry: The power of apology in mediation. *Mediation Quarterly, 17* (3), 265–280.

Schroth, H. A., Bain-Chekal, J., & Caldwell, D. F. (2005). Sticks and stones may break bones and words can hurt me: Words and phrases that trigger emotions in negotiations and their effects. *The International Journal of Conflict Management, 16* (2), 102–127.

Silsbee, D. (2010). *The mindful coach: Seven roles for facilitating leader development* (Rev. ed.). San Francisco, CA: Wiley.

Singer, L. (2001). Best practices when training mediators. In R. M. Schoenhaus (Ed.), *Conflict management training: Advancing best practices* (pp. 22–24). Washington DC: United States Institute of Peace.

Slaikeu, K. A. (1996). *When push comes to shove: A practical guide to mediating disputes.* San Francisco, CA: Jossey-Bass.

Sockalingam, S., & Williams, E. (2002). *Culture, conflict, consensus: Culturally competent mediation.* Association for Conflict Resolution Annual Conference, San Diego, CA.

Standards for private and public mediators in the state of Hawaii. (2002). Retrieved from http://www.courts.state.hi.us.

Stephenson, M. O., & Pops, G. M. (1991). Public administrators and conflict resolution: Democratic theory, administrative capacity, and the case of negotiated rule-making. In M. K. Mills (Ed.), *Alternative dispute resolution in the public sector* (pp. 13–26). Chicago, IL: Nelson-Hall.

Supreme Court of Texas. (2011). Approval of amendments to the ethical guidelines for mediators. Docket Number 11–9062.

Susskind, L. E., & Field, P. T. (1996). *Dealing with an angry public: The mutual gains approach to resolving disputes.* New York, NY: Free Press.

Syukur, F. A., & Bagshaw, D. M. (2013). Court-annexed mediation in Indonesia: Does culture matter? *Conflict Resolution Quarterly, 30* (3), 369–390.

Umbreit, M. S., & Armour, M. P. (2010). *Restorative justice dialogue: An essential guide for research and practice.* New York, NY: Springer.

Umbreit, M. S., Coates, R. B., & Roberts, A. W. (2000). The impact of victim-offender mediation: A cross-national perspective. *Mediation Quarterly, 17* (3), 215–229.

United States Institute of Peace. (2001). *Conflict management training: Advanced best practices.* (R. M. Schoenhaus, Trans.). Washington, DC: Author.

Ury, W. L., Brett, J. M., & Goldberg, S. B. (1988). *Getting disputes resolved.* San Francisco, CA: Jossey-Bass.

Van Kleef, G. A., De Drue, K. W., Pietroni, D., & Manstead, A. S. R. (2006). Power and emotion in negotiation: Power moderates the interpersonal effects of anger and happiness on concession making. *European Journal of Social Psychology, 36* (4), 557–581.

Van Slyke, E. J. (1999). *Listening to conflict: Finding constructive solutions to workplace disputes.* New York, NY: American Management Association.

Vreeman, R. C., & Carroll, A. E. (2007). A systematic review of school-based interventions to prevent bullying. *Archives of Pediatrics & Adolescent Medicine, 161* (1), 78–88.

Wall, J. A., & Dunne, T. C. (2012). Mediation research: A current review. *Negotiation Journal, 28* (2), 217–244.

West, R. L., & Turner, L. H. (2010). *Introducing communication theory: Analysis and application* (4th ed.). New York, NY: McGraw-Hill.

Wildau, S. T. (1987). Transitions: Moving parties between stages. *Mediation Quarterly, 16* (3), 3–13.

Wissler, R. L. (2004). The effectiveness of court-connected dispute resolution in civil cases. *Conflict Resolution Quarterly, 22* (1/2), 55–88.

Wolvin, A. D., & Coakley, C. G. (1993). A listening taxonomy. In A. D. Wolvin & C. G. Coakley (Eds.), *Perspectives on listening* (pp. 15–22). Norwood, NJ: Ablex.

Wolvin, A. D., & Coakley, C. G. (1996). *Listening* (5th ed.). Madison, WI: Brown and Benchmark.

Index

Abstract ideas, 148, 182–183

ADR. *See* Alternative Dispute Resolution

Advocacy needs, 71

Agenda, 26, 31, 32, 90, 104, 113, 124, 142–151, 193

Agenda list, 146–150

Agreement testing, 33

Agreement to mediate, 66–67, 107

Agreement writing, 26, 27–28, 33, 109, 178–187

Alternative Dispute Resolution, 2

Analysis, 39 (table)

Anger, 10, 41, 47, 91, 131 (table), 135, 157, 169, 194

Apology, 131 (table), 165–166, 170, 172

Arbitration, 13–14

Assertiveness, 119

Attacking, 132

Attribution error, 118, 133

Attribution theory, 118–119

Balanced mediation model, 23–24, 28–34

Bargaining chip, 71

Bargaining range, 166–167

Barriers to settlement, 31

BATNA . *See* Best alternative to a negotiated agreement

Behavioral framing, 143

Best alternative to a negotiated agreement, 64, 156, 159, 168, 169, 171

Bias to settle, 20

Blaming, 133, 155

Boundaries, 38, 63–64, 69

Brainstorming, 23, 27, 159–160, 171

Business mediation, 7, 28, 39

Caucus. *See* Private meeting

Causes of conflict, 91–94

Child custody mediation, 39, 84

Civility, 108, 136

Closure, 33

Coaching, 162, 171, 172, 200

Co-construction of meaning, 117

Cold call, 61

Cold-mediation session, 91

Collective solicit, 158

Collectivist culture, 35

Columbo, 128–129

Co-mediation, 67, 192–193

Common ground. *See* commonality

Common value, 163

Commonality, 32, 113, 125–126, 131 (table), 144–145, 156, 171

Communication accommodation theory, 41–42

Communication anxiety, 127

Communication style, 91, 131 (table)

Community circle model, 89

Community mediation, 3, 6, 22, 193

Competitive bargaining, 155, 162–167

Competitive conflict escalation cycle, 92

Competitive worldview, 148

Compromise, 155

Concessions, 148, 155, 158, 161, 163, 166

Conciliation, 23

Concrete ideas, 129, 143, 148, 182–183

Confidentiality, 25, 31, 67, 83, 87, 101, 102 (table), 105, 106, 107, 168, 169

Conflict causes, 131–132

Conflict of interest, 86

Consistency, 118

Constituency, 45, 88

Content paraphrasing, 49–50, 123, 157

Contingency agreements, 35, 162, 164, 170, 171, 183–184

Continuing relationships, 149

Controlling the process, 41–42, 111, 135, 136–137, 146

Convergence, 41

Cooperative negotiation, 155–156, 158–162

Cooperative worldview, 148

Cost-cutting, 162

Court-annexed mediation, 7, 22, 35

Credibility, 29, 30, 64–65, 100, 102 (table), 103–104, 110–111

Criteria, 123, 131 (table), 147, 148, 159, 163, 185
Crying, 136
Cultural conflict styles, 34
Culture, 22, 34–36, 41, 54, 55, 67, 76, 81, 84, 92, 94–95, 103, 132 (table)

Deadlocks. *See* Impasse
Debriefing, 188, 197
Defensive climate, 45 (table)
Defensiveness, 45, 51, 121, 133, 135
Demographic information, 67–68
Denotative meaning, 52
Direct language in agreements, 179–181
Direct speech, 34
Directiveness, 157
Disputant roles, 88
Dispute resolution continuum, 15 (figure)
Distributive bargaining, 155
Divergence, 41–42
Dual roles, 83, 85, 87

Early commitment, 166
Emotion, 10, 22, 26–27, 34–35, 44, 46, 91, 131 (table), 134–137, 156, 168, 170
Emotional contagion theory, 41
Emotional intelligence, 44, 119–120, 125
Emotional paraphrase, 25, 26, 47–49, 51, 52, 131 (table), 137 (table)
Empathy, 39 (table), 43, 47, 120 (table)
Equidistance
Ethics, 56, 64–66, 76–77, 82–88, 173, 197
Ethnocentrism, 35
European-American model, 34
Evaluative mediation model, 157
Evidence, 137
Experts, 109
Extended pre-mediation, 193–194
Eye contact, 103

Face, 81, 95, 158, 169, 170, 171–172
Facets of mediation model, 23
Facilitation, 200
Facts, 129
Family mediation, 5, 23, 71
Fear, 91, 121, 168, 194
Fractionate, 89, 164

Functional models, 22–23
Future focus, 128, 131 (table), 162, 182, 184

Gems, 165
Generalizations, 133–134
Gender, 93
General inquiry questions, 127–128
Generations, 91
Goals, 92
Good faith, 168
Government mediation, 7
Grievance story, 162
Ground rules, 39 (table), 100, 101, 102 (table), 107–108, 111, 134

Happiness, 129 (table)
Hearing, 42
Hidden agenda, 127, 168, 169
Hidden costs, 186
High-low exchange, 165
Humor, 130
HURIER model, 44

"I" statement, 125, 131 (table), 133, 188
Impartial framing, 151, 182
Impartial regard, 106
Impartiality, 15, 31, 34, 35, 40, 81, 82, 83–84, 87, 101, 102 (table), 105–106, 142, 173
Impasse, 73, 130, 162, 170–171
Inclusive language, 136
Individualistic culture, 35
Information, 91, 132 (table)
Informed choice, 3, 64, 70, 86, 87, 88, 99, 104, 186
Informed consent, 70, 83
In-group, 35
Intake, 25, 60–77
Interests, 3, 10 (table), 11–12, 15, 32, 50, 88, 112 (table), 116, 122–124, 127, 128, 132, 133, 144, 155–156, 164, 168, 170, 185
Internal attributions, 133
Internet mediation, 194–195
Interruptions, 25, 88, 107, 121, 127, 134, 136
Intrusiveness, 40, 145, 157, 173
Issue list, 73, 113, 116, 127, 142
Issues

distributive, 25
emotional, 4, 10 (table), 124
identification, 26, 31–32, 62 (table)
linking and unlinking, 161
negotiable, 143
packaged, 148, 156
procedural, 11, 73, 124, 146, 171
psychological, 11, 27, 73, 171
relationship, 4, 8, 31, 156
substantive, 5, 11, 21, 26, 31, 50, 51, 73, 119, 124, 146, 156, 170, 171
vs. interests, 39 (table)

Linchpin, 146, 147, 148
Linking issues, 161
Listening, 5, 42–52, 110
Listening barriers, 44–45, 121
Litigation, 12–13
Logjam, 171
Logrolling, 161
Lying, 55, 168, 169

Med-Arb, 14
Mediation
   appropriateness, 69
   benefits of, 3–5, 195–201
   certification, 195
   codes of practice, 195
   contexts, 39
   defined, 14–15
   environment, 75–76
   location, 74
   models, 20–24, 104, 157
   moves, 27
   panel, 22
   parties, 3
   phases, 26
   philosophy, 20–22
   plan, 90–91
   problem solving, 21–22
   reasons to, 1–5
   small claims, 22
   transformative, 20–21, 81, 194
   types, 5–8
   variables, 24–28

Mediator
   abilities, 39 (table)
   competence, 84, 87, 126, 197–199
   employment, 196
   ethics, 56, 65–66, 82–88
   privilege, 67
Mediator monologue. *See* Opening statement
Memorandum of understanding, 107, 178–187
Metacommunication, 136
Mixed motive conflict, 155
Monologue style, 99–100
Mulling, 136, 168
Multitasking, 38
Mutual gains negotiation, 69, 155
Mutual framing, 150, 159

Need to be heard, 121
Negative labeling, 51
Negative peace, 8, 9 (table)
Negotiable issues, 143
Negotiated rule-making, 7
Negotiation, 26, 31, 32, 53, 154–173
Neutral framing, 151
Neutrality, 15, 31, 34, 35, 63, 81, 82–84, 87, 101, 102 (table), 103, 105–106, 132, 134, 137, 142, 173
Nonagreement, 187
Nonverbal communication, 52–53, 98, 143
Notetaking, 31, 101, 106–107, 111–113, 143

Observable framing, 143
Offers, 32
On-line dispute resolution, 194–195
Opening statement, 30–31, 88, 98–111, 193
Overaccommodation, 42
Out-group, 35

Packaged issues, 148–149, 156
Panel mediation, 193
Paraphrasing feelings. *See* Emotional paraphrase
Peer mediation, 6, 23
Perceptual bias, 44
Personality, 91
Perspective taking, 130, 161
Pitfalls, 132–137

Positions, 11, 50, 63, 122–124, 155, 159, 163, 166, 168, 171
Positive homework, 136
Post-mediation, 33–34
Postpone, 135, 136
Power, 8, 9 (table). 29, 38, 39 (table), 41, 67, 71, 72, 81, 83, 91, 92, 93, 95, 110, 132, 136, 155, 182
Power chairs, 75
Power distance, 35
Pre-mediation, 24–25, 29–30, 88, 90, 193–194
Privacy management theory, 42
Private meeting, 22, 25–26, 75, 83, 86, 101, 102 (table), 105, 108, 134, 162, 165, 167–169, 171
Private value, 163
Probing questions, 136
Problem solving, 5, 22, 27, 32, 40, 158–167
Promise, 155

Questions
  being Columbo, 128–129, 137 (table)
  closed-ended, 53
  future-focused, 128, 137 (table)
  general inquiry, 127–128
  genuinely curious, 54
  open-ended, 53, 137 (table), 168
  probing, 136, 137 (table)
  specific inquiry, 128, 129
  vision, 128
  whole picture, 128

Rapport, 110–111
Reality testing, 119, 168–169, 185–186
Recency, 73
Reconciliation, 20, 23
Referrals, 66
Reformulation, 56
Reframing, 5, 25, 50–52, 121, 130, 137 (table), 157, 158, 158, 171
Relationship, 46, 149, 166, 170
Relative value, 165
Respect, 31, 68, 101, 108, 123, 143
Restraining orders, 72
Retaliation, 8, 9 (table)
Restitution plan, 89

Restorative justice, 6, 60
Rights, 9–11
Ripeness, 73
Role reversal, 161–162
Roles, 31, 80–82, 105

Safety, 98, 120–121, 123, 135, 169
Saving face, 55
School mediation, 6
Seating, 75–76
Second party paraphrase, 133
Selective attention, 44
Self-determination, 20, 42, 64, 70, 76, 87, 104
Self-serving bias, 118
Settlement, 32, 33
Settlement range, 166–167
Shuttle, 27, 34, 169, 171
Siding. *See* Taking sides
Signing ceremony, 186
Silence, 55–56
Sliding scale, 165
Soft agreement, 172, 181, 187 (table)
Special education, 39
Specific inquiry question, 129
Specificity, 33
Stakeholder, 72, 89–90, 101, 104
Standards of practice, 16, 173, 195, 197
Stereotypes, 35
Storytelling, 22, 26, 31–32, 53, 110, 113, 117–139, 143
Structure, 69, 91, 131 (table), 134
Style, 92
Subpoena waiver, 67, 102 (table)
Summary, 137
Supervisor mediation, 7, 81
Supportive climate, 45 (table)
Symbolic interaction theory, 117–118

Take-it-or-leave-it offer, 166
Taking sides, 134, 168
Third party, 2
Time, 164–165
Timing, 73–74
Tit-for-tat, 155
Transformation, 56, 118, 129
Transformative mediation, 20–21, 27, 81, 194

Threat, 50, 70–71, 155, 163, 171
Trust, 29, 43, 47, 53, 60, 61, 69, 98, 103, 110, 124, 130, 133, 149, 151, 168, 170, 182
Trusting the process, 40, 127
Truthfulness, 86
Two-way commonality statement, 144–145

Unauthorized practice of law, 64, 105, 178
Uncertainty avoidance, 35
Unexpected consequences, 185
Uniform Mediation Act, 27, 67, 82
Uniqueness, 118
Unlinking issues, 161

Validation, 25, 44, 47, 51, 63, 116, 121, 127, 131 (table), 134, 136, 171, 188

Values, 91, 93, 131 (table), 170
Verbal aggression, 69
Victim Offender Dialogue, 6
Victim Offender Mediation (VOM), 6, 23, 25, 39, 68, 71, 89, 100, 116, 133, 194
Violence, 70–71
VOM. *See* Victim Offender Mediation

WATNA. *See* Worst alternative to a negotiated agreement
Whole picture questions, 128
Withdrawing from a case, 87
Withholding information, 169
Workability, 33
Worst alternative to a negotiated agreement, 64, 168

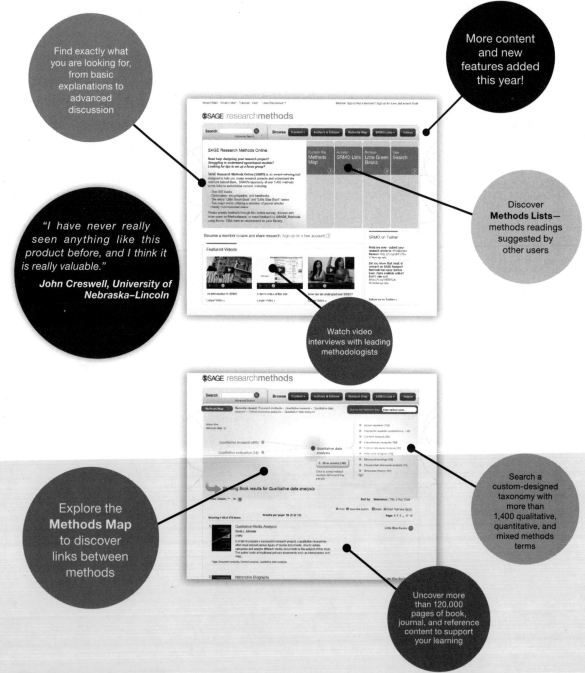

⑤SAGE research**methods**

The essential online tool for researchers from the world's leading methods publisher

Find exactly what you are looking for, from basic explanations to advanced discussion

More content and new features added this year!

Discover **Methods Lists**— methods readings suggested by other users

"*I have never really seen anything like this product before, and I think it is really valuable.*"

John Creswell, University of Nebraska–Lincoln

Watch video interviews with leading methodologists

Explore the **Methods Map** to discover links between methods

Search a custom-designed taxonomy with more than 1,400 qualitative, quantitative, and mixed methods terms

Uncover more than 120,000 pages of book, journal, and reference content to support your learning

Find out more at
www.sageresearchmethods.com